Brian J. Robb is the *New Y*[...] bestselling biographer of L[...] Depp and Brad Pitt. He's also written acclaimed pop culture books on silent cinema, the films of Philip K. Dick, Steampunk, J. R. R. Tolkien, Wes Craven and Laurel and Hardy, and the TV series *Doctor Who* and *Star Trek*. He is co-editor of the popular website Sci-Fi Bulletin and lives in Edinburgh.

A BRIEF HISTORY OF

Gangsters

Brian J. Robb

ROBINSON

RUNNING PRESS
PHILADELPHIA · LONDON

ROBINSON

First published in Great Britain in 2014 by Robinson

Copyright © Brian J. Robb, 2014

1 3 5 7 9 10 8 6 4 2

The moral right of the author has been asserted.

A CIP catalogue record for this book
is available from the British Library.

ISBN 978-1-47211-054-1 (paperback)
ISBN: 978-1-47211-068-8 (ebook)

Typeset in Stempel Garamond by TW Typesetting, Plymouth, Devon
Printed and bound by CPI Group (UK) Ltd, Croydon, CR0 4YY

Robinson
is an imprint of
Constable & Robinson Ltd
100 Victoria Embankment
London EC4Y 0DY

An Hachette UK Company
www.hachette.co.uk

www.constablerobinson.com

First published in the United States in 2015 by Running Press Book Publishers,
A Member of the Perseus Books Group

US ISBN: 978-0-7624-5476-1
US Library of Congress Control Number: 2014941632

9 8 7 6 5 4 3 2 1
Digit on the right indicates the number of this printing

Running Press Book Publishers
2300 Chestnut Street
Philadelphia, PA 19103-4371

Visit us on the web!
www.runningpress.com

CONTENTS

PART ONE: AMERICAN GANGSTERS BEFORE PROHIBITION

I

LAWLESSNESS IN THE OLD WEST

Gangsters. The word conjures up a world of crime, gun molls, and corrupt political power. It also suggests a certain amount of glamour: the fedora hats, trench coats, the 'rat-a-tat-tat' of Tommy guns, the nightclubs and speakeasies, the gambling dens and the dames in flowing gowns. That image comes more from the thrilling gangster movies of the 1930s than the actual gangsters themselves, although some of them did live up to it.

The modern use of the term 'gangster' originated in an Ohio newspaper of 1896 and simply referred to a group of people involved in organized crime. It seems to have had a maritime origin, going back to the seventeenth century – according to the *Oxford English Dictionary*. Famous gangsters range from Italian-Americans like Lucky Luciano, Meyer Lansky and Bugsy Siegel to those found around the world, such as Britain's notorious Kray Twins,

France's Jacques Mesrine, and the Triads and Yakuza gangs of the Far East.

Gangsters – especially the romanticized American gangster of Prohibition and the Depression era, a time when America's rulers failed their people – have proved to be resilient and attractive figures, somehow glamorous in their law-breaking lifestyles. They have transcended the time and place of their origins and have become archetypal figures, a repository of ordinary people's dreams about the romance of crime.

With a strong focus on the American archetype, *A Brief History of Gangsters* explores the histories, both personal and criminal, of key figures in the worlds of organized crime. The book closes with a study of the gangster in popular culture, particularly in film and television. As recent hit TV series such as *The Sopranos* and *Boardwalk Empire* and blockbuster movies like *Public Enemies* (2009) and *Gangster Squad* (2013) show, the gangster is here to stay.

Although the infamous figure of the American gangster is largely associated with the period of the 1920s to the 1940s – roughly from Prohibition through to the Second World War – there are deeper roots. In an American context, the rise of the gangster – that is, someone who is part of or who runs an organized crime network – really begins in the Old West.

During the 1800s the notoriety of the proto-gangster 'outlaw' figure was spread through the rise of newspapers that, often gleefully, chronicled their misdeeds. Members of organized gangs of outlaws, such as the James Gang; the group led by Billy the Kid known as 'the Rustlers'; the Doolin–Dalton Gang; and the 'Wild Bunch', all became public figures.

The untamed wilderness of the Western half of the United States attracted a certain type of rugged, self-reliant settler, while the lack of law (initially, at least) made the

West a particularly attractive place for those of a criminal bent, many of whom were fleeing the authorities in the East. The spread westwards by settlers who first arrived on the continent of North America in the East developed from the early seventeenth century and ran through until the early twentieth century. The American frontier – the 'Old West' or 'Wild West' – described this expansion westwards, largely in the second half of the nineteenth century.

General lawlessness was common, with personal crimes slowly giving way to organized criminal activity carried out by groups of people (usually, but not exclusively, men). Commonplace crimes included horse stealing, highway robbery, and currency counterfeiting. Pioneer families were often targeted for their goods and supplies, as the relatively few lawmen struggled to cope. Stagecoaches would most often escape attack if they carried armed guards, but small criminal gangs – often comprising no more than two or three people – could easily target relatively unprotected homesteaders. Due to the nature of these crimes, with many seen as being against the struggles of the expanding nation itself, punishments were often extreme.

Centres of the cattle business, such as Dodge City, and mining towns, like Tombstone, Arizona, became attractive to the increasingly organized crime gangs of the Old West. Cowboys resting up in large towns would spend the money generated from months on the cattle trail, so were frequent targets for bandits, as were miners, who dealt in silver and gold, and the wealth those minerals created. Key events of Western legend, such as the 1881 gunfight at the O.K. Corral, were examples of the lawlessness of the time. Although often seen as bandits themselves, the three Earp brothers – Virgil, Morgan and Wyatt – were in fact investors in a local mine and local law officers when they killed a trio of outlaws during the confrontation.

Separated from family or community, the (mostly) young men who strived to find new lives on the American frontier often found themselves in areas where law enforcement was difficult to maintain or next to non-existent. Some of the key members of outlaw gangs had experienced the violence of the Civil War in the 1860s, while others who attacked banks, stagecoaches and trains had fallen upon difficult times having failed to make a success in the cattle industry or in other fields after the war. Some were simply individualists, those for whom organized society held no attraction, and who were determined to go their own way in life (perhaps a basic trait of the American frontiersman), even if that meant falling foul of the law.

Often the only opposition to such activity came not in the form of legally designated lawmen and their deputies, but in the shape of informally organized community 'posses', where armed men set out to pursue or dissuade the bandits from their local activities. In California in the mid-nineteenth century, criminal activities flourished. Infamous outlaw gangs were responsible for much of the crime that terrorized the frontier, and it is in these groups that the roots of America's later gangsterism is to be found.

Jesse James and the Western Gangs

Perhaps the most notorious American outlaw of the Old West was Jesse James, whose exploits became the stuff of legend and myth within his own lifetime, thanks to newspaper coverage and dime novels embellishing his story. Born in Missouri in September 1847, Jesse Woodson James was the son of a man who was both a Baptist minister and the founder of a college. His father died of cholera in 1850, when Jesse was only three years old. He had an older brother, Alexander Franklin – known simply as Frank – and a younger sister, Susan. His mother eventually remarried (for the second time) to a doctor in 1855 – they had four further children together.

Growing up prior to the Civil War in the north/south 'border' state of Missouri, where Jesse's family were originally farmers and slave owners, he experienced some of the growing anti-slavery movement's activities that sometimes led to outbreaks of violence. The resulting Civil War, which came about largely due to the South's resistance to the North's desire to outlaw slavery, did much to shape the rest of Jesse James' criminal life.

Aligned with the Confederate side, representing the Southern States, the James family witnessed some of the battles between Unionist militia known as 'jayhawkers' and secessionist guerrilla fighters dubbed 'bushwhackers'. Frank James joined a local secessionist military group, resulting in a revenge attack on the James farm in May 1863 by Unionists, during which Jesse's mother and stepfather were tortured. This served to radicalize Jesse, who joined his brother as part of 'Bloody' Bill Anderson's Confederate raiders (several members of that group would go on to become members of the James Gang).

Jesse saw much action during the civil conflict, and learned about weapons and warfare on the job. He and his brother were participants in several notorious actions, including the Centralia Massacre of September 1864, in which many unarmed Union troops were killed or injured. As a result of the brothers' activities, the James family were driven out of Clay County in Missouri and had to move south into Nebraska.

Shot (for the second time) while intending to surrender to a Union patrol near Lexington, Jesse James was – according to legend – left for dead, only to rise again as an outlaw. As he was presumed dead, he was never granted an amnesty at the end of the conflict in 1865. In the chaos that followed, Jesse was able to disappear, embarking upon his criminal exploits around 1866.

It wasn't until 1869 that Jesse James, along with his brother Frank, were identified as wanted men following a bank robbery in Gallatin, Missouri. As with most criminals of their type, public opinion was solidly against them and their activities, with the community keen to see the pair of outlaws brought to justice. However, Jesse was smart enough to begin using the media that vilified him and his brother to try to change public opinion. He wrote an 'open letter' to the *Liberty Tribune* newspaper, published on 24 June 1870, asserting the James brothers' innocence and claiming instead that they were the victims of political persecution following their wartime service for the Confederacy.

There followed a decade of propaganda, on behalf of and against Jesse James, while the criminal activities of his gang continued. A sympathetic newspaper editor, John Newman Edwards, did much to create an unearned Robin Hood image for Jesse James, portraying the proto-gangster as an avenger who struck wealthy railroad bosses and venal bankers on behalf of the common folk, although he kept the resulting loot for himself and his gang members.

Jesse James had set about creating his own myth as a 'good guy' outlaw. During one train robbery, the James gang distributed copies of an account of the event then underway to passengers to pass onto the media in the aftermath. The main concerns of this pre-written 'history' were to exaggerate the height of the gang members to point out that the hands of the passengers were studied so the gang would avoid robbing 'working folk'.

Jesse cultivated a cult of the personality, making his marriage to Zerelda Mimms in April 1874 a matter of public interest through the pages of the *St. Louis Dispatch* newspaper – now this modern Robin Hood had found his Maid Marian. Further sympathy for Jesse was generated when Pinkerton Agency detectives, charged with his capture, raided the James' family home in January 1875. A device intended for illumination was thrown into the house through the window, but it exploded, killing Jesse's nine-year-old half-brother. This, and other incidents, were built up to depict Jesse and his outlaw gang as righteous folk, fallen on hard times as a result of the political situation following the Civil War, suffering persecution. The gang became famous, robbing stagecoaches, trains and banks, often in front of large crowds of witnesses: the gang members even took to 'performing' theatrically for the gathering public crowds during their daring 'daylight robberies'.

The politicization of crime would be a hallmark of later gangster organizations, of which Jesse James was a pioneer. Pleading for a pardon for his actions, Jesse succeeded in setting the Democrats and Republicans, and their respective 'tame' press organizations, against one another over his fate. However, the bank raid in Northfield, Minnesota (subject of the 1972 Philip Kaufman movie *The Great Northfield Minnesota Raid*), in September 1876 turned the tide against the James Gang. Three of the gang members were killed and the Younger brothers, James Gang associates, were wounded and apprehended. Following a concentrated manhunt, of the whole gang only Frank and Jesse remained at large.

While Frank adopted a new identity and attempted to 'go straight', the restless Jesse continued his criminal activities, and in 1879 recruited a new gang, many of whom were aware of their leader's fame as an outlaw, and who were not 'battle-hardened' in the way Frank and Jesse had been by the Civil War. The new James gang returned to train hold-ups. The robberies became more violent, and these more undisciplined gang members frequently turned on one another, making Jesse paranoid that one of his own gang might kill him.

That's exactly what happened in April 1882 (as seen in the 2007 movie *The Assassination of Jesse James by the Coward Robert Ford*), when James gang member Robert Ford shot the thirty-four-year-old Jesse in the back of the head, while he was hanging a picture on the wall in their remote hideaway. Jesse's body was identified through his two previous chest wounds and the missing tip of his middle finger. Instead of gaining the reward he thought was his, Ford was charged with murder, although later pardoned. Along with his brother Charley, Ford then toured the country putting on a vaudeville show in which they re-enacted the killing of Jesse James in front of paying crowds.

Such was the notoriety and legend of Jesse James, many refused to believe he was really dead. The *New York Daily Graphic* had declared Jesse James to be 'the most renowned murderer and robber of his age', so it was unlikely his folk legend would fade quickly. Several later criminal figures claimed they were actually Jesse James, or used his name to justify their crimes in the wake of his death. Even as late as 1951, the 101-year-old J. Frank Dalton claimed that he was in fact Jesse James, having survived the assassination attempt of 1882. The body buried in 1882 was exhumed in 1995 and DNA testing proved it was indeed the corpse of notorious outlaw and proto-gangster, Jesse James.

In a similar style to Jesse James, Billy the Kid – born in November 1859 as William Henry McCarty Jr, also known as William Bonney – was a veteran of war who turned to crime. Billy's war was the Lincoln County War of 1878, after which he became an outlaw on the American frontier, surrounded by myth.

Billy grew up in a mining encampment called Silver City in New Mexico, only turning to crime after his mother's death in 1874. He first became a horse thief, then – aged just seventeen – killed for the first time when he ran into a bully who'd been tormenting him. The Lincoln County War suited Billy as a time and place where he could become lost, and as a way of learning the use of weapons and the consequences of violence. Various shoot-outs, assassinations and targeted killings followed.

After the war, Billy was briefly a cattle rustler. After a failed attempt to win an amnesty, he was captured by Sheriff Pat Garrett (who'd also participated in the Lincoln County conflict) following a gunfight in 1880. Found guilty of murder for his part in the gang slaying of Sheriff William J. Brady, Billy avoided the noose in April 1881 when he killed two of Garrett's deputies who were guarding him, and escaped. He would be free from the law for three months, hidden by Hispanic sheep herders. However, Garrett was on the Kid's trail, tracking him to Fort Sumner, where in the summer of 1881 he shot him dead at the age of just twenty-one.

Billy the Kid's criminal career was short-lived, but his fame spread far and wide across the United States. The 1881 price on his head – a $500 bounty – issued by the Governor of New Mexico, helped make him notorious, although exaggerated accounts of his feats helped. The Kid's youth and quickness on the draw were built up, especially in the kind of dime novels he'd grown up reading, and so another proto-gangster legend was born. Public opinion turned against Garrett, seeing his killing of 'the Kid' as an unfair act. During his short-lived crime spree, Billy the Kid was said to have killed between fifteen and twenty-six men – the legend prefers the total of twenty-one, one for each year of the Kid's life. As with Jesse James, others claimed to be Billy the Kid after his death; DNA testing of his remains was thwarted by court proceedings in 2004, with the state of New Mexico preferring to protect Billy the Kid's legacy as a tourist draw over verifying the facts.

The equally youthful Sam Bass ran a criminal gang in the 1870s and robbed the Union Pacific Railroad gold train from San Francisco in September 1877, taking $60,000, still the largest ever robbery from that still-existing railroad service. The Bass Gang staged various robberies, most often netting less than $500 each time, before they moved up to more risky stagecoach robberies and then railroad trains. Holding up four trains within twenty-five miles of

Dallas brought the Bass Gang to the attention of Pinkerton agents, who were teamed with a special company of Texas Rangers to track them down.

By threatening his ill father, the Rangers were able to turn a member of the gang, Jim Murphy, into an informer. While an ambush of Sam Bass's next planned raid was being prepared by the Rangers, Bass shot and killed a local sheriff who'd noticed him while he was scouting the Williamson County Bank. Attempting to escape, Bass was mortally wounded by a pair of vigilant Texas Rangers. Sam Bass died the following day – his twenty-seventh birthday.

The pattern was repeated in the tales surrounding other such proto-gangsters of the Old West, including the Dalton Gang, Black Bart, and Butch Cassidy and the 'Wild Bunch'. During a two year period from 1890, the Dalton Gang – comprising three Dalton brothers and five others – specialized in train and bank robberies. The three Dalton brothers – Gratton, Bob and Emmett – started out as lawmen like the Earps, but turned to crime when they were not paid (a fourth brother, Bill, was part of the Wild Bunch). They recruited others into the gang, pulling their first job in a raid on a casino in Silver City, New Mexico. Thereafter the Dalton Gang held up passenger trains, stole horses and raided train stations to rob waiting passengers. Ambition got the better of Bob Dalton who decided he wanted to go one better than Jesse James and rob two banks in broad daylight at the same time.

Wearing fake beards, the gang attempted the double deed in Coffeyville, Kansas in October 1892. Despite the disguises, they were recognized by locals who quickly gathered together an armed posse while the gang were still in the banks; a frantic shoot-out ensued as they attempted a getaway. At least three townspeople and a marshal were killed, as were four members of the gang: two Dalton brothers – Gratton and the recognized leader, Bob – as well as Dick Broadwell and Bill Power. Of the five participants in the bank raids only Emmett Dalton survived, but he had been seriously wounded: reportedly, around twenty bullets were removed from him. He was tried and imprisoned in March 1893. Later, he would write books about his experiences as an outlaw in the Dalton Gang and enjoyed a career as an actor in Hollywood – in 1918, he played himself in a movie – before dying at the age of 66 in 1937.

Black Bart – born Charles Earl Bolles in Norfolk, England in 1829 – was an Old West outlaw who became known for the poetic messages he left behind after some of his raids. He robbed Wells Fargo stagecoaches around Northern California and Southern Oregon between the 1870s and 1880s. Although he only actually left poems behind after two raids, it became known as his trademark. Frightened of horses, Black Bart was a bandit who got around only by foot, never fired a gun during his raids, and was always polite, using good manners and no foul language, leading to him becoming known as a 'gentleman bandit'. He controlled his victims by pretending to talk to his 'gang' hidden in nearby bushes, but he always operated alone.

Wounded during his final robbery, Black Bart made his escape, but dropped several personal items including a handkerchief. A laundry mark led Wells Fargo detectives to a cleaning company, where they got Bart's address. Arrested and convicted, despite his protestations, Black Bart went to San Quentin prison for four years. Released in 1888 and in failing health, he went straight, apparently dying around 1917.

The charisma and notoriety of later gangsters can be seen in an earlier form in Butch Cassidy, the bank and train robber and leader of the 'Wild Bunch' gang. Robert Leroy Parker was born in 1866 in Utah and worked on several ranches, acquiring the nickname 'Butch'. He took the surname Cassidy from his mentor, dairy farmer and cattle rustler Mike Cassidy (itself an alias). It wasn't until 1889 that Butch Cassidy took up a life of crime full time, stealing $21,000 from a Telluride bank in co-operation with two other outlaws. Horse thieving and the operation of a protection racket – demanding money with menaces – followed, leading to an eighteen-month jail term.

Released from jail, Butch Cassidy involved himself even further in the criminal underworld, rising to become leader of a group of bandits known as the Wild Bunch. A spate of bank robberies followed, and in 1896 Harry Longabaugh joined the gang and became known as the 'Sundance Kid'. Payroll thefts and stagecoach ambushes followed, with an ever growing manhunt making the gang's criminal activities increasingly more difficult to conduct. After each raid the gang would split up and later reconvene at their 'hole-in-the-wall' hideaway, a secluded area in Dubois, Wyoming. In 1900 five members of the gang, including Butch and Sundance, cheekily posed for a studio group photograph, which they then mockingly mailed to the pursuing Pinkerton detectives. The lucrative raids continued, but the heat on the gang got too much, so Butch Cassidy and the Sundance Kid headed for South America, hiding out in Buenos Aires in Argentina.

Failing to change their ways after trying to run a legitimate ranch in Patagonia, the pair of outlaws continued to raid banks in South America, bringing them to the attention of Argentine law enforcement who in turn brought in the Pinkerton agents already on their trail. Fleeing their pursuers – and continuing to stage robberies on the way – Butch and Sundance ended up on the run in Chile. Although their deaths were never confirmed, in 1908 in Bolivia two unknown bandits were trapped in a house in San Vicente by members of the Bolivian army. Under siege, one bandit killed the other (who had been fatally wounded in the shoot-out with the army), before turning the gun on himself. The local police did not know the bandits identities, and they were buried locally in unmarked graves.

Legend has it that these graves were the final resting places of Butch and Sundance.

Their story is also the story of the end of the Old West: in evading the ever reaching long arm of the law, they had to flee further than most, all the way to South America. The myths, legends and tales that surround these often flamboyant and theatrical figures were the reading matter of many of the men who went on to become the key names of the true era of the classic American gangster. Many were born in the final quarter of the ninteenth century, and they would define the criminality of the first half of the twentieth century. The mythologizing of the outlaws of the Old West would be carried on to the urban gangsters who replaced them.

2
ORGANIZED CRIME BEFORE PROHIBITION

The American gangster is largely an urban figure. The gangsters and their organized crime networks arose alongside the growth of American cities in the late-nineteenth and early-twentieth centuries. Just as the cities spread, grew, and their skyscrapers reached ever higher, so did the tentacles of organized crime spread, infecting the commerce and politics of the modern city and dominating the underworld. Most large American cities were infested with the disease of crime from their inception. It was the arrival of Prohibition – the nationwide ban on the manufacture, transportation and sale of alcohol between 1920 and 1933 – that led to a boom in gangsterism across and between the major US cities. The early history of organized crime in a trio of major American cities illustrates the trends.

New York

New York developed from Algonquian Native American lands settled by European colonists throughout the sixteenth and seventeenth centuries. Originally called New Amsterdam, New York was a British-controlled trading port in the early 1700s, and a centre of the slave trade. Following the American Revolutionary War, the city remained a British military and political base of power until the evacuation of 1783. By 1785 New York was the American national capital (before it settled in Washington D.C. in 1790), and in 1789 America's first President, George Washington, was inaugurated in the city. Slavery was abolished there in 1827, although racial discrimination would continue for many decades.

The nineteenth century saw New York boom thanks to waves of European immigration, especially a large number of Irish immigrants fleeing the famine of the late-1840s and early-1850s. The American Civil War of 1861–5 caused disruption in New York, although the effects of the conflict were felt most strongly elsewhere. It wasn't until 1898 that the modern city of New York was properly formed, incorporating Brooklyn and several other counties. The city took on its modern shape of the five boroughs of the Bronx, Brooklyn, Manhattan, Queens and Staten Island. It was the ideal urban breeding ground for organized crime and the rise of the gangster.

While outlaws were making the most of their freedoms in the Old West, mass immigration from Europe brought a new kind of criminal to the East. All sorts arrived in the ports of New York across the better part of a century, and among the virtuous settlers arrived criminals. They came from all over, fleeing the pogroms, famines, wars, suppression and revolutions in their homelands, heading to the 'new world' for a fresh start, by fair means or foul. With low-level crime, there also came high-level corruption.

One example is La Mano Nera, or The Black Hand, a

loose association rather than an organization, often confused with the Italian Mafia. The name applied to one of
the key crimes pursued by gangsters: extortion. Developed
in mid-eighteenth-century Sicily, the 'Black Hand Society'
appeared in the American press from the 1890s through
to about 1915. The scheme was simple: money would be
demanded from individuals, often by letter, and if payment
was not forthcoming, violence would follow. The letters
featured colourful, often threatening, graphics, including
depictions of deadly weapons, skulls, smoking guns or a
hangman's noose. They'd be signed with the symbol of an
open hand, printed in thick black ink – which is why *The
New York Herald* newspaper dubbed them 'Black Hand'
letters. The majority of practitioners came from Italian
immigrant stock, who brought this shakedown of America
with them.

Those who failed to pay up would be punished in various ways. Straightforward violence was the minimum
response, but other options included the fire-bombing of
commercial premises and even the kidnapping of family
members to force payment. By 1900, police had compiled
reports of Black Hand threats from not just New York,
but Chicago, New Orleans and San Francisco. It was
estimated that up to 90 per cent of Italian immigrants in
New York had received Black Hand threats at one time or
another.

One famous victim was tenor Enrico Caruso, who
received a Black Hand letter demanding he hand over
$2,000 – rich or famous people were obvious targets.
Caruso paid up, and was then repeatedly targeted with
a batch of letters totalling demands of up to $15,000. He
reported the situation to the police, who co-operated with
the singer in a sting that captured two Italian-American
'businessmen' who were behind that particular scam.

When threatened, Black Hand groups would turn to
assassination to remove troublesome officials, and their

involvement was suspected in the killings of New Orleans police chief David Hennessy in 1890 and anti-crime crusading New York Police Department lieutenant Joseph 'Giuseppe' Petrosino in 1909. By the mid-1920s, with the arrival of Prohibition, the Black Hand gangs had faded out in favour of other, rather more subtle, forms of extortion and intimidation practised by the newer gangsters and organized crime groups.

A social club that became a political machine and then a source of institutional corruption, New York's Tammany Hall became a by-word for organized subversion from the eighteenth century until as late as the 1960s. It began as a social organization for 'pure Americans', known as the Society for St Tammany, or the Columbian Order. Established in 1786, this fraternal group became the Tammany Society after three years, and like the Freemasons, it existed to help its members get on in life, business and politics.

The group came to dominate the Democratic Party locally in New York, and then nationally with the election of John Adams as President in 1800. Immigrants, mainly Irish, were aided by the society to rise high in politics, especially from the 1840s onwards. Political patronage, as a form of organized corruption, blossomed through their auspices. The leaders of the society organized the new arrivals as mass voting blocks, ensuring their control over local government and services.

The most infamous Tammany leader was 'Boss' William Tweed, who between 1854 and 1871 controlled the Irish vote and could bend it to his will. His influence was spread far and wide through his membership of various political groups, councils and organizations, including the United States Senate from 1867. He kept his voting block happy by ensuring that expansive municipal works, which created jobs, were conducted primarily in their areas. Despite attempts at reform, exposure of his own financial and political corruption, and even a jail term, 'Boss' Tweed survived and maintained his influence until his death in 1878, aged 55.

Tammany Hall exemplified a rarefied form of gangsterism, one in which the legitimate tools of state and society were corrupted from within by a group of self-interested, well-connected people, whose main interests were power and money. While there was much corruption and vice, there was rarely any of the violence usually associated with America's more straightforward gangsters. That didn't mean there were not alliances between political extortionists and raw gangsterism, such as that exhibited in the Five Points district of New York [see chapter 3].

To ensure the voter turned out and voted in the 'correct' way, intimidation and violence were used. Elections could cost lives, but none of the politicians themselves would be directly implicated. The phrase 'vote early, vote often', supposedly coined by gangster Al Capone, epitomized the electoral corruption practised on behalf of Tammany Hall members, with organized teams of voters altering their physical appearance between numerous assaults on the ballot box. In some elections, even the dead were pressed into voting.

Although graft and political corruption were rife for many decades under the effect of Tammany Hall, eventually its influence began to wane. In 1932, the Tammany Hall-sponsored Mayor Jimmy Walker was forced from office, and Democratic President Franklin D. Roosevelt campaigned to remove the organization's Federal patronage. Republican Fiorello La Guardia was elected Mayor on an anti-Tammany ticket in 1933, taking office in January 1934. He tackled corruption head-on, and reforms installing a merit-based civil service followed, greatly reducing Tammany Hall's organizational influence. La Guardia would go on to become a thorn in the side of many of the city's established gangsters in the 1930s.

Tammany Hall was much reduced, its influence circum-scribed, and its members and practitioners side-lined. It wasn't until the 1950s that there was a brief resurgence in the group's influence, with the arrival of Carmine DeSapio as leader. He managed to orchestrate several elections, just as the group had done many times in the past, ensuring his influence and patronage was felt far and wide. However, the opposition was swift in its retaliation, attacking DeSapio's links with organized crime, especially senior mobster Frank Costello, the self-appointed successor to the infamous 'Lucky' Luciano. Despite attempting to present himself as a reformer, DeSapio was exposed as an old-time Tammany Hall 'boss', and was driven out of power.

By the middle-1960s, the Tammany Hall machine had all but ceased to exist. With no obvious leadership, and dramatic shifts in control of the Democratic Party, the organization that had dominated New York's politics and much of its crime for so long, simply faded away. The name lived on, though, as a shorthand way of describing any form of political corruption, influence-peddling, or 'machine' politics that set out to gain and exercise power through manipulation of elections, criminal associations and abuse of patronage.

Chicago
The 'Windy City' of Chicago was incorporated in 1837, and experienced rapid growth throughout the nineteenth century. Like New York, it was an ideal breeding ground for crime, corruption and early gangsterism. The 'Chicago Outfit' – known more simply as 'The Outfit' – was the main Italian-American Mafia organization in the city that eventually fell under the control of Johnny Torrio in the 1920s [see chapter 6]. Its history, however, dates back to the very earliest days of the twentieth century.

As the city grew, so did its need for the forces of law and order. By 1850, with a population of 80,000, Chicago still had no properly organized police force; just a handful of 'watch marshals' charged with keeping order. Within five years a very limited formal policing force was established. Built over swamplands, the city was raised on stilts in the later 1850s to avoid sinking, creating a network of tunnels and subterranean lairs which would become the notorious haunts of those who wished to evade the watchful eyes of the law.

In these new tunnels beneath the city, a five-foot tall English immigrant called Roger Plant and his wife ran a combined saloon, gambling den and brothel between 1858 and 1868, named 'Under the Willow' for the tree on the surface that signified its subterranean location. It was known to the police as 'the Barracks'. Gangs of criminals, pickpockets, thieves, human traffickers and pimps would congregate throughout 'the Willows'. As a result, the entire area beneath Chicago became known simply as the 'under-world', a term that would soon become associated directly with wider criminal networks of gangsters and broader criminal activities.

Chicago was described as the 'gem of the prairie' by gang historian Herbert Asbury (author of *The Gangs of New York*, later filmed by Martin Scorsese). One of the area's 'gems' was the Sands, north of the Chicago River and out to Lake Michigan, packed with gambling dens, whorehouses and boarding rooms. In April 1857, newly elected Chicago Mayor 'Long John' Wentworth led a raid by police and firefighters on the Sands, in the hopes of eliminating some of the city's key crime dens. Gamblers and prostitutes were evicted, and up to fifteen buildings were demolished as a result.

The Civil War brought professional gamblers to Chicago in large numbers. As the economy of the South collapsed, 'gentleman' gamblers moved north, with many making their fortunes in Chicago during the war years. While others were fighting, criminal elements were busy making money.

Chicago also became a supply centre for the Union Army, presenting plenty of opportunity for corruption, graft and sharp practice. Members of the armed forces who passed through the city became fair game for the area's organized criminals, just as in the Old West when recently paid cattlemen had been targeted. The area around Clark Street and between Randolph and Monroe, known as 'Gamblers' Row', also became known as 'Hair Trigger Block', due to the preponderance of gunfights that broke out following disputed games of chance. One particular street corner, nicknamed 'Death's Corner', was a key ambush point where those who had not paid up to the notorious Black Hand blackmail gangs were assaulted. Between 1910 and 1911, there were up to thirty-eight Black Hand-related murders in the Little Italy district of Chicago, many carried out by a notorious figure known only as the 'shotgun man' who was never identified.

The real-life Mickey Finn, whose name came to be associated with drugged alcohol that renders the drinker unconscious, was an early Chicago gangster. He operated a saloon in the city in the 1870s. His 'Mickey Finn Special' contained a secret 'voodoo powder' as one of its main ingredients. Once knocked out, Finn would rifle through his victim's pockets and wallet, removing coins, notes or any other valuables found there.

The Chicago fire of October 1871 wiped out much of the city, destroying many of its original wooden buildings, and creating conditions ripe for looting and widespread criminal activity. The city began attracting the criminal element from other areas, including New York – many moved further west to escape others of their kind or in the hope of finding fresh fields to exploit. By 1879, Michael Cassius McDonald had become established as Chicago's first 'crime lord'. As well as bringing in his criminal associates from other places, McDonald sought political influence, exerting control over his successful mayoral candidate,

Carter Harrison, Sr, who served four terms until 1887. As payback, McDonald was awarded the bookmaking and gambling rights for the city and the entire state of Indiana, running his crime empire from a tavern known locally as 'The Store'. McDonald's own criminal henchmen adopted the phrase 'The Syndicate' for their organization.

During McDonald's reign he had control of various politicians and officials, such as Chicago Police Chief William McGarigle. The chief's association with proto-mobsters saw him tried for 'graft' (meaning political corruption, or payment for political favours), and he later fled to Canada to evade both the law and the Mob (as the American Mafia became known). McDonald had his rivals, such as the Valley Gang, a group of pickpockets and armed robbers who operated on the city's south side (they would later become allied to Al Capone). By 1900, the Valley Gang were functioning as muscle for hire to violently enforce the rule of the city's crime bosses.

McDonald was top dog of his criminal empire until his death in 1907. Others followed in his pioneering wake, including 'Big Jim' O'Leary, gambler Jacob 'Mont' Tennes, and Chicago First Ward Aldermen (a type of councilman) Michael 'Hinky Dink' Kenna and 'Bathhouse' John Coughlin. Political office and crime, especially gambling, continued to be closely associated throughout the city. These four men practically split the city between them, running profitable criminal gambling operations and staying out of each other's way.

The rise of the popularity of horse racing and the arrival of the telegraph changed the nature of the gambling business, with betting on horses (then legal) and the quick communication of winners and losers connected by the 'numbers racket'. Control of the racket and the information about race winners became key to the city's criminal enterprises. On the back of the numbers racket arose the protection racket, in which pay-offs were made to avoid raids on premises (known as 'policy shops') or attacks on the bookmakers' 'runners', young men who took the numerous collected gambling slips between betting parlour venues and the criminal headquarters.

From 1890, the growth of the 'red light' Levee area near the city docks provided another outlet for criminal activities, with rampant prostitution leading to the establishment of almost 200 brothels with names like The Little Green House or The House of All Nations. The area also boasted the Everleigh Club, a night spot for the city's elite, straight and criminal, run by the infamous brothel-keepers, the Everleigh Sisters.

An anti-vice reform movement gained ground in the city, led by the Civic Federation. Churches and social reformers alike joined forces in a futile attempt to rid Chicago of vice. By 1910, a formal Vice Commission had been established. Tales of 'white slavery', in which hundreds of women were said to be sold into prostitution in the city, formed the basis for a moral panic. As a result, the transportation of women for the purpose of prostitution became a Federal offence through the Mann Act (a law movie comedian Charlie Chaplin would fall foul of in the 1940s, as part of a smear campaign against him orchestrated by the FBI's J. Edgar Hoover). By 1914 the majority of the known bordellos in Chicago had been closed down, including the Everleigh Club, although this would only be a temporary state of affairs.

The victories of the Chicago reform movements would be short-lived. Vice and other criminal activities would continue in the city, but increasingly under the wire. Someone had to co-ordinate things, and first to fill the void was 'Big Jim' Colosimo, an Italian-American crime boss who took over the prostitution racket in the early 1900s and built a criminal empire on the back of it. His tendency to wear ostentatious diamonds also gave rise to the nickname 'Diamond Jim'.

His restaurant, Colosimo's Café, on South Wabash in the Levee became the social centre of the city's new rising criminal underworld. Due to his growing notoriety, and presumed wealth (from criminal enterprises), Colosimo and his key men fell victim to an outbreak of Black Hand extortion letters. Perceiving the threat from the Black Hand as a danger to his status and control over the city's criminal networks, Colosimo summoned a relative from New York, Johnny Torrio, to help him, and so kicked off a whole new era for gangsters in Chicago.

San Francisco

Immigration from China and the Far East to the west coast of the United States was largely to San Francisco, and with the law-abiding immigrants came the Chinese gangs, known as 'Tongs'. Spanish colonists had originally established San Francisco in 1776, but the California gold rush of the 1840s and 1850s had brought about sudden growth and wealth – and where there's wealth, crime surely follows.

This boom had given rise to the Barbary Coast, a 'red light' district and lawless area running from Pacific Street down to the docks. The saloons, dance halls and whorehouses here were home to much of the city's organized crime, including gambling, graft, vigilantism and prostitution. A gang called the 'Hounds', consisting of veterans of the Mexico–America war, as well as refugees from New York's Five Points and Bowery districts, ran much of the Barbary Coast area at first. They later became known as the Regulators, and would patrol the area, persecuting those of Spanish or Chinese ethnic origin and engaging in extortion. Chinese immigrant workers in the city came under attack, so they formed supportive groups which soon evolved (in some cases) into criminal enterprises. As a way of raising funds, the Tongs, offshoots of the home-grown Chinese Triads [see chapter 20], would create gambling houses and expand from there into other criminal activities, including extortion and protection rackets backed by violence.

A prime Tong leader was 'Little Pete', Fung Jin Toy, who was born in China in 1864 but emigrated along with his family to San Francisco in 1870. As a child he witnessed Tong warfare, especially a conflict between the Kwong Docks and Suey Sings gangs, inspiring him to study their methods and tactics. By 1885, Fung was a member of the Som Yop Tong, engaged in gang warfare over the opium trade. To protect himself against attack from the traditional Chinese weapons of cleavers and knives, he wore a chain mail vest and a reinforced hat.

By 1890, at the age of twenty-five, Fung was the overall leader of the Som Yop Tong, supervising the organization's interests in not only drug trafficking, but also gambling and prostitution. It was claimed that in his rise to power, and in his attempts to protect that power, 'Little Pete' had killed around fifty fellow gang members. He was given his nickname by the local newspapers, who became aware of his power over elected officials through generous bribery payments.

Fung was a well-known figure in San Francisco, especially when he began to wear his signature chain mail openly around town, accompanied by a pair of ostentatious bodyguards. He attracted the attention of rivals, who conspired to have him eliminated. Hired Tong assassins Lem Jung and Chew Tin Gop got to 'Little Pete' by abandoning traditional Chinese weaponry and adopting American-style firearms. Fung was shot five times on 23 January 1897, dying in a San Francisco barbershop. His assassins returned to China wealthy men.

Another San Francisco criminal gang were the Sydney Ducks, largely made up of ex-convicts from Australia (then Britain's penal colony), whose area of dominance became known as 'Sidney Town' [sic]. Between 1849 and 1851, the Sydney Ducks set fire to large parts of San Francisco in

order to disguise their criminal activities. Growing vigilantism on behalf of ordinary citizens and a gradually
better organized police force would bring an end to gangs
like the Sydney Ducks.

By 1871, San Francisco was a growing port town, but
it had only around a hundred policemen – roughly one
officer for every 1,500 people living there. The April
1906 earthquake and resulting fire razed much of the city,
destroying up to three-quarters of the buildings. Although
the city was rapidly rebuilt, the conditions were such that
in the aftermath of the earthquake, crime and looting ran
rampant. Much of Pacific Street and the Barbary Coast was
destroyed, allowing the city 'fathers' the chance to rebuild
the area as a law-abiding entertainment district known as
'Terrific Street'. The newly gentrified area didn't eliminate
crime altogether, but it did much to mitigate its extent.

In 1911, new Mayor James Rolph took office for what
would be the first of ten terms of governance, dedicated to
major reform – supported by William Randolph Hearst's
San Francisco Examiner newspaper which launched
an anti-crime and graft crusade in the city in 1913. One
result of this activity was the Red Light Abatement Act
that resulted in the closure of most of the city's brothels in
1917. Like most large American cities, however, organized
crime would return to San Francisco with a vengeance
with the arrival of Prohibition in 1920. [For Los Angeles,
see chapters 9 and 10].

3

THE FIVE POINTS GANGS

Prohibition – the restrictions on the availability of alcohol imposed upon the United States from 1920 – didn't come out of nowhere, but it certainly provided a boost for the rising gangsters of New York and Chicago. Since the turn of the century, criminal gangs had formed in both cities, producing leaders and kingpins who would be in prime position to capitalize on the banning of alcohol by sating a national thirst through criminal activities.

The Five Points Gangs

As a breeding ground for organized crime gangs and would-be gangsters, the Five Points area of New York became notorious. The area fell within the Sixth Ward of Manhattan and comprised the meeting point of five individual streets: Mulberry, Anthony, Cross, Orange and Little Water (some have since changed names or disappeared altogether). Falling between Broadway and the

Bowery, Five Points linked New York high society with underworld criminality. Members of the main gang that controlled the area were largely of Italian-American origin, and some would mentor future key gangland figures such as Al Capone, 'Lucky' Luciano and Johnny Torrio.

By the 1820s, the area around the district was home to waves of Irish immigrants, some of the later ones fleeing the famine of the 1840s, and it was largely made up of gambling dens and brothels. The original tenements built in the area were established over a landfill that barely contained an old sewage pond that frequently leaked into the buildings, spreading disease. Land values failed to grow, and residents were encouraged to move out and move on, making way for each new set of transient occupants. No one invested financially, spiritually or morally, in the Five Points area, so it was left to rot and the people with it.

Over the next fifty years, Italian and Eastern European Jewish immigrants filled the district, adding to the ethnic mix and sparking off a street war between the different immigrant gangs. Initially, many of the gangs were organized in self-defence, aiming to protect new arrivals from the predations of others. However, these self-defence units would soon turn aggressively hostile to other, newer waves of immigrants who threatened to move in on their turf.

There were many gangs operating in New York in the years leading up to Prohibition. Among the most prominent early groupings were the Forty Thieves, one of the earliest gangs of Irish immigrants active from the early 1820s for the better part of twenty-five years, along with the Kerryonians, made up exclusively of immigrants from County Kerry in Ireland, and the Roach Guards, who originally formed to protect local liquor merchants but who soon turned to wider criminal pursuits, including robbery and murder – they engaged in an ongoing feud with the Dead Rabbits, whose emblem was a dead rabbit impaled upon a spike and carried into battle.

The middle of the century saw a shift in power to such gangs as the Bowe Brothers, who controlled the waterfronts and dockyards of the East River between the 1840s and the 1860s; the Patsy Conroy gang of river pirates who operated from about 1860 to 1874; the Swamp Angels, who dominated the New York Harbour area from the 1850s into the post-Civil War period, and who used the sewers to move contraband goods and men in and out of the city, eventually merging with the White Hand Gang by the end of the century; and the Grady Gang, made up of Civil War veterans who operated around Broadway in the 1860s, modelling themselves after Old West outlaws like Billy the Kid.

Ethnic Irish gangs operating in Five Points included the Whyos, a post-Civil War grouping that controlled much of the area and its criminal enterprises between the late 1860s and the early 1890s. Their odd name came from the greeting members would call to one another, a version of 'Why-Oh', modelled after the sound of birds or owls. They'd grown out of an earlier gang known as the Chichesters, consisting of up to one hundred members who were allied with the Dead Rabbits gang (particularly active through the 1850s) against the Bowery Boys (a largely anti-Catholic grouping based north of Five Points) from the 1820s. Many of these earlier gangs were amalgamated or absorbed into larger groupings like the Whyos after the Civil War.

The later years of the century, up to the arrival of Prohibition, saw other groupings rise to prominence, like the 19th Street Gang, an anti-Protestant Irish group of pickpockets, muggers and thieves, big in the 1870s; the Gopher Gang, who came out of the Manhattan neighbourhood of Hell's Kitchen (also home to the Rhodes Gang) to dominate much of the area's bordellos and gambling dens by the 1890s until about 1910; and the Hudson Dusters, a successor to the Gopher Gang, who took on the gangs from the West side, such as the Potashes and the Boodles, and who were in turn replaced by the Marginals, whose members declined due to inter-gang assassinations and police crackdowns between 1915 and 1919.

The gang fights sometimes became an end in themselves in Five Points, with violence rivalling money as the point of gang life. More often than not, the individual gangs would temporarily put aside their own differences to team up for assaults on the forces of law and order: regular running battles in the streets between police (largely Irish) and various gangs were not uncommon. Five Points gangs were sometimes employed by the corrupt politicians from Tammany Hall to form the muscle they needed to enforce their will at the ballot box. The connections between the gangs and the politicians would only be strengthened, not weakened, by the imposition of Prohibition in 1920.

Kelly versus Eastman

Some individuals were bigger than the gangs: often the men who led them or at least co-ordinated and benefited from their illicit activities, the gangsters. The first in a long line of hoodlums who rose to become a gangster leader was the Five Points Gang founder, Paul Kelly.

Italian-born Paolo Antonio Vaccarelli adopted the more Irish-sounding name of Paul Kelly in America when he became a professional boxer in the early 1890s. His prizefight winnings allowed him to invest in New York property, including bordellos in the Bowery and athletic clubs, which served as front organizations for the gangs of street kids that formed the nucleus of his Five Points Gang. His headquarters were two connected buildings at 57 and 59 Great Jones Street (they are still there, and were the site of artist Jean-Michel Basquiat's drug-overdose death in 1988), comprising the Little Naples Café and the New Brighton Athletic Club. From this base, Kelly would mastermind his operations in the area west of the Bowery, including hiring his men out to Tammany Hall politician

'Big Tim' Sullivan to 'motivate' voters to cast their ballots in the 'right' way and keeping those inclined to vote for rival candidates away from the polling booths, by intimidation or violent means if necessary.

Kelly was always well-turned out, concerned with his appearance, despite his pugilist past. He liked to surprise people who made assumptions about him as a gangland kingpin, fluently speaking a variety of languages including Italian (of course), but also French and Spanish. His deceptive dress sense disguised an individual ready to turn violent at the drop of a hat if it helped him get his way. He'd established the New Brighton Athletic Club to take advantage of a loophole in the law that allowed boxing matches in private clubs – the next door café existed to feed and water the patrons of his boxing bouts. It soon became a key hang-out for hoodlums and gang members from all over New York.

Kelly's main rival in gangsterdom was Monk Eastman, head honcho of the Eastman Gang who operated largely east of the Bowery and were among the last of the gangs to dominate the Five Points area in the lead up to Prohibition. Born Edward Eastman in 1875, the son of a Civil War vet, Monk was a tough-looking thug with even more of a pugilist's mug than Kelly.

As well as the usual extortion and prostitution rackets, Eastman had other early interests including a bike rental scam and the 'stuss' card game, a Jewish variant of 'faro' played in saloons which died out before the First World War. Having at one time set up a pet shop with the help of his grandfather, Eastman would always list 'bird seller' as his occupation on official forms – he was often accompanied in his activities by his tame pigeons. He was first arrested in 1889, but the three months he spent on Blackwell's Island penitentiary for larceny proved to be a very useful criminal education. Eastman worked as a bouncer at the New Irving Hall on Broome Street, near his pet shop. This was a hang-out for Tammany Hall politicians, who would often put Eastman's gang to work strong-arming voters during elections. He lived on East Fifth Street, just two blocks from Kelly's New Brighton Athletic Club.

The feuding between Kelly and Eastman and their respective gangs came to a head in September 1903 with a lengthy gunfight on Rivington Street that involved dozens of gangsters. At least one was killed and another wounded fatally as a result of the mêlée; civilians were injured and members of Eastman's gang arrested. To solve the problem, Tammany Hall politicians stepped in, as they had active interests in both gangs. A one-on-one boxing match was arranged between one-time professional fighter Kelly and the novice Eastman, who only looked like he'd been a boxer in the past. An old barn in the Bronx was the location of the two-hour bout in 1903. Unfortunately, the outcome was a square draw with both men suffering heavy injuries. The gang warfare picked right up again as though nothing had happened.

Early the following year, Eastman attempted a stick-up robbery of a wealthy-looking young man on Broadway and 42nd Street. Unfortunately his target was being followed by Pinkerton detectives who'd been hired by the young man's parents to keep him safe. Eastman shot at the detectives while trying to make his getaway, but was captured by a patrolling policeman. Seizing the opportunity to end the Eastman–Kelly gang war, the men of Tammany Hall refused to provide Eastman with the customary protection and he went down for a decade, but only served five years. His gang splintered in his absence.

With Eastman out of the picture, Paul Kelly had control over Five Points and beyond. However, he was the target of a hit attempted by former lieutenants of Eastman's gang, Razor Riley and James 'Biff' Ellison. The attack at Kelly's Great Jones Street headquarters killed his bodyguard, Bill Harrington, and wounded Kelly, who escaped. The negative publicity caused by the armed raid saw New York Police Commissioner William McAdoo close down the club.

Eastman served in the First World War after his jail time, returning to a life of petty crime afterwards, but with no gang power base behind him. He partnered with a corrupt Prohibition agent who shot and killed him in a squabble over money on the morning of 26 December 1920. Kelly reverted to his birth name of Paul Vaccarelli and moved from street crime into labour relations as Vice-President of the International Longshoreman's Association, organizing strikes and – in an echo of his old ways – providing muscle for labour disputes into the 1920s. He died on 3 April 1936, just at the height of classic American gangsterism. The long war between Eastman and Kelly was finally over, and there were no winners.

The coming of Prohibition

The organized gangs of the Old West and the political and social corruption that followed in the developing cities of the mid to late-nineteenth century saw crime and criminal gangs flourish, with the forces of law and order sometimes struggling to keep up. There would, however, be one major piece of American legislation that would truly give rise to the age of the American gangster: the Prohibition of alcohol instituted between 1920 and 1933.

Although the 18th Amendment to the American Constitution banning the manufacture, transportation and sale of alcohol took effect overnight, between 16 and 17 January 1920, it had been decades in the making. The battle to turn the United States into a 'dry' nation had been raging almost since the Colonial period of the seventeenth century. After all, the Puritans had brought wine with them in their ships that journeyed to the 'new world' in the 1630s. However, as early as May 1657 the General Court of Massachusetts had declared the sale of strong liquor to be illegal.

Alcohol itself was never really the problem. It was the abuse of alcohol, the problems of behaviour caused by drunkenness and the related social problems that made it an issue for government. Some of the strongest anti-alcohol campaigns were run by religious groups and pro-suffrage women's groups. Alcohol and the American government would be closely entwined, largely down to the fact that the majority of government tax revenue was generated from alcohol sales. By 1910, the Federal government made $200 million in alcohol taxes, 30 per cent of all Federal revenues overall.

Almost as soon as America gained independence from the United Kingdom, battles over the control of alcohol began. The Whiskey Rebellion of 1791 in Western Pennsylvania began as a protest against taxes on the alcohol Pennsylvania farmers made from their excess grain and corn – it was far easier and cheaper to transport in the form of distilled liquid. The new taxes imposed were part of a deliberate extension of government power, partly as a way to pay down debts from the Revolutionary War that the Federal government had assumed after individual states failed to pay. Violence erupted during attempts by officials to collect the taxes, culminating in an armed stand-off between US Marshals and a 500-strong rebel militia in 1794. Conflict was avoided, although there were arrests, and the tax was eventually repealed in 1801.

There were three main waves of campaigning for nation-wide Prohibition of alcohol in the 1840s, the 1880s and the 1910s. The American Temperance Society (ATS), formed in 1826, pioneered the 'dry' crusade. Its 1.5 million members, up to 60 per cent of whom were women, took the 'pledge', a declaration of abstinence from drinking alcohol. Although focused on the 'demon drink', the ATS swept up many committed to wider reforms in American society, including abolitionists against slavery, and those pursuing various rights for women, including the right to vote.

By the 1840s there was a stronger religious tinge to those who campaigned against alcohol. This abstinence drive was championed by several devout groups, but especially the Methodists. Slowly, though, it seemed abstinence alone was not enough and the campaign broadened to take in 'satanic saloons' and the 'sins' engendered by alcohol. The places where drink was sold to willing patrons became associated with other dubious activities, such as prostitution.

There were some early successes, such as the 1851 state-wide prohibition in Maine, a move quickly followed by up to a dozen other states. These provisions, however, were all repealed by the end of the middle decade of the nineteenth century due to social unrest and opposition riots. A new drive to tax alcohol developed around the time of the American Civil War of 1861–5, seen by government as a way of raising the funds to pay off another war debt – it would take until 1916 to clear those loans. So-called 'moonshine' – home brewed liquor – remained untaxed, hence its prevalence, particularly in the South. By 1875, 20 per cent of Federal revenues came from these new nationwide excise taxes on alcohol sales.

Two organizations drove the cause forward in the 1880s: the nationwide Prohibition Party, founded in 1869; and the Women's Christian Temperance Union (WTCU), created in 1873. The WTCU saw abuse of alcohol, primarily by men, as a threat to the American family, although their organization embraced several other, particularly Socialist, causes. By 1881, as a result of such campaigns, Kansas had outlawed alcohol in the State's Constitution, suggesting a new legal way forward for those who wished to see such a ban enforced nationwide – an amendment to the United States' Constitution. Among the prominent leaders of the campaign were Frances Willard of the WTCU and Carrie Nation, a campaigner who took the struggle into her own hands by attacking saloons' stocks of whisky and beer with an axe. Other, more refined ladies stuck to prayer and non-violently picketing places where drink was consumed. Slowly others would follow the example of Texas in becoming 'dry states', including Iowa in 1882, North Dakota in 1889, Oklahoma in 1907, Mississippi and Georgia in 1908, North Carolina and Tennessee in 1909, and West Virginia in 1914. During the First World War other states – mainly in the South – would follow, preparing the way for the imposition of nationwide Prohibition from 1920.

By the end of the nineteenth century there had been a notable drop-off in alcohol consumption in America, with fermented beer replacing distilled whisky, a change driven by the tastes of the working men of immigrant populations. Eighty per cent of saloons across America – whose numbers tripled between 1870 and 1900 – were owned by 'first generation' Americans. In San Francisco there was almost one saloon for every 100 men.

The rise of the saloons also gave rise to the Anti-Saloon League (ASL), an organization formed in 1893 that effectively superseded the Prohibition Party and the WCTU It campaigned against the places where working men gathered, taking them away from their families and tempting them into drink – the attraction of a 'free lunch', food laid on by the saloon owners, was often enough to get men inside. The brewers attempted to argue that beer was less harmful than distilled whisky, in the hope they would escape the sanction of campaigners. Brewers often owned saloons, known as 'tied houses', paying for their extravagant decoration, and they also became involved in such political machines as that run by the Democrats in New York that manipulated the working men to vote their candidates into office.

This electoral strategy worked both ways, however. Church networks became just as organized in their opposition to the saloons and to alcohol, and co-ordinated their supporters and congregations to vote against 'wet' office

holders. Wayne Wheeler of the ASL was particularly effective in arranging the election of pro-Prohibition candidates
by organizing voters to focus on that single issue at the
expense of everything else they might or might not advo-
cate. The same combination of religious groups (including
Baptists, Quakers and Lutherans), women's groups, and
rural and ethnic groupings were the driving force behind
the campaigns of the 1880s through to the turn of the century. The 'wet' opposition consisted largely of Protestant
and Roman Catholic groups who did not support a role for
government in defining personal morality.

Crime was seen as a symptom of the influx into the
newly developing urban cities on the East coast of immigrant ethnic groups who frequented the saloons, where
their votes were bought en masse by the big-name political operators known as 'bosses'. Prohibitionism was driven
by racist and nativist (the Anglo-Saxon 'divine right' that
founded America) beliefs, and a reforming zeal that united
social reformers and the socially repressive together in the
same cause.

For government, the biggest problem of the rising
Prohibition tide was the potential loss of revenue from
alcohol taxes: no legal alcohol meant no tax revenues. The
answer came in the 1913 adoption of the 16th Amendment
to the Constitution that established a nationwide federal income tax. That same year saw the movement for
National Prohibition adopt the concept of achieving their
aim through a further amendment to the Constitution.
The women's movement would win a victory with the 19th
Amendment, passed in 1920, that prohibited any citizen
being denied the vote on the basis of sex. The Prohibition
movement and the female suffrage cause had long been
entangled.

The 65th Congress, convened in January 1917, had
– largely as a result of campaigns by the likes of Wayne
Wheeler – seen 'drys' outnumber 'wets' by over two to

one in both the Republican and Democratic parties. The involvement of America in the First World War served both to sideline the issue of Prohibition as an immediate concern, while also offering another reason for its adoption – resources used to make alcohol, such as grain, would be better directed towards the war effort.

The eventual Resolution for a Constitutional Amendment banning alcohol was adopted in both houses of the US government in December 1917. By 16 January 1919 the required majority of thirty-six states (of the forty-eight states that then made up the union) and a two-thirds majority in both houses of Congress and the Senate had ratified the new amendment. In October that year, Congress voted to pass the Volstead Act, named after lawyer Andrew Volstead who chaired the House Judiciary Committee that managed the legislation, that would enforce the 18th Amendment. From midnight on the evening of 16 January 1920, it would be illegal to manufacture, transport or sell alcohol anywhere in the United States (although neither Connecticut nor Rhode Island ratified the 18th Amendment).

From 17 January 1920, the fifth largest industry in the United States was outlawed. Just over 1,500 newly established Federal Enforcement Agents were charged with upholding the new law across the United States, an almost impossible task. The adoption of Prohibition would lead directly to the establishment of the first American nationwide criminal syndicate and the rise of the gangster class.

PART TWO: PROHIBITION AND AFTER: RISE OF THE AMERICAN GANGSTER

4

'LUCKY' LUCIANO: THE MAN WHO ORGANIZED CRIME

His nickname was 'Lucky', but it turned out to be something of a misnomer. Salvatore Lucania, born in Sicily in 1897, was the gangster who would become known as 'the man who organized organized crime'. His family immigrated to the United States in 1907 when he was aged ten, settling in the Lower East Side of Manhattan among many other immigrant Italian communities. Young Salvatore quickly began making a name for himself as a tough guy. He was a regular truant from school (his lack of English held him back) where he extorted his fellow pupils, demanding two cents each day with the threat of a beating. During 1914 his despairing parents sent him to a special educational institution for two months. He finished with school and took up his one and only legitimate job as a delivery boy for a hat maker, earning $7 per week.

It was games of chance that led Lucky to a life of crime:

he won $244 in a dice game, quickly quit his job and decided he could earn more money through street scams. That saw him forming a street gang that included two school friends as members: Meyer Lansky and Benjamin Siegel. One of his first business interests was an extension of his school activities, offering Jewish youngsters protection from Italian and Irish gangs at the rate of ten cents per week. He also spent some time running with the Five Points Gang, becoming friendly with Paul Kelly's second-in-command Johnny Torrio, who'd recruited him. His powerful allies couldn't protect Lucania from an opium trafficking arrest in 1916 and he served six months in a youth reformatory. His other gang-related activities included robbing pawn shops and moneylenders, as well as hitting low-level banks on the Lower East Side. Around then he adopted an easier to say name. It was certainly easier for the cops, who repeatedly arrested him, than his birth name: so was created Charles Luciano.

The substantial demand for alcohol that still existed in the wake of Prohibition from 1920 gave Luciano a new focus for his criminal activities. An alliance with Lansky and Siegel was hugely profitable from its inception. Luciano's bootlegging business – for which he imported Scotch from Scotland, rum from the Caribbean and whisky from Canada – was boosted by the patronage of Arnold 'the brain' Rothstein. Reputed to have fixed the 1919 baseball World Series (having won big by betting against the 'losing' favourites, the Chicago White Sox), Rothstein was engaged in reshaping organized crime in New York to make it more businesslike and less thuggish.

Born in New York in 1882, Rothstein came from a well-off background but turned to crime while his older brother studied to become a rabbi. A mathematical prodigy with a talent for numbers, Rothstein became addicted to gambling and figured out how he could make money from it. By the age of twenty-eight in 1910, he had his own casino that served as the base for his criminal operations involving the fixing of horse races. He was reputedly a millionaire by the age of thirty. Rothstein sensed great business opportunities in Prohibition, and wanted to sign up an operator like Luciano to help bring in 'the product' to serve his chain of speakeasies – illegal underground public drinking dens that had sprung up nationwide in the wake of Prohibition. Luciano also acquired his sense of style from Rothstein who was always something of a snappy dresser.

By 1925, 'Lucky' Luciano was grossing $12 million each year and making around $4 million personal profit through bootlegging liquor. He reinvested his cash in other criminal enterprises, such as gambling dens and labour racketeering (simply another form of extortion). In partnership with Lansky and others, Luciano boasted of the biggest bootlegging operation in New York, one that extended as far as Philadelphia. He was one of the 'Big Six' bootleggers that included his cohorts Lansky and Siegel, as well as Louis 'Lepke' Buchalter, Jacob 'Gurrah' Shapiro, and Abner 'Longy' Zwillman. Luciano's time in the sun was coming to an end, however. His criminal mentor and protector, Arnold Rothstein, was assassinated in November 1928, apparently over an unpaid gambling debt.

In the resulting power vacuum following Rothstein's death, Mafia rivals Guiseppe 'Joe the Boss' Masseria and Salvatore Maranzano tried to bring Luciano into their respective organizations, planning to subsume his bootlegging business within their wider organizations. Both objected to him being in cahoots with Jews like Rothstein and Lansky rather than Italians, and death threats followed to make Luciano toe the line. He eventually came down on the side of Masseria, resulting in near-deadly reprisals from Maranzano's gang that gave Luciano his facial scars and drooping left eye, and the nickname 'Lucky' as he was one of the few who survived being 'taken for a ride' by Maranzano's men, as happened to him in 1929.

In the late 1920s, Luciano was Masseria's chief lieuten-ant during the early days of the 'Castellammarese War' that ran on until the spring of 1931. The power struggle between Masseria and Maranzano (who'd been born in the Castellammarese del Golfo region in Sicily, so giving the conflict its name) was over who would control the lucrative crime syndicate then emerging in New York on the back of Prohibition. Luciano was one of the leading players who would continue to build his own criminal power base amid the fighting.

Both Masseria and Maranzano were regarded as 'old timers' who had started their criminal careers back in the 'homeland' of Italy. Known as 'Mustache Petes' (Sicilian Mafia members), they had failed to adapt to the new ways of doing things in America taken up by the 'young Turks' who'd either been born in the US or arrived when they were very young, like Luciano, and who were happy to work in concert with fellow gangsters of Jewish or Irish origin.

Establishing a national crime network

Luciano attempted to secure his position by forging inter-state alliances with other criminal kingpins. One of seven he set up in a loose organization known as the 'Seven Group' (Luciano was superstitious about certain numbers) involved Enoch 'Nucky' Johnson, the real-life mobster who inspired the character of Nucky Thompson in HBO's gangster television series *Boardwalk Empire* (2010–14). Johnson ran Atlantic City on the New Jersey coast – an area where Prohibition essentially remained, for all prac-tical purposes, unenforced – and spanned the worlds of organized crime and corrupt politics to his own advantage and that of his friends and associates. His various political and social positions helped him effectively disguise his role as Atlantic City's biggest bootlegger during Prohibition, making him and his team obvious partners for Luciano's squad. In defence of his actions, Johnson once said: 'We have whiskey, wine, women, song and slot machines [in Atlantic City]. I won't deny it and I won't apologize for it. If the majority of the people didn't want them they wouldn't be profitable and they would not exist. The fact that they do exist proves to me that the people want them.'

Other members of Luciano's 'Seven Group', besides himself and Johnson, were the Lansky–Siegel gang, covering New York City; Joe Adonis, operating in Brooklyn; Long Island and Northern Jersey 'bosses', Longy Zwillman and Willie Moretti; Boston's 'King' Solomon, who looked after New England; and Harry 'Nig' Rosen, who dominated the Philadelphia operation. By 1929, the 'Seven Group' between them had struck up arrangements with up to twenty-two different organized groups smuggling alcohol (and engaging in other criminal activities) from Florida to Maine and as far west as the Mississippi River.

Even this geographical dominance was not enough for Luciano, who in concert with Meyer Lansky took a far more capitalistic, businesslike approach to the world of organized crime, following the example set by Rothstein. Rather than being in violent competition with one another, Luciano floated the idea of a national organization in which all the mobsters would co-operate in dividing up the lucrative illicit trade that Prohibition had unwittingly created. He called for a 'national convention' of crime bosses, but it took months to arrange, although the most suitable venue never seemed to be in doubt: Atlantic City. All the main names attended the May 1929 summit, from Chicago's Al Capone (whose gang of attendees included 'Waxey' Gordon), then a rising star of crime, to Moe Dalitz, Lou Rothkopf and Charles Polizzi from the Cleveland outfit, as well as most of the members of Luciano's 'Seven Group' (Lansky also took the opportunity to combine the trip with his honeymoon).

First item on the agenda was a huge party, with the

majority of the 'delegates' having brought wives and girlfriends (or both) with them for the occasion. The serious stuff would not begin until the second day when the assorted gangsters held their summit on the beach, removing their socks and rolling up their trouser legs to walk along the water's edge. In complete privacy, America's top crime bosses collaborated in the establishment of a national network of their organizations, with pledges made to avoid violent confrontations between the gangs – if they could organize things right, claimed Luciano, there was no reason why everyone should not benefit equally well from Prohibition. 'There was business enough to make us all rich,' Capone claimed to have explained to the other gangsters. 'It was time to stop all the killing and look on our business as other men look on theirs . . .'

The Castellammarese War

The Castellammarese War – or more accurately 'wars', as there were multiple inter-gangster conflicts in the period from early 1928 until April 1931 – was the battle between Joseph Masseria and Salvatore Maranzano for control of the Italian-American Mob. For most of the 1920s, Masseria was the undisputed boss of the New York Mafia, the crime families who'd relocated to the city mainly from Sicily. As well as Luciano, he had Vito Genovese, Albert 'Mad Hatter' Anastasia, Joe Adonis, Alfred Mineo, Willie Moretti and Frank Costello as 'underbosses' on his side.

Sicilian crime boss Don Vito Ferro wanted a slice of Masseria's action, especially when Prohibition proved to be so lucrative for America's gangsters. He sent Maranzano to take control – by fair means or foul – of all Mafia operations in the United States, starting with Masseria's outfit on the East coast. On Maranzano's side of the equation were Stefano 'The Undertaker' Magaddino, Joseph 'Joe Bananas' Bonanno, Joe Aiello and Joseph Profaci. Although initially a fight between these two old-time crime lords for control over the rich pickings the late 1920s had to offer, the conflict also turned into an opportunity for the 'young Turks' to take on the older generation and thereby supplant them. That's when Luciano saw his opportunity.

To begin with, hostilities between the factions largely consisted of hijacking each other's liquor trucks, transporting the booze down from Canada or in from boats moored off the coast. As time passed, however, things turned more violent. In early 1930, Masseria ordered a 'hit' on Gaspar Milazzo, followed by a takedown of one of his own men, Gaetano Reina, who'd switched sides to support Maranzano. The remaining Reina family unsurprisingly threw their lot in with Maranzano, and the gangster shooting war began in earnest.

Maranzano's forces began taking out Masseria's men, with two executed in August and one in September. By then, Masseria had wiped out Maranzano ally Joe Aiello in Chicago, a killing that Al Capone attempted to take credit for. The reprisals against Masseria's gang were swift, including the murder of his key ally Steve Ferrigno. Several nervous members of Masseria's remaining squad swiftly defected to the Maranzano side.

Luciano and Vito Genovese opened a channel of communication to Maranzano himself, offering to topple Masseria from within his organization, if only to bring an end to the debilitating conflict. On 15 April 1931, while eating at the Nuova Villa Tammaro restaurant in Coney Island, Joe Masseria was gunned down, along with two henchmen. Luciano, who'd set up the hit, was there, but just before the pre-arranged shooting he had gone to the bathroom. Four gunmen – Genovese, Albert Anastasia, Joe Adonis and Benjamin 'Bugsy' Siegel – were said to have taken part to ensure the job was done properly. Masseria died from gunshot wounds to the head, back and chest.

The Castellammarese War was over, but the killings hadn't finished. Luciano took over what was left of the

Masseria gang, and recognized Maranzano as the 'capo di tutti capi' or 'boss of all bosses'. In a shake-up of the organization, Maranzano established the 'Five Families' of the New York 'American Mafia' (distinct from the Sicilian original), with Luciano in charge of what would eventually become the Genovese crime family – the other families were the Profaci (which later became Columbo), Gagliano (later Lucchese), Maranzano (later Bonanno) and Vincent Mangano (later Gambino). The other major cities, such as Chicago, would each have a single Mafia family in charge.

Maranzano didn't have long to enjoy the fruits of his new organized crime structure. On 10 September 1931, he was shot and stabbed to death in his Park Avenue office in Manhattan by a team of Jewish hitmen who had been recruited for the task by Meyer Lansky, and included Bugsy Siegel. They gained entry by pretending to be tax inspectors who wanted to see Maranzano's accounts. Luciano had struck before Maranzano could come after him. There followed the legendary 'Night of the Italian Vespers' during which many of the older Mafia members were eliminated, leaving Luciano as the undisputed kingpin of all the New York crime families – although there is some doubt as to whether more than a handful of mobsters were actually eliminated in this so-called Mafia 'purge'. Five years of relative peace between the gangs would follow as members of the Syndicate toed the line and split the wealth of Prohibition peacefully among themselves.

The Dewey days
The attack on Luciano back in 1929 that had given him his distinctive scar had also made his name in the press. Although things were considerably quieter after the end of the Castellammarese War, the police still had a vested interest in depicting people like 'Lucky' Luciano as criminal masterminds to be feared by the public. In 1935, prosecutor Thomas E. Dewey was appointed by the State Governor

as a special district attorney in Manhattan with a remit to aggressively pursue the Mob and political corruption. He rapidly recruited a staff to aid him, including investigators, process servers, administrators and clerks. He had access to a squad of police officers arranged by New York mayor Fiorello LaGuardia.

Dewey's primary interest was in organized crime that had grown out of Prohibition (which ended in 1933), activities on a large scale that were orchestrated and could cross county and even state lines, including such activities as extortion, the 'numbers' racket and prostitution. He also set out to eliminate or reduce the political corruption built around the Tammany Hall machine that often had connections with the kind of gangsters who were also behind much organized crime.

Dewey's first target was Dutch Schultz who had been tried twice before, but had always escaped conviction. Born Arthur Flegenheimer in 1901, Schultz started his criminal life as a burglar (which put him behind bars for a while) before turning to bootlegging booze following Prohibition, opening a string of speakeasies across the Bronx, and running trucking operations that brought alcohol into the city. He moved into other neighbourhoods, coming into conflict with Jack 'Legs' Diamond in Manhattan. Diamond was driven out when he survived a machine-gun attack in 1929. Schultz's rapid expansion then brought him both to the attention of Luciano – who attempted to control him – and Thomas Dewey, who pursued him for tax evasion.

Schultz threatened to deal with the Dewey situation in the simplest way possible: he'd have Dewey killed. For Luciano, who was making the most of this 'quiet period' where his organized crime schemes could flourish without spates of killing, this public declaration was far too high-profile. Before Schultz could act and bring further heat down on the Five Families and their activities, Luciano and the members of The Commission (as the group meeting of the family heads was known) had Schultz killed instead. On 23 October 1935, thirty-four-year-old Dutch Schultz was shot in the bathroom of his headquarters at the Palace Chophouse in Newark, New Jersey – he died later in hospital. His two bodyguards and his accountant were also killed in the attack.

These killings only served to turn Dewey's interest directly upon Luciano and his co-conspirators. Dewey arranged for a huge number of brothels in the New York area to be raided, with the prostitutes and the 'madams' who ran them arrested. He was convinced that in this way he could connect the illegal earnings from prostitution directly to Luciano. Dewey was able to coerce testimony from a trio of prostitutes – in return for their immunity from prosecution – implicating Luciano as the overall controller of organized prostitution in the New York and New Jersey area. In a heated atmosphere, Dewey was able to secure the conviction of Charles Luciano in 1936 for 'white slavery' with sixty-two counts of 'compulsory prostitution'. It now appears that in his zeal to win a conviction, Dewey was himself corrupt in procuring false testimony under oath from witnesses. His need to win successful convictions overrode his scruples, it seems.

Luciano was convicted for a period of between thirty and fifty years and sent to Dannemora prison (now the Clinton Correctional Facility) in Clinton County, New York, where he served ten years. Dewey's career prospered, with him securing further high-profile convictions, such as that of the former president of the New York Stock Exchange for embezzlement. He would prosecute American Nazi leaders during the Second World War and become New York's District Attorney. That was only a stepping stone to a successful political career as the New York State Governor and eventual Republican United States Presidential candidate in 1944 and 1948.

The Second World War made strange allies of law

enforcement and the Mob. Luciano was just one of several gangsters recruited by Naval Intelligence to help mitigate waterfront sabotage on the East coast, and thwart the efforts of German spies. The mobster was transferred to a jail near Albany with instructions to gather information on enemy activities from jailed dock racketeers and relay it to the authorities. Information obtained in this way led to the June 1942 arrest of eight German agents who'd landed on the East coast from a U-boat. Documents found on them outlined a planned two-year campaign of sabotage at defence plants, bridges and railroads along the East coast. Luciano was also useful, under the codename 'Operation Underworld', in supplying the names of contacts abroad who could help the Allied invasion forces who landed in Sicily in 1943. After the war the US government denied they'd colluded with gangsters to achieve war aims; there was even some speculation that some dock sabotage, including a series of fires, had been carried out by the Mob themselves so that Luciano could volunteer to help.

At long last, Luciano's nicknamed proved briefly accurate. He was granted executive clemency by the very man who had convicted him: Thomas Dewey, then New York's Governor. As he'd never bothered to become a US citizen, Luciano was deported to Italy in February 1946. Before the end of that year he was in Cuba running new criminal enterprises, including a casino with Meyer Lansky. The US, claiming Luciano was now a major drug trafficker using Cuba as a base to smuggle heroin into America, put pressure on Cuba to send Luciano back to Italy, which they did in early 1947. That didn't stop his activities, though, and he continued to shift drugs from Corsica and Turkey into America. He began collaborating with French mobsters, sowing the seeds of the post-war 'French connection' in drug trafficking.

Luciano initially lived well in Italy, generating income from his drug smuggling and being paid homage by his successors still active in the United States. However, by the 1950s, Luciano and his like were regarded by the new names in organized crime as 'Mustache Petes' themselves, just as he'd looked upon Maranzano and Masseria back in the 1920s. The money stopped flowing and his authority ebbed away. Luciano began planning a 'tell-all' memoir of his days in the Mob, a move that irritated the still very much active Meyer Lansky, who was based in Florida and Cuba. He was behind at least one attempt to rub out his old boss with an assassination attempt in Naples. Again, on that occasion Luciano was indeed Lucky.

It was a heart attack that finally felled Salvatore Lucania aka Charles Luciano aka 'Lucky'. He died aged 64 in an airport in Naples on 26 January 1962, while waiting to meet a film producer to discuss a biographical movie. His last wish was to be buried in New York City, where he'd made his mark as the man who finally 'organized' crime. However, the US authorities did their best to block such a move. Finally, a Federal court unexpectedly ruled in Luciano's favour – he was still not an American citizen, even in death, but the court ruled that a corpse could not be a citizen of any country and so could not be subject to immigration rules. His siblings arranged for his remains to be interred in the family vault in St John's Cemetery in Queens, New York. Even in death, 'Lucky' Luciano was still running rings around those in America who made the rules.

5

MURDER, INC.: LANSKY, SIEGEL AND THE MOB ASSASSINS

It was a catchy tag. 'Murder, Inc.' was the buzz phrase the American press dreamed up as shorthand to refer to the organized crime groups who conducted a series of high-profile assassinations (more often than not of fellow mobsters) throughout the 1930s and 1940s. Two of the founders of the group were a pair of Charles 'Lucky' Luciano's top lieutenants: Meyer Lansky and Benjamin 'Bugsy' Siegel. Together they created the 'enforcement arm' of the American Mafia that was responsible for anywhere between an estimated 400 and 1,000 contract killings across two decades.

Murder, Inc. emerged from the establishment of the Syndicate at the May 1929 meeting of Mob bosses organized by Luciano. Following good business practice, a protocol was developed to deal with 'problems' that could only be handled through assassination, whether it was an over-zealous Mob boss, an out-of-control low-level gangster, or a high-profile politician who wasn't co-operating. A single, specialized unit was established to carry out directed killings nationwide, although local 'family' heads would still retain the right to execute local 'hits'. The big fish, though, would be taken care of by Murder, Inc., but only following a majority vote of agreement by the Syndicate's ruling council – known as The Commission – especially if the target was another Mob boss.

Meyer Lansky

Meyer Lansky never really escaped the shadow of 'Lucky' Luciano. He had first met Luciano at school, where Lansky's attempts to resist Luciano's intimidation made them lifelong friends. Like Luciano, Lansky had been born in Europe – not in Italy but Grodno (present-day Belarus). Majer Suchowlioski, as he was then called, arrived in New York's Lower East Side with the rest of his family at the age of nine (his father had made the move separately two years before). At school – on those few occasions when any of them bothered to attend – he'd hooked up with Luciano and Benjamin 'Bugsy' Siegel, the only one of the three actually born in the United States. This trio found New York's street life of hustlers and gamblers much more interesting than anything they were being taught in the classroom. Their schoolyard gang would continue through to adulthood when they'd dominate American organized crime across the country, from New York to Florida and Los Angeles. The alliance between the Italian and the two Jewish boys worked for all three, but Luciano was always the boss.

The arrival of Prohibition in 1920 made Lansky's name and fortune. He set up a car and truck rental company as a front for his bootlegging activities, moving alcohol over the Atlantic, straight into harbours in New York and New Jersey. Initially he was working with Arnold Rothstein, but he soon partnered up directly with his old pal Luciano, bringing Siegel and his younger brother Jake Lansky into the business. Anyone was fair game for extortion by 'the Bugs and Meyer mob', including Jewish moneylenders and store keepers, and Italian and Irish shop owners.

Their major allies during the 1920s were the Joe Adonis mob, based on Broadway, and a major supplier of alcohol to the area's illegal speakeasies, among them the 21 Club on West 52nd Street, established in 1922, and ex-bootlegger Sherman Billingsley's Stork Club that had opened in 1929. Their key selling point was the high quality of the liquor they supplied, far better than the usual 'rotgut' available throughout New York. Lansky and Siegel supplied the armed escorts for the trucks bringing in shipments from the coast.

The two leaders of the Bugs and Meyer mob had also established themselves as willing killers early on, when they operated as Luciano's personal gunmen. Contract murders became their speciality. Lansky, especially, was instrumental in planning Luciano's daring 1931 assassinations of Joe Masseria and Salvatore Maranzano during the Castellammarese War. He was rewarded with high positions within the overall American Mafia's New York family, despite not being Italian.

Active as members of the Bugs and Meyer mob were such New York underworld figures as Abner 'Longy' Zwillman, Moe Sedway and Louis 'Lepke' Buchalter, who'd go on to be a key figure as part of Murder, Inc. Some gang members were specifically designated as hitmen, including Red Levine, Abraham 'Bo' Weinberg and 'Bugsy' Siegel himself, who was reputed to take on such jobs simply because he enjoyed them. These wise guys, among several other members, made up the muscle, working as enforcers for Luciano and his right-hand man, Frank Costello, during the 1920s and into the 1930s. Luciano ruthlessly used the Bugs and Meyer mob in his quest to subordinate, consolidate and eventually dominate the various gangsters operating in the wider New York area.

Lansky built a network up and down the East coast and into the mid-West, as well as in Cuba and the Caribbean, from where he imported alcohol, sowing the seeds of wartime and post-war contacts. As well as bootlegging, Lansky was politically active during the early 1930s, using his criminal experience and contacts to battle American Nazis. The German-American Bund or Federation (previously the Friends of New Germany, which began in 1933) was established in 1936 to promote a favourable view of Nazi Germany throughout America. Jewish street gangs organized by Lansky disrupted Bund activities, meetings and rallies. 'We wanted to show them that the Jews would not always sit back and accept insults,' Lansky later said of his anti-Nazi activities.

It was, however, crime and the opportunities of Prohibition that most concerned Lansky. The loss of that income upon repeal of Prohibition in 1933 saw him move into equally lucrative but also illegal businesses such as gambling in casinos he owned or co-owned, from New Jersey to Florida and New Orleans. Lansky, with other partners, established the Plantation casino near Miami. His facility with numbers came in useful here as he devised a way of managing his gambling operations so the house would always come out on top, and he used the Mob connections built during Prohibition to supply security for his venues, protecting them and their patrons from the attentions of other gangsters, as well as the law.

The 1936 imprisonment of Luciano put Lansky in place as head of the New York Syndicate. In that role he was a major co-ordinator of 'Operation Underworld', the anti-Nazi action by criminals and gangsters that helped reduce Luciano's prison time and saw uneasy co-operation between Naval Intelligence and the country's top gangsters extend into the Cold War era. It was Lansky who set Luciano up in Cuba following his 1946 release, as his connections with Batista ensured the Cuban dictator welcomed Mob money when invested in casinos and prostitution, while tolerating the growing heroin trade between Cuba and America. In December 1946, major Mob figures, including Luciano and Lansky, met in Havana where they were entertained by an up-and-coming young singer, Frank Sinatra. Lansky was also instrumental in setting Siegel up in business through the Flamingo hotel and casino in Las Vegas, a major area of expansion for the Mob in the 1940s [see chapter 9].

In the early 1950s a more mature Lansky was called to testify before the Congressional committee looking into interstate organized crime in the United States. His identification on the public stage as a key Mob figure saw local investigations in Florida and New York take place into his activities. As a result, Lansky faced indictments in 1953 for gambling and conspiracy, which resulted in his casinos being closed down. Although he was never convicted of anything, there was continued official harassment for the rest of his life by bodies such as the Internal Revenue Service, the Immigration Service and the Federal Bureau of Investigation. Despite this scrutiny, Meyer Lansky continued to develop his interests in Cuba until the Castro revolution of 1959, following which the casinos were nationalized and Lansky lost all his remaining investments.

By then he'd cannily expanded into the Bahamas, with casinos in Nassau that kept him in business throughout the 1960s. By 1970, tired of American government persecution (as he saw it) and facing renewed tax evasion charges, Meyer Lansky relocated to Israel where he applied for citizenship (which was denied in 1972). He was expelled from Israel three years after arriving and then embarked upon an international tour seeking a new home, which included a failed attempt to secure asylum in Paraguay. His offer to various nations of a $1 million payment for sanctuary was repeatedly rebuffed.

In the end, Lansky returned to the United States where he was finally put on trial and faced the testimony of

Vincent 'Fat Vinnie' Teresa, a loan shark with little credibility who'd turned informer. Lansky was acquitted of all
charges in 1976 and retired to Miami Beach, where he lived
until his death of lung cancer in 1983 at the age of eighty,
one of the longest lived American gangsters.

Lansky's legend was no doubt built up by the press, the
statements of other mobsters, and claims that he played
a more central role in the establishment of the modern
American Mafia than he really did. However, along with
Luciano he was a key figure in consolidating various
competing bootlegging operations into one supremely
well-organized and lucrative enterprise. Due to continuing official secrecy, there is much debate over his war work
and how beneficial it might have been to American interests, as well as his own and those of his gangster friends.
Along with Bugsy Siegel, he was one of the founders of
Las Vegas, which became the fastest-growing American
city in the years after the Second World War. Just before
his death, Meyer Lansky was listed alongside fellow mobster Moe Dalitz on *Forbes* magazine's first ever 'Rich List'
with an estimated fortune of $100 million. Lansky was a
numbers guy, hence his labelling as the 'Mob accountant',
but overall he was a smart American entrepreneur whose
undoubted skills were put to the service of a host of criminal enterprises rather than into legitimate business.

Benjamin 'Bugsy' Siegel

He was one of the most notorious and well-known gangsters of his time, but Benjamin 'Bugsy' Siegel hated the
nickname he's still best known by today. Explosive of
temper and dangerous to know, Siegel was the third of the
Luciano–Lansky–Siegel triumvirate who met in childhood
and did so much to shape organized crime in America
through the 1930s and into the 1940s. While Luciano was
the organizing brains and Lanksy worked the numbers,
Siegel was the muscle, the gunman, the killer-for-hire who

had no compunction about 'rubbing out' rivals and whose ambition eventually got the better of him in Las Vegas. He was a driving force behind Murder, Inc.

Born in 1906 in Williamsburg, Brooklyn, Siegel was a native New Yorker who could trace his ancestry back through poor Jewish families to the part of the former Russian empire that is now Ukraine, although other sources put his family's origins in Austria. Benjamin Hyman Siegelbaum (his surname was soon shortened to 'Siegel') quickly became a teenage hoodlum whose outbreaks of temper and tendency to 'bug' people saw him acquire the lifelong nickname of 'Bugsy'. Of the three childhood friends, Siegel was by far the toughest and most vicious: he claimed his earliest arrest in 1926 was for rape. He ran a protection racket on Jewish pushcart merchants in the local neighbourhood, with threats to burn their goods unless they paid up. During the trio's early exploits in extortion, it would be Siegel who'd first raise his fists to hammer their victims into line.

Their small-time protection rackets, drug-dealing and gambling enterprises were mere training for the opportunities Prohibition brought the trio. They moved on to large-scale rum-running, supplying speakeasies, and from street crap games to owning and operating illegal casinos and more down-market 'gambling dens'. Initially under Arnold Rothstein's tutelage, and then Luciano's, Siegel and Lansky operated their truck rental business as a front for bootlegging. Luciano was the link man between the older Mafia bosses from Sicily and the non-Italian rising stars of the criminal underworld in the United States, prime among them being the leaders of what became the Bugs and Meyer mob. Contract murder became their focus, although Siegel was more often the on-the-spot trigger man than Lanksy, who was more of a back-room facilitator.

It was Masseria's insistence that Luciano drop the non-Italian Jews from his organization that saw Luciano turn on him: Lansky planned the hit; Siegel was one of those who pulled the trigger on the Mob boss.

Bugsy Siegel married in 1929 and would go on to have two daughters, but there were questions over his sanity. One story has him killing an opponent in a card game, supposedly for cheating. He then replaced the corpse in the chair, continued playing and dealt a new set of cards. Bugsy then shot his opponent once more, supposedly for his failure to 'ante up'. Upon examining the dead man's cards, Siegel is reputed to have declared the dead man 'nutty' for not betting when he had a full house. Lanksy took advantage of Siegel's instability, hiring him out to other Mob bosses as a willing hitman. Fellow mobster, and member of the Bugs and Meyer mob, Joseph 'Doc' Stacher recalled of Siegel: 'Bugsy never hesitated when danger threatened. While we tried to figure out what the best move was, Bugsy was already shooting!'

However, Bugsy Siegel didn't have Lansky's luck when it came to avoiding the law. He was arrested on charges of illegal gambling and bootlegging in 1932, but avoided jail by paying a fine (probably on Lansky's advice). With the end of Prohibition in 1933, Siegel and Lanksy supplemented their illegal gambling earnings with a completely legal sideline. They invested with fellow gangsters Joe Adonis and Frank Costello in Capitol Wines and Spirits, a now legal liquor distributor, one of the largest and most lucrative in New York.

Siegel was restless, though, and he saw his opportunities on the East coast or in Chicago as rather limited since others had them all sown up – he also feared for his own safety, believing he'd become a target for other Mob bosses after his Murder, Inc. activities. He looked West, to southern California and more specifically Hollywood, for new criminal opportunities. Trading on his undoubted charisma (when he kept his explosive temper under control), Siegel had long associated with movie actor George Raft since they'd grown up together on the Lower East Side. Raft (who featured in *Scarface*, 1932, based on Al Capone's rise) provided Siegel's entrée into Hollywood high society in the mid-1930s. The gangster could see there were rich pickings to be had in Tinseltown, as the movie-making capital of the world had come to be known to millions of moviegoers worldwide.

Initially, he set up a series of floating crap games that moved around town from home to home to evade the law, and then hooked up with Los Angeles mobster and former Black Hander Jack Dragna whose control of the local scene was slipping. Siegel successfully ran legal bookmaking operations based around the Santa Anita race track (which he declared as earnings on his tax returns, learning from Capone's mistakes; see chapter 6) and illegal offshore gambling ships located along the California coast. A new network of criminal enterprises opened up on the West coast of America, largely independent of the original empire builders back East.

Siegel became the newly nicknamed 'King of the Sunset Strip', friends with movie stars such as Clark Gable, Cary Grant and Gary Cooper, as well as studio executives like Jack Warner of Warner Bros. and Louis B. Mayer of MGM. Jean Harlow was a close friend of Siegel's and godmother to one of his daughters. The mobster threw extravagant Hollywood parties, attracting young up-and-comers in the entertainment business such as Frank Sinatra. Despite these friendships (or perhaps facilitated by them), Siegel couldn't resist running an extortion racket on movie producers. He also got involved with the unions, such as the Teamsters and the Screen Extras Guild, and had them stage strikes forcing the studios to pay him off, adding labour racketeering to his list of criminal endeavours. Siegel, notoriously, 'borrowed' large amounts of money from his movie star friends, but never paid them back and none of them dared demand he did so.

During his time in Hollywood, Siegel built an alliance with Cleveland mobster Mickey Cohen who acted as his chief lieutenant [see chapter 9]. Dragna, fearing Siegel's reputation for violence and under instruction from the imprisoned Luciano, agreed to take a subordinate role to the two new criminal kingpins of California. Siegel dominated the local numbers racket, using his earnings to establish a drug trade route from Mexico into Los Angeles, partly run through the Chicago Outfit.

Siegel's interest in Las Vegas grew out of his Hollywood experience and his desire to make a mark for himself by establishing something that would rival anything built by his East coast competitors. In 1941, a decade after the state of Nevada had legalized gambling, he invested in a series of small casinos. This gave him a foothold in the area and formed the basis for his greater ambition. He petitioned his former East coast acquaintances, including Meyer Lansky, to invest in casino and hotel properties in Las Vegas, including El Rancho Vegas, the area's first popular hotel.

Siegel's big opportunity came when property developer Billy Wilkerson – a major Hollywood figure who owned newspapers and restaurants – ran short on funds to build his planned gambling haven, the Flamingo Hotel and Casino on Las Vegas Boulevard. The ever-ruthless Siegel moved in, using Mob money from the East coast to oust Wilkerson and take over the development of the Flamingo, which then grew in size and scope under his supervision.

Siegel's extravagance was to be his downfall. He spent much more money on the Flamingo than his East coast investors ever intended, with construction costs ballooning from just over $1 million to nearly $6 million. Luciano and those around him suspected Siegel of syphoning off funds for himself, an activity he and others had been adept at back in the days of Prohibition. The Mob, however, didn't appreciate such tactics being used on them by one of their own.

The Flamingo's grand opening in December 1946 was supposed to be a star-studded Hollywood-style event, but turned into a washout as bad weather grounded the charter flights that should have brought the high-spending Hollywood rollers over to Las Vegas. In the early days, the Flamingo lost huge amounts of money. Siegel quickly closed it down, revised his approach and re-opened three months later as a money-making venture – but by then the East coast Mob's patience with Bugsy had worn very thin.

On 20 June 1947, an unknown assassin fatally shot Siegel at the Los Angeles home he shared with Virginia Hill. The would-be king of the Mob was riddled with bullets, including two shots to the head. Who organized the hit has never been confirmed – no one was ever charged with the murder and it remains officially unsolved to this day. Fingers were pointed to the East coast, with Siegel's former friends Lansky, Joe Adonis and the then-exiled-to-Italy 'Lucky' Luciano voting on The Commission to exterminate their West coast 'problem'. This was backed by the fact that the day after Siegel's killing, the Syndicate's representatives seized control of the Flamingo, eventually turning it into one of the biggest attractions in Las Vegas. Others suggested Jack Dragna and his Chicago allies had struck back at Siegel for the years of humiliation he'd heaped upon the mobster who once thought of himself as the 'big man' in Hollywood. In 1987, Eddie Cannizzaro, a driver for Dragna, claimed he'd carried out the hit on Siegel. Finally, a third option makes the killing a more personal matter. In this version, Cleveland mobster Moe Dalitz killed Siegel in a fight over their shared 'moll' Virginia Hill, in whose house Siegel was killed (Hill was conveniently abroad at the time). Former Los Angeles chief of police Clinton H. Anderson addressed the question in his autobiography: 'We spent many man hours investigating the Siegel case and were convinced he was killed by his own associates. There was never sufficient evidence to pinpoint the identity of the assassin.'

Bugsy Siegel was the least accomplished of the three school friends who rose to the top of the gangster world, but he is perhaps the most well known and mythologized, partly due to his spectacular assassination, but also thanks to his role in the development of Las Vegas. A bust of Bugsy stood in the chapel at the Flamingo for many years after his death, and countless films and documentaries have charted his rise and fall, including 1991's *Bugsy* starring Warren Beatty. Bugsy Siegel was a ruthless killer who claimed to have personally pulled the trigger on up to twelve men, but who lacked the smarts that Luciano and Lansky used to secure their positions. His ambition, temper and inability to bend to the will of others ultimately sealed his fate, dead at forty-one, probably killed on the orders of his old schoolyard friends.

The rise and fall of Murder, Inc.
Murder, Inc. was the vehicle that 'Lucky' Luciano, Meyer Lansky and 'Bugsy' Siegel used to secure and enforce their dominance over the American Mob, running from the 1930s through to the 1950s. Hundreds were killed by operatives acting for Murder, Inc. and many different methods of killing were used, from simple gunshots through to knives, strangulation, burial alive and the ice-pick, a deadly favourite of many mobsters. Those charged with Mob assassinations went about their business in a quiet but ruthless manner, determined not to draw too much attention to their activities. In the end, it would be one of their own who would bring the organization down.

Masseria and Maranzano were gone by the mid-1930s, and Luciano was firmly in charge. He had a discipline problem, though, and wanted to ensure his authority was clearly stamped upon every American Mafia endeavour, coast to coast. The Syndicate was organized along legitimate business lines, so Luciano saw no reason why its enforcement wing shouldn't be run likewise. He put Meyer

Lansky and Bugsy Siegel in charge of setting it up, allowing them to draw upon their former associates in the Bugs and Meyer mob for manpower.

Louis 'Lepke' Buchalter was charged with hands-on day-to-day operation of Murder, Inc. Targets would be decided by the 'board' of the Syndicate at their meetings, then the orders handed on to Buchalter to execute. He and his men were paid a regular salary that was topped up by a 'bonus fee' for each operation successfully concluded. Buchalter was supported by Albert 'Mad Hatter' Anastasia, and among their most trusted operatives were Martin 'Buggsy' Goldstein and Abe 'Kid Twist' Reles. Joe Adonis, a long-standing Lanksy–Siegel associate, and Jacob 'Gurrah' Shapiro were also key lieutenants. They operated out of the Black Rose candy store in Brooklyn, and Harry 'Pittsburgh Phil' Strauss was said to have been their most accomplished hitman, responsible for in excess of a hundred killings.

The targets of Murder, Inc. were largely fellow mobsters who'd stepped out of line, informers, or law officials who got in the gangsters' way. Ironically, one of the major drivers of Murder, Inc.'s activities was prosecutor Thomas E. Dewey and his campaign against organized crime begun in 1935. Witnesses and suspected informants who were helping the Dewey investigation were among the hit squad's first targets.

As already seen, the shooting of Dutch Schultz on 23 October 1935 came about because he was determined to eliminate Dewey himself, and the mob feared that such an overt action would just bring the wrath of the law down upon them even harder. To prevent Schultz acting alone against Dewey, The Commission had set Murder, Inc. on to him. Hitmen Emanuel 'Mendy' Weiss and Charles Workman shot Schultz, but he didn't die until the following day. Weiss fled the scene along with getaway driver Seymour Schechter, leaving Workman behind to make his own way back to Brooklyn. Workman filed a complaint against his fellow killers to the Syndicate board, and Schechter was soon also rubbed out by Murder, Inc. personnel. Only Workman would be sent down for the Schultz killing, serving over two decades in Sing Sing prison, and Weiss would be tried and executed in 1944 for an entirely different murder.

Schultz was only one of many mobsters targeted by the teams of killers that made up Murder, Inc. Three other victims in 1935 alone were Mob chauffeur and bodyguard Morris Kessler, and brothers and gang leaders Louis and Joseph Amberg, all killed as part of a gang war with Buchalter's crew. In 1937, loan shark George Rudnick was killed when it was suspected he was an informant, and Buchalter's ex-associate Max Rubin was shot and wounded by Murder, Inc. personnel after he refused to leave town to avoid being summoned by Dewey as a witness against the Mob.

Dewey did secure the co-operation of several witnesses, including Harry Rudolph, 'Dukey' Maffetore, Abraham Levine and Abe Reles, who were willing to speak out about the unsolved murder of nineteen-year-old small-time hood Alex 'Red' Alpert in 1933. They all felt that they might be future targets of Murder, Inc. themselves (some were even part of it), so had turned informant before the Mob could catch up with them. Their testimony was to be the basis of a series of first degree murder indictments issued in New York and resulted in a variety of trials that threw public light on a series of explosive gangland killings.

Among the killings that the participants were convicted of were the 1935 Dutch Schultz killing, the 1936 murder of candy store owner Joe Rosen, the 1937 ice-pick slaying of George 'Whitey' Rudnick in a Brooklyn parking garage, and the 1939 strangulation of bookmaker Irving 'Puggy' Feinstein. Those convicted and then executed included Charles Workman, Frank Abbandando, Harry Stauss,

Martin Goldstein, Irving Nitberg and Emanuel Weiss. The biggest fish nailed by Dewey's actions was Louis Buchalter himself, the original head of Murder, Inc. He was convicted in November 1942, and despite appeals, was executed in Sing Sing prison in March 1944.

Abe 'Kid Twist' Reles didn't live to see the convictions that he'd helped secure. Held in police 'protective custody' in the Half-Moon Hotel in Coney Island, Reles fell or was thrown from his room window early on the morning of 12 November 1941. A 1951 grand jury concluded the death was accidental, but the suspicious circumstances left it open to speculation that the Mob had had their revenge and his police guards may have been involved. Thereafter, Reles became known in the press as 'the canary who could sing, but couldn't fly'.

With many of its top men imprisoned or executed, Murder, Inc. had lost its potency by the mid-1940s. Luciano, Lanksy and Siegel had all moved on to other things, while Albert Anastasia had been in charge since Buchalter's arrest for involvement in the killing of Joe Rosen. The newspapers, fascinated by the revelations that came out of the Dewey trials, made memorable larger-than-life characters out of a group of largely petty criminals and ruthless murderers. It was the papers that dubbed Anastasia the 'Lord High Executioner of Murder, Inc.' and he went on to become the boss of the Gambino crime family for much of the 1950s. Anastasia finally met his end in a barber shop at the Park Sheraton Hotel in October 1957, when he was shot and killed by his own Murder, Inc. 'executioners', although no one was ever convicted of his killing. Following his death, the remaining organized crime bosses held a summit in Apalachin, New York to divide up his rackets. As ever in organized crime, when one boss is wiped out, several more spring up to take his place.

6

GET CAPONE! – THE LIFE AND TIMES OF 'SCARFACE'

Known by his enemies as 'Scarface', Al Capone would become the widest known of the American gangsters who came to prominence in the 1930s and 1940s, partly because unlike many of the others, he lived a more public life – a decision that would contribute to his ultimate downfall. His name alone would come to personify the period and its key underworld figures. Although born in Brooklyn, New York, it would be in Chicago that Capone would make his mark.

Alphonse Gabriel Capone was born on 17 January 1899, the son of Italian immigrants – his father had been a barber from Castellammare di Stabia, south of Naples. He was one of nine children, and two of his brothers – Ralph and Frank – would join him in his criminal career. Although a promising student in his early years, Capone was expelled from school at the age of fourteen for hitting a teacher, and his future seemed set to be a life of working odd jobs, with early positions including working in a bowling alley and a candy store.

Despite running with several early street gangs, including the Junior Forty Thieves and the Bowery Boys, Capone's Neapolitan roots excluded him from full membership of the Sicilian Mafia then establishing itself in New York. He graduated to the Brooklyn Rippers and was even in the Five Points Gang for a while, but being merely a member of someone else's gang didn't suit Capone.

In his early days he was mentored by two prominent gangsters: Frankie Yale and Johnny Torrio. Yale had built a protection racket around Brooklyn's ice delivery business, and opened a bar called the Harvard Inn on Coney Island with the proceeds. Capone worked in Yale's bar as a bartender and bouncer, while learning the ropes of organized crime. It was in the Harvard Inn in 1917 that the eighteen-year-old Capone gained the three facial scars that gave him his notorious nickname. Small time hoodlum Frank Gallucio slashed Capone's face with a knife after Capone attempted to chat up Gallucio's sister. Although the three scars added to his tough reputation, Capone would go to great lengths in his attempts to cover them up in later life using make-up – no one dared call him 'Scarface' in his presence. Ironically, Gallucio would later become one of Capone's many bodyguards.

Capone's other mentor was Johnny Torrio. From southern Italy, Torrio had come up through the street gangs to become Paul Kelly's right-hand man in the Five Points Gang. Torrio tried to run his criminal enterprises as though they were legitimate businesses, avoiding unnecessary violence wherever possible. His interests included the numbers racket, loan sharking and opium trafficking. Torrio took a shine to Capone, who was newly married and had become a father in 1918, as he felt he showed promise in organized crime.

Torrio relocated to Chicago to partner with his uncle, restaurant owner James 'Diamond Jim' Colosimo, who'd built a network of nearly one hundred brothels in the city but was facing ever-increasing extortion demands from local Black Hand gangs. It was Torrio's role to eliminate the blackmailers, and he then stayed on as Colosimo's major-domo. Capone also fled New York in 1919 after his role as a gunman for Yale saw him facing a double murder charge. Torrio brought him to Chicago, as the wily mobster was hatching plans of his own. Seeing the possibilities inherent in looming Prohibition, Torrio lobbied Colosimo to get into bootlegging, but the older gangster refused, not wanting to risk what he'd already built up by drawing extra heat on his operations. Seeing the easy money from Prohibition as too good to miss, Torrio decided he didn't want to be second-in-command when he was more than capable of running things in Chicago by himself.

In May 1920, while awaiting a delivery at his restaurant, Colosimo was shot dead – no one was ever charged with his murder, although initial suspicion fell upon his second wife, actress and singer Dale Winter. However, since then it has been determined that it was more likely Torrio who ordered Colosimo's assassination, possibly hiring Frank Yale to do the job. Yale was initially a police suspect, but a lack of evidence forced them to let him go. The fact that Al Capone stayed on in Chicago as Torrio's right-hand man while he took over Colosimo's 'outfit' suggested that he was also involved in planning the Colosimo killing; Torrio saw Capone as the muscle to his brains.

As Torrio took over the Chicago Outfit, Capone brought out his brothers Ralph and Frank to help with the gang's expansion into bootlegging, while maintaining their other interests in prostitution, gambling, and clubs such as The Four Deuces. The gang quickly controlled the supply of liquor to the Downtown Loop speakeasies, and expanded into the city's South Side. A further expansion into the

North Side and Gold Coast areas was resisted by fellow bootlegger Dion O'Banion and his North Side Gang. The resulting conflict claimed several lives before the parties came to a short-lived compromise during 1923.

A double-cross in a business deal between O'Banion and Torrio over the ownership of a brewery left Torrio $500,000 out of pocket and under arrest by the Chicago police. Reluctantly, Torrio decided the only way forward was the removal of O'Banion. The gangster was killed in his North Side flower shop by a trio of gunmen (one of them Frank Yale) in November 1924, sparking yet another gangland war. The 'great beer war' brought Chicago mayor William Dever into action against the corrupting influence of bootleggers and gangsters, and he launched a new determination to enforce Prohibition.

As a result, Torrio and Capone relocated their Outfit to suburban Cicero, Illinois, a small town to the west of Chicago, where they fixed the 1924 election. Although their selected town council candidates won, the violence surrounding the attempted voting fraud claimed the life of Capone's older brother, Frank, who was shot dead by police on election day. Control of the council allowed for the immediate expansion of their speakeasies, gambling dens and brothels in the area, but Torrio's success would be short-lived.

Very early in 1925, an assassination attempt was made on him, led by some unruly North Side Gang members in retaliation for the hit on O'Banion. Caught in a hail of gunfire that saw him sustain wounds in his jaw, lungs, legs and abdomen, Torrio nonetheless survived. Following emergency surgery, he was visited by Capone who placed several men around his room and the hospital to protect their gang leader from any further attacks. Torrio decided he'd had enough, and he passed control of the Chicago Outfit to Al Capone, telling his replacement: 'It's all yours, Al. Me? I'm quitting. It's Europe for me.' Following some time in prison for Prohibition violations, Johnny Torrio moved back to Italy later in 1925, leaving Al Capone as the king of Chicago's underworld. Although he'd later return to the United States and become involved on the fringes of gangsterdom, Torrio would never again attain the same amount of power.

Chicago's 'beer wars'

By 1925 Al Capone was in sole control of the Chicago Outfit and as a result controlled much of Chicago's boot-legging business, bringing in around $100 million each year. Prohibition was big business for those who knew how to take advantage of it. Capone's organization was run by four 'senior partners' that included himself, his older brother Ralph, their cousin Frank Nitti and Jack Guzick, with the profits from their illegal enterprises split more or less evenly. Their headquarters, where Capone and his entourage would hang out, was in the Metropole Hotel from 1925 and later the Lexington Hotel, a location nick-named 'Capone's Castle'.

Alcohol would come into Chicago from Canada and the East coast, as well as from Midwestern moonshine opera-tors and previously closed local breweries that the gang took over and surreptitiously put back into production. Corruption of local politicians and police meant that more often than not, the law would look the other way. New Chicago mayor William Hale Thompson, who replaced the anti-crime crusading Dever from 1928, was on the Capone payroll from the beginning, meaning that the gangster's casinos and speakeasies operated largely free from the intervention of any authorities.

Capone made the most of his newfound wealth, dress-ing the part of a man about town, paying for expensive cigars and gourmet food and drinks from his ill-gotten gains. His favourite drink was Templeton Rye from Iowa. It is from Al Capone that the idea of gangster as celebrity emerged. Predecessors and contemporaries, like Lucky Luciano, Meyer Lansky or Bugsy Siegel, mostly wanted to keep their names out of the papers – although during his time in Los Angeles, Siegel would begin to think himself as much of a celebrity as the movie stars he hung out with. Capone attracted huge media interest, so he adopted a public persona, presenting himself not as the criminal and killer he really was, but as a more acceptable Robin Hood figure. As Prohibition was largely unpopular in big cities like New York, Chicago and Los Angeles, the public had a very different view of Al Capone than law enforcement: he was providing a much appreciated service in supplying alcohol that the state was denying the people. Capone was cheered by the crowds at sporting events, such as the baseball games he attended, while President Herbert Hoover was booed by the same crowds. The gangster was often seen cruising the streets of Chicago in his armoured car, and would make a point of offering big tips to waiters who served him, all the better to further spread his image as a champion of the people. It all served to disguise his real purpose and activities, while Capone himself became addicted to the attention that fame brought him.

The four-year period after Capone took over the Chicago Outfit from Torrio was one marked by increasing violence that was to culminate in the notorious 1929 St Valentine's Day Massacre. Following the death of mobster O'Banion came the 1926 assassination of Assistant State Attorney William H. McSwiggin. A Cicero native, McSwiggin had grown up with the O'Donnell brothers, Myles and William, and Jim Doherty, who made up the core of Chicago's West Side Gang. The West Siders were allied with Torrio against O'Banion's North Side Gang, which had been taken over by George Moran following O'Banion's killing. McSwiggin was a tough prosecutor who never went easy on gangsters (his nickname was the 'Hanging Prosecutor'), except in the case of his childhood friends, the O'Donnells. McSwiggin was killed in April 1926 in their company, probably on Capone's instructions.

Moran and his North Side mob were a constant threat to Capone, his associates and his 'business' interests. George Clarence Moran, known to everyone as 'Bugs', started running with the Chicago gangs as a teenager – he was jailed three times before he reached the age of twenty-one. Although of French Catholic descent, Moran allied himself with O'Banion's predominantly Irish gang rather than with Torrio and Capone's Italian South Siders. After O'Banion's death, Moran swore vengeance on Torrio and Capone, and when his assassination attempt on Torrio failed, he focused his efforts on the Outfit's new leader, Al Capone. Just as Capone used the press to burnish his image, so Moran attempted the same tactics to cast doubt on the gangster's so-called Robin Hood pursuits, claiming 'Capone is a lowlife'.

Moran invented the drive-by shooting: he and his men would drive around the city hoping to find Capone. The one time they did spot him, Moran's henchmen opened fire on Capone and his associates while Moran drove past them. Capone survived that attack, although his driver was injured and his car bullet-ridden. From then on, he adopted the use of a specially armoured vehicle.

When they couldn't get to Capone, Moran and his men would hit the gangster's bodyguards, kidnapping one and torturing him, before killing him and dumping the body. Moran made a second direct attempt on Capone's life in Cicero itself, attacking his hotel with Thompson sub-machine guns. (Although invented in 1918, it was only in the mid-1920s that the 'Tommy gun' rose to prominence as the gangster's weapon of choice. The compact but powerful weapon allowed for a high volume of shells to be fired rap-idly – the Federal Bureau of Investigation would officially adopt the weapon from 1933.) Again Capone was unhurt, though shaken, although the ground floor restaurant they were in was shredded by the brutal gunfire. A 1926 'peace treaty' between the two gangs held for less than two months.

Moran was first to break the fragile truce, by hijacking Capone's liquor shipments and selling the stolen alcohol directly to the area's speakeasies. Capone retaliated by arranging for the destruction by fire of Moran's popular Chicago dog-racing track. The tit-for-tat action continued, with Moran then targeting friends and gang members associated with Capone. More bodyguards provided temporary protection, but Capone was gradually coming to the conclusion that something drastic would have to be done to get Moran out of his way. Each leader was losing men and profits at an accelerating pace.

As part of his spreading criminal empire, Capone had taken control of the Unione Siciliana, a fraternal association that became the Italian-American equivalent of the Tammany Hall Democratic political machine. To do so, he'd killed his one-time mentor (and Torrio's likely assassin) Frankie Yale. Although formally barred from membership of the Mafia (due to his place of birth), Capone was able, through control of the Unione Siciliana, to organize other 'pure' Mafia groups – such as the Genna brothers and his rival Joe Aiello – as part of his overall syndicate, a crime organization that involved not just Italians, but Jews, Irish and Poles. When Moran targeted and killed Antonio Lombardo and Pasqualino Lolordo, Capone's friends and heads of the Unione Siciliana, it was the final straw following Moran's raids on his shipments. Al Capone decided to wipe out the North Side Gang once and for all.

The St Valentine's Day Massacre

Moran received a fateful phone call on 13 February 1929 informing him that a truckload of whisky from Detroit was available at a bargain price, if he wanted it. It was an offer the mobster couldn't resist, so he arranged for the delivery of the whisky to take place the following day – St Valentine's Day – at the garage of S.M.C. Cartage Company at 2122 North Clark Street, where Moran stashed his boot-legging trucks. Unusually, Moran would be late getting to the garage that day – that was the only reason he missed being killed alongside the seven victims of what the press would label the 'St Valentine's Day Massacre'.

The garage had been under surveillance for some time by men holed up in an apartment across the street – men thought by police to be in the pay of Al Capone. They monitored the trucking warehouse that doubled up as Moran's base of operations, planning the best time to strike. On 14 February, two men dressed as Chicago police officers, accompanied by three others dressed as civilians, entered the garage, rounding up the five members of the Moran gang who were present. Also having the misfortune to be there at the time were a Moran hanger-on (not officially a gang member) and the garage handy man. All seven men were lined up facing the garage wall, and the five raiders let rip with their Tommy guns, spraying the men and the wall with bullets. The gangsters swung their guns back and forth, hitting the men in the head, chest and legs. Shotguns were then used to ensure the victims would not survive. The ferocity of the firepower was such that some of the victims' limbs and heads became detached from their bodies. The attackers then fled the scene, leaving six men dead and one dying. Only the garage mechanic's dog, a German shepherd named 'Highball', survived the massacre. The aftermath was discovered by two women who'd heard the barking of the distressed dog (tied by a leash to a truck) from their boarding house across the street.

Al Capone made sure he was out of town when the attack happened, although there can be little doubt he ordered it. Moran had arrived at the garage, along with his lieutenant Ted Newberry, just in time to see what he believed to be policemen entering the premises – fearing he'd been set up, he fled the scene. The men who'd entered the garage that morning were hired contract killers, not the usual Mob figures, so as to distance the attack from Capone and his associates. At least some were believed to have belonged to Egan's Rats, a gang based in St Louis, Missouri, formed by Thomas Kinney and Tom Egan. The gang had largely broken up by 1924, thanks to the convictions of many members due to the actions of an informer. Those who remained at large scattered across the country, but one crew reformed around Fred 'Killer' Burke, reportedly hired by Capone for the St Valentine's Day action in Chicago.

The victims included four North Side Gang members: brothers Frank and Peter Gusenberg, both Moran gang enforcers; Albert Kachellek (AKA 'James Clark'), Moran's major-domo; and Adam Heyer, the gang's accountant. Reinhardt Schwimmer was an optician by trade whose gambling obsession had brought him into the orbit of the Moran gang, while Albert Weinshank ran several dry-cleaning operations for Bugs Moran, and looked so much like the gangster the hitmen may have mistaken him for their target. Finally, the garage mechanic John May simply had the misfortune to be keeping the wrong type of company. Frank Gusenberg was the only one to (briefly) survive, but following the Mafia code of omertà – the code of silence – he repeatedly insisted 'Nobody shot me' when asked, despite the fourteen bullets in his body.

Although he saw it as a necessary action – and it succeeded in removing Moran's North Siders as an active faction in Chicago – the public backlash against the ferocity of the St Valentine's Day Massacre damaged Capone's wider reputation, especially his public Robin Hood status. The photos of the aftermath of the massacre, run without censorship by a gleeful press, served to associate Capone firmly with destructive, bloody violence. Even though he had a carefully arranged alibi – he was in Florida, in the company of an impeccable witness, Miami's Dade County

solicitor Robert Taylor – covering the period of the massacre, it was widely believed by the public that Capone had
ordered the hit on his rivals. Bugs Moran himself was in no
doubt, saying of the deadly action against his men, 'Only
Capone kills like that'.

The police investigation of the St Valentine's Day
Massacre initially focused on Detroit's Purple Gang, associates of Capone's who were supposedly supplying the
Moran gang with illegal alcohol on that day. Two landla-
dies of the rooming houses opposite the garage identified
police photo 'mug shots' of members of the Purple Gang as
men who had taken rooms with them in the weeks before
the attack. It was believed by police that they were keeping an eye on the comings and goings at the garage prior
to planning the attack. Several members of the gang were
brought in for questioning, but none was ever formally
charged. A 1927 Cadillac Sedan car, believed by police to
have been used by the killers, was found at a Wood Street
garage fire on 22 February. The car was eventually traced
to Claude Maddox, a former St Louis gangster with ties to
the local Egan's Rats gang and to Capone's organization.

No one was ever charged with taking part in the St
Valentine's Day Massacre. One of the weapons discovered
by police was thought to have been used in Michigan. They
arrested Fred Burke, who'd also been identified by witnesses
who saw the 'police' car arrive at the garage. One of Burke's
well-known M.O.s (modus operandi, or 'way of working')
was to dress as a policeman, a trait shared with fellow mobster James Ray. The charges didn't stick, but Burke was later
prosecuted and jailed for the killing of a local Michigan
policeman in December 1929. He died in prison in 1940.

Others attempted to increase their own underworld
credentials by claiming to have been involved in the notorious gangland massacre, such as Fred Goetz, a small-time
bank robber. Just in case he was involved and might talk,
however, his fellow gangsters rubbed him out in 1934.

There was a gruesome postscript to the St Valentine's Day Massacre. Al Capone's second-in-command, Sicily-born Jack 'Machine Gun' McGurn, who had reportedly been involved in planning the Moran gang massacre was himself killed exactly seven years later on 14 February 1936 – the unknown gunmen involved left a St Valentine's Day card near his corpse. McGurn had also been arrested in connection with the original St Valentine's Day hit, but he had a 'blonde alibi' in the shape of his glamorous wife, Louise Rolfe. It was widely believed that one of the trio of killers of McGurn had been James Gusenberg, brother of Frank and Peter, victims of the St Valentine's Day Massacre.

Public Enemy Number One

The 1929 massacre brought new attention to Al Capone from the forces of law and order. In April 1930, Chairman of the Chicago Crime Commission Frank J. Loesch released his list of 'Public Enemies'. Top of the list was Al Capone, Public Enemy Number One. His brother, Ralph, was placed at number two on the list of twenty-eight of Chicago's most-wanted criminals. Loesch intended the list to be a warning that the people named were now under constant watch by the police, and it would be the aim of Chicago's law enforcers to catch and lock up each one of them. (Later in the 1930s, J. Edgar Hoover's Federal Bureau of Investigation – the FBI – would appropriate the term 'Public Enemies' and compile a new list of urgently wanted criminals, including John Dillinger, Baby Face Nelson, Bonnie and Clyde, Pretty Boy Floyd, Ma Barker and Alvin Karpis.)

A concerted effort was begun to bring Al Capone to justice, notably by Bureau of Prohibition agent Eliot Ness and Internal Revenue agent Frank J. Wilson, who set out to target Capone for violations of income tax. Capone had largely relocated to Florida by then, while his lieutenants continued to supervise the day-to-day activities of his

criminal networks in Chicago. Capone's Florida neighbour – President Herbert Hoover – was so disturbed by
the gangster's wild parties that he authorized the all-out
action to bring Capone to justice.

The US Treasury Department followed through with the
two-front attack on the gangsters of Chicago. Ness, whose
investigators came to be known as the 'Untouchables',
raided Capone's illegal distilleries and seized his cargoes
of bootleg whisky imported from Canada or the East
coast. Meanwhile, Wilson's men began following the
money, hoping to prove Capone's vast income from his
illegal activities and looking to charge him with evading
payment of taxes. It was this painstaking work, analysing
the paper trail and putting together the financial information, that would finally connect the mobster to his illegal
empire. The authorities managed to get Capone jailed
for ten months in 1929–30 after he was caught changing
trains in Philadelphia carrying a concealed weapon while
on a return trip from a bootleggers' conference in Atlantic
City – an arrest believed to have been organized by the
East coast Mob to allow Capone time to 'cool off' after the
St Valentine's Day Massacre, as his actions were bringing
unwanted attention upon all gangsters.

Finally, in 1931 gangster Al Capone was indicted for
the mundane crime of income tax fraud, essentially non-
payment of taxes due on income. Initially, Capone hoped
to plead guilty in order to receive a more lenient sentence,
but as insurance he had his 'associates' arrange for the jury
members attached to his trial to understand the personal
implications for them and their families of a 'guilty' ver-
dict. Capone's attempt at jury tampering, however, was
thwarted by Ness's Untouchables, who uncovered his plans
and were able to arrange for his jury to be switched at the
last-minute with one due to sit on a completely different
case. Capone withdrew his guilty plea, and a lengthy trial
followed. In mid-October 1931, the federal jury found Al

Capone guilty on five out of the twenty-three charges he faced – three counts of tax evasion, and two counts of failure to file tax returns. Attempted appeals were denied, and much of his property was seized, including his armoured car which was later used by President Franklin D. Roosevelt in the early years of the Second World War. Capone was sentenced to eleven years in prison, and ordered to pay court costs and fines: 'Scarface' had finally been caged.

Sentenced in May 1932, Capone was first locked up in the Atlanta US Penitentiary, then in Lincoln Heights Jail. In August 1934 he was transferred to the newly opened Alcatraz, an island in San Francisco Bay which had been converted from a military fort and prison to serve as a civilian prison. Capone was largely isolated during his time at Alcatraz, which was known as 'The Rock', and that, along with the repeal of Prohibition in 1933, served to greatly reduce his power which he attempted to continue to exercise from behind bars.

Capone was often targeted by other inmates, and developed a long-running jailhouse feud with Texas bank robber James Lucas. Assigned to janitorial duties, Capone was derided by other prisoners as 'the wop with the mop'. In 1938, he was diagnosed by the jail's physician as suffering from syphilis of the brain, a long-time ailment he had not attended to. His good behaviour and deteriorating mental condition saw Capone serve out the final year of his sentence in a Baltimore mental hospital. He was released in November 1939, retiring to his remaining property on his Palm Island estate in Florida, with his wife and son. He died of a stroke in January 1947, aged 48. Ironically, five days before – at the age of 87 – Andrew Volstead, who gave his name to the Volstead Act that had introduced Prohibition to America, from which Capone had enriched himself and his friends and caused so much mayhem, had also died. With the death of Al Capone, the legends surrounding 'Scarface' began.

7

PUBLIC ENEMIES: THE JOHN DILLINGER GANG

Replacing Al Capone as Public Enemy Number One in the 1930s was John Dillinger, the 'dustbowl desperado' nick-named 'snake eyes' who robbed two dozen banks, escaped from jail twice, and regularly wore a bulletproof vest to protect himself in his frequent shoot-outs with the police across the Midwest. He even had the chutzpah to rob a pair of police stations. Dillinger followed in Capone's footsteps in more ways than one, becoming a media celebrity whose post-Prohibition criminal exploits were celebrated as often as they were condemned by newspapers closely following his trail of havoc. He was just the most well-known of a group of Depression-era rural gangsters who captured the American imagination that included Baby Face Nelson, Pretty Boy Floyd, and the romantic outlaw pairing of Bonnie and Clyde.

Those Dillinger days

John Dillinger epitomizes the violent, constantly on-the-run gangster of the Depression, evading the law for over a year and leading Federal agent Melvin Purvis on a chase that took in multiple states including Oklahoma, Ohio, Kansas, Missouri and Arkansas. During 1933 and into 1934, this seemingly bulletproof outlaw became a hero to some and a villain to others. His bravado, daring exploits and colourful public persona created a series of myths around a figure who was, in reality, a violent, unrepentant bad guy. His habit of athletically leaping over bank counters during robberies became a trademark. It was his exploits, however, that would lead to significant improvements in nationwide policing, with J. Edgar Hoover developing a more sophisticated Federal Bureau of Investigation to take down gangsters like Dillinger.

Born in Indianapolis, Indiana on 22 June 1903, John Herbert Dillinger was destined to become the quintessential American gangster of the 1930s. His parents were of French and German-Prussian descent, but Dillinger was American all the way. He and his older sister, Audrey, endured a tough childhood with a strict grocer father who didn't spare them physical punishment whenever he felt it was necessary, and he felt that often. Dillinger's almost pathological negative reaction to authority figures, which plagued him all his life and led to many of his later troubles with the police and the law in general, may have started in childhood with his own father.

Dillinger's mother died just before he turned four years old, and his father remarried, leaving the boy's then seventeen-year-old sister to look after him. As a teenager, young Dillinger was almost as much of a tearaway as he would become as an adult. He constantly got into fights at school and was regularly pulled up by his teachers and supervisors for petty theft. Like many who have been bullied, Dillinger himself became something of a bully, often picking on school children younger and smaller than himself, knowing he could easily dominate them. As soon as he could, Dillinger got out of school and found a job in an Indianapolis machine shop, then worked in a furniture factory. Although a hard worker, his lack of discipline led to him staying out all night at raucous parties.

His father took the decision to move the family out of the city – which he feared was corrupting his seventeen-year-old son – to rural Mooresville, Indiana in 1920. The move did little to calm Dillinger down: he was arrested for auto theft in 1922, causing his always-rocky relationship with his father to worsen. Acting upon a widely-held belief, Dillinger's father thought a spell in the military might sort young John out, so he was enlisted in the United States Navy in 1923 and served aboard the battleship USS *Utah*. He only lasted a few months, taking the opportunity of time in port at Boston to desert just before Christmas. The Navy eventually gave up trying to turn John Dillinger into a serving sailor, resulting in a dishonourable discharge shortly thereafter.

Reluctantly returning to Mooresville, twenty-year-old Dillinger found romance with sixteen-year-old Beryl Hovious; the pair were quickly married in April 1924 and moved to Indianapolis. Attempting to do the right thing and settle down to family life in a new city, Dillinger was quickly frustrated and overcome with wanderlust once more. He couldn't hold down a decent job for long, and his marriage rapidly crumbled, leading to divorce by 1929 (initiated by Hovious after Dillinger was jailed). During his marriage Dillinger had felt under pressure to find a way to make money fast. On a night out with a friend, pool shark Ed Singleton, the drunken pair found their thoughts turning to robbery as a quick and easy way to raise some much needed cash. The seeds were sown for Dillinger's career in crime.

The first job John Dillinger pulled was in September

1924. With Singleton, he robbed a Mooresville grocery store, escaping with just $50 between them. In their haste to escape, the two would-be gangsters were spotted by a local minister, who recognized them and reported what he'd seen to the police. The next day the pair were arrested. On trial, Singleton pleaded not guilty, while Dillinger's father – also a Mooresville church deacon – convinced his son to plead guilty in the hope of avoiding a long prison sentence. Regardless, Dillinger was convicted of assault and battery with intent to rob, and conspiracy to commit a felony. Expecting lenient treatment thanks to a deal he believed his father had made with the county prosecutor, Dillinger was taken aback to be sentenced to ten to twenty years in prison (Singleton, however, only got two years). As a result, he staged his first attempt to escape custody, but it was short lived and the twenty-one-year-old was quickly recaptured.

Locked up in the Indiana Reformatory from 1924, and then Pendleton Jail in Indiana, and finally in Indiana State Prison in Michigan from 1929 until 1933, Dillinger put his time behind bars to good use – learning to become the best criminal he could. The harsh sentence caused Dillinger to become unrepentant, determined not to follow society's accepted rules. Associating with other more experienced criminals in Indiana State Prison, he learned how best to pull off bank heists and the 'dos and don'ts' of a successful criminal career. In particular, Dillinger paid close attention to a robbery technique outlined by German bank robber Herman Lamm, one he'd adopt himself for many of his later bank jobs. A former Prussian soldier, Lamm approached robbing a bank as a military operation, timing each action down to the second. He pioneered the idea of 'casing' a prospective bank to scope out its security precautions and to anticipate any obstacles. Lamm would draw up detailed floor plans, showing the location of safes, and highlighting escape routes. Each member of the gang would have a specific job to ensure the robbery was carried out as efficiently as possible. Many of Dillinger's later robberies showed just such meticulous attention to detail in the planning, if not always in the execution.

Released at the height of the Depression in May 1933, there was very little prospect of the now jail-educated John Dillinger going straight and finding a legitimate job. Instead, he applied all he'd learned from older, more experienced criminals, pulling off his first bank robbery just one month after he was released. The day before his thirtieth birthday, Dillinger struck at the New Carlisle National Bank in Ohio, making off with around $10,000. He hit four other banks in Indiana or Ohio between July and September 1933, netting a total of approximately $47,000. The would-be career criminal was careless, however, allowing himself to be tracked down by the Dayton, Ohio police. He was quickly captured and returned to prison in Lima, Ohio, but not before the police confiscated papers that outlined what appeared to be a fully worked out prison escape plan.

The plan was genuine, one that Dillinger had developed during his near-decade in Indiana State Prison, along with other prisoners, such as Harry 'Pete' Pierpont, Charles Makley, Russell Clark and Homer Van Meter, the people who'd given Dillinger such a top-notch criminal education. Four days after Dillinger was locked up in Lima, a version of his escape plan was put into action resulting in Pierpont, Makley and Clark, along with several others, breaking out of Indiana State Prison, using smuggled shotguns and rifles. During the escape, the gang shot two guards. Pierpont, Makley and Clark with parolee Harry Copeland then turned up at Lima jail disguised as police officers, claiming they'd come to extradite Dillinger to Indiana for parole violations. Asked by Sheriff Jess Sarber for their credentials, Pierpont shot the man dead and the gang broke Dillinger out of his cell, where he was awaiting trial. They then locked the Sheriff's wife and his deputy in Dillinger's cell. The four outlaws headed to Indiana where they joined the other escaped criminals, Ed Shouse and Canadian John 'Red' Hamilton. Together they would form the core of the Dillinger gang.

So began a spree of cross-country bank robberies by the Dillinger gang and an epic chase by the forces of law and order that took place over ten months between September 1933 and July 1934. According to a later FBI tally, the gang killed ten, wounded seven, robbed banks and police arsenals, and staged three jailbreaks during their reign of terror across America's Midwest. At the same time, much of the Depression-struck public came to regard John Dillinger as a wayward hero, who hit the banks that had wrecked the economy but never stole from the local farmers who were waiting to deposit money in those same crooked banks. When he appeared in newsreels unspooling in cinemas where he'd hit the local banks, audiences applauded Dillinger rather than the forces of law and order who sought to capture him.

The gang hit three banks between October 1933 and January 1934 in Indiana and Wisconsin, getting away with just over $120,000 in total. To pull off the robberies, they needed weapons, so hit state police weapons arsenals in Auburn and Peru (both in Indiana) stealing several machine-guns, rifles, revolvers, ammunition and police-issue bulletproof vests. While hiding out in Chicago in December 1933, Dillinger gang member John Hamilton shot and killed a police detective. In response, the Chicago police department organized a dedicated forty-man-strong 'Dillinger Squad'. Traps established by the police repeatedly failed to capture Dillinger, who would inevitably shoot his way out. John Dillinger was now declared to be Public Enemy Number One, and people were warned to be on the look-out for the armed-and-dangerous outlaw. The following month Dillinger killed a police officer during a shoot-out while conducting a robbery of the First National Bank of East Chicago, Indiana. The gang fled to Florida, before moving on to Tucson, Arizona. While there, on 21 January 1934, fire erupted in the Congress Hotel in which they were laying low, and the firemen evacuating the hotel residents recognized Clark and Makley as wanted Dillinger gang members. They were arrested, along with Harry Pierpont and Dillinger himself. Cash from the East Chicago robbery and a cache of weapons were also seized.

Dillinger was sent to Lake County Jail in Crown Point, Indiana, to be held for trial for the killing of the police officer during the East Chicago robbery. Pierpont, Makley, and Clark were sent to Ohio to be put on trial for the killing of Sheriff Jess Sarber during the breakout of Dillinger from Lima jail. Dillinger gang member Ed Shouse gave prosecution testimony that saw the trio convicted in March 1934, with Pierpont and Makley given death sentences, while Clark was to be jailed for life. During another escape attempt, Makley was shot dead by prison guards and Pierpont was wounded. He was put to death by the state shortly thereafter. Clark served his time, eventually being released in 1968, only to die from cancer a few months later.

Locked away in Crown Point, which newspapers – echoing police boasts – claimed was escape proof, Dillinger spent his time whittling an imitation gun from wood, then blackened it with shoe polish. That March he threatened guards with his fake weapon, and managed to escape along with another inmate, Herbert Youngblood (who'd be killed in a police shoot-out just two weeks later) and two hostages they'd taken. Jail officials claimed the weapon had been real, smuggled in to Dillinger by his attorney, but later FBI reports make it clear it had been manufactured from wood from a shelf in Dillinger's cell and modelled after a Colt .38 pistol. This latest escape was too much for J. Edgar Hoover, then forming his Crime Division into the

Federal Bureau of Investigation (which would be formally established as such in 1935). Dillinger had stolen a sheriff's car during his escape, and crossed state lines to Chicago in the stolen vehicle, so committing a Federal offence. Hoover put one of his best agents, Melvin Purvis, onto the Dillinger case with instructions to bring his crime spree to an end, one way or another. Purvis formed a dedicated team of 'G-Men' and set out on Dillinger's trail. They were said to have used life-sized photographs of Dillinger's face for target practice.

With a new gang, including Lester 'Baby Face Nelson' Gillis and Eddie Green, Dillinger was up to his old tricks, robbing banks in Sioux Falls, South Dakota and Mason City, Iowa, escaping with over $100,000 in total, although Dillinger and 'Red' Hamilton were wounded. The gang almost fell into an FBI trap in St Paul, Minnesota, but Dillinger, his girlfriend Evelyn Frechette, and Homer Van Meter shot their way out. Eddie Green was wounded and captured by the FBI. While in a delirious state he revealed much information that proved very useful to Dillinger's pursuers. As a result, Frechette was captured by Purvis while in a tavern in Chicago, but Dillinger escaped his pursuers once again.

Dillinger and Van Meter raided another police weapons store in Warsaw, Indiana and continued to evade their determined pursuers, with Dillinger, Hamilton and Nelson embroiled in yet another shoot-out following another failed FBI trap at the Little Bohemia Lodge near Rhinelander, Wisconsin. In the gun battle, Nelson killed one FBI agent, while the FBI only managed to kill an unfortunate innocent civilian bystander. Hamilton was fatally wounded in the mêlée, with Dillinger burying his body on the outskirts of Oswego, Illinois.

In May 1934 new Federal laws allowed for the indictment of Dillinger and his associates for conspiracy, and substantial rewards were offered for information leading to

their capture, with the FBI offering $10,000 and five indi-
vidual states offering another $10,000 in total. In response,
Dillinger and Van Meter were said to have undergone plastic surgery in May in Chicago in order to change their
appearance. Dillinger paid the German-born Dr Loeser to
remove his fingerprints and alter his facial appearance. An
accidental overdose of ether almost killed the gangster on
the operating table. Disappointed with the results, which
had barely changed the way he looked at all, Dillinger
decided to lie low for a while. By June, US grand juries
had further indicted Dillinger on a host of new charges,
just in time for the outlaw's thirty-first birthday, which he
celebrated in a nightclub in Chicago with new girlfriend
Polly Hamilton. Through Hamilton, Dillinger then met
Romanian prostitute and madam Anna Sage.

There was no let up, with the Dillinger gang striking again
in South Bend, Indiana, killing another policeman during a
bank raid that netted them $30,000. Returning to Chicago,
Dillinger reunited with Sage, whose real name was Anna
Cumpanas. Fearing she might be deported for running a
brothel, Sage, through an intermediary, had approached
FBI agent Melvin Purvis, letting him know that on 22 July
Dillinger was intending to take her and Polly Hamilton to
see a movie at the Biograph Theater on Lincoln Avenue.
Purvis immediately assembled a large team of specialist
FBI agents and Chicago policemen, planning to surround
the cinema and grab Dillinger as he exited. Appropriately,
the wanted gangster was watching a gangster movie,
Manhattan Melodrama, starring Clark Gable and William
Powell. When the outlaw appeared in the theatre's foyer,
the assembled lawmen let loose, shooting him in the head
and his left side. Within minutes, notorious gangster John
Dillinger lay dead on the sidewalk.

Or did he? The details of the killing of John Dillinger
were muddled at the time, and they remain so today. There's
no record of who actually fired the fatal shots. Anna Sage

has been transformed into a mysterious 'woman in red' who led Dillinger to his downfall. One of the Chicago policemen in attendance was Mark Zarkovich, supposedly linked to Sage, who helped himself to the money in Dillinger's pockets. Sage was then deported, as she feared, in 1936. Melvin Purvis, the agent who successfully brought Dillinger's crime spree to an end, mysteriously resigned from the FBI in 1935, just as the newly formed organization was finding its feet and learning lessons from the Dillinger debacle. Most importantly of all, was it really Dillinger who was shot outside the Biograph Theater?

The resulting autopsy report disappeared for over thirty years. It revealed the dead man's eyes were brown, where Dillinger's were recorded as blue. The corpse had suffered from rheumatic heart disease from childhood, which Dillinger, apparently, had not. More obviously, the corpse as described was both shorter and heavier than John Dillinger, and none of his identifying marks – such as easily noticed birthmarks and scars from gunshot wounds – were ever properly recorded. The dead man didn't even look like Dillinger, a discrepancy explained away through the plastic surgery story, which remains unconfirmed. Was the FBI's trophy corpse in fact a completely different small-time crook – one who'd been seen around locally during the period Dillinger was locked up in prison in Michigan City, Indiana? Did Dillinger actually escape the forces of law and order for one last time in 1934, having learned his lesson as an on-the-lam fugitive, and finally settled for a more quiet life out of the limelight? Whatever the truth, the legend of John Dillinger would live on for decades after his death, whether genuine or faked.

Baby Face and Pretty Boy
John Dillinger wasn't the only notable gangster operating in the American Midwest during the 1930s: there was also his one-time gang member and associate Baby Face

Nelson, as well as Pretty Boy Floyd, who each gained their own kind of lasting criminal notoriety.

Born Lester Joseph Gillis in 1908, George Nelson was to go down in history as 'Baby Face' Nelson, the nickname he was given due to his youthful looks and small stature. Nelson was one of the gang who helped John Dillinger in his second jailbreak in Crown Point, Indiana, and he joined Dillinger on the United States' 'Most Wanted' list as part of the gang declared Public Enemy Number One. He was reputed to have the dubious distinction of having been the gangster who killed more FBI agents in the line of their duty than any other criminal individual. Perhaps fittingly, it was agents of the FBI who finally gunned 'Baby Face' down in November 1934, aged twenty-six.

Nelson was first arrested at the age of twelve after he shot a fellow child in the jaw with a pistol he claimed to have found. As a result he was sent to the state reformatory. The second arrest of this precocious criminal came the following year when he was picked up for car theft and joyriding – this time he got a further eighteen months of juvenile detention.

Aged nineteen, it looked like Nelson was on the straight-and-narrow, working at a Standard Oil gas station in his neighbourhood. Unfortunately for the easily led Nelson, the station was also the main base of a gang of 'tyre strippers' who regularly stole tyres from vehicles parked locally. He quickly fell in with the gang, becoming acquainted with many of the key figures in the wider local underworld and soon had a driving job, delivering bootleg alcohol to Chicago speakeasies. That led to him joining the suburban Touhy Gang, led by Irish-American bootlegger Roger Touhy, a Chicago rival of Al Capone. Touhy was regularly intimidated by Capone as the gangster wanted to take over his operation.

Within two years, Nelson had his own gang and had stepped up his criminal activities to include armed robbery.

In January 1930, Nelson and his gang invaded the home of magazine publisher Charles M. Richter, tying him up and ransacking his home. They escaped with $25,000 worth of jewellery. That became the gang's M.O., and they did the same at the home of Lottie Brenner Von Bulow two months later, escaping with $50,000 in jewels. The gang's habit of tying their victims up with adhesive tape saw Chicago newspapers dub them 'The Tape Bandits'.

In the winter of 1931, the Tape Bandits were all captured, including Nelson. He was sentenced to a year in the state penitentiary at Joliet, Illinois but escaped in February 1932 during a prison transfer. His underworld connections saw him find shelter with Reno, Nevada crime boss William Graham. He then headed west and spent some time working for bootlegger Joe Parente in Sausilito, California. While working in the San Francisco Bay area, Nelson hooked up with John Paul Chase, Tommy Carroll and Eddie Green, who formed the core members of his gang. Also along for the ride was Helen Warwick, whom Nelson had married in 1928. They had a son, Ronald, and a daughter, Diane, and Nelson insisted in attempting to maintain a 'normal' family life while he evaded the law, even if it was funded from the proceeds of crime.

By 1933 the Nelson gang had moved onto bank robberies, alternating them with their home invasions of prominent people, audaciously including that of Chicago mayor 'Big Bill' Thompson. They made off with his wife's jewellery, valued at $18,000. She described her assailant as having 'a baby face. He was good looking, hardly more than a boy . . .' That was enough for the press to coin the nickname 'Baby Face' for Nelson, which quickly stuck. In the summer of 1933, Nelson teamed up with bank robber Eddie Bentz, when they knocked over the Grand Haven Bank in Michigan that August. The gang made a point of ripping up mortgage agreements and loan paperwork, while distributing cash to public onlookers, so creating a seemingly inevitable and entirely self-justifying Robin Hood myth. Nelson added to his gang, recruiting sometime Dillinger associate Homer Van Meter from the St Paul's Green Lantern Tavern. They raided the First National Bank of Brainerd, Minnesota, getting out with $23,000, but not before the hot-headed Nelson sprayed passers-by with random machine-gun fire.

In March 1934, Nelson and his associates helped spring John Dillinger from jail in Crown Point, Indiana, throwing his own gang in with Dillinger's full time. The merged outfit resumed their bank-robbing activities, but while Dillinger was methodical in his approach, Nelson was more wild with a hair-trigger temper, liable to start shooting at the slightest provocation. After the death of Eddie Green, the Dillinger–Nelson gang fled to hide out at the secluded Little Bohemia Lodge by Manitowish Waters, Wisconsin. Lodge owner Emil Wanatka claimed not to know the new arrivals were wanted men, but he did notice they were all 'packing heat', meaning they had guns, during a late-night card game. The next day, while Nelson's wife and children were away, Wanatka, through a friend, brought the men's presence at his Lodge to the attention of the FBI. Melvin Purvis and his agents organized a rush-raid on the Lodge, believing the gangsters were preparing to leave the next morning.

There was chaos as the hasty FBI agents opened fire on departing guests, killing a civilian, wounding others and alerting the gangsters – who were still inside – to their presence. Most of the gang members, including Dillinger, escaped the location through a variety of means, but true to character Nelson grabbed a machine-gun and began attacking the FBI agents head-on, exchanging direct fire with Purvis. He then escaped in a stolen car, taking several people hostage, including Wanatka. During the escape, Nelson wounded two FBI agents and killed another. He then made his getaway in the FBI vehicle, before hiding out in the woods until things quietened down. Nelson's wife Helen was captured and interrogated by the FBI, then convicted on charges of harbouring a fugitive and released on parole. Nelson later re-connected with the remaining Dillinger mob and his wife in the summer of 1934, determined to lie low in various tourist camps in the Chicago area.

By the end of June, Nelson, Dillinger, Van Meter and another accomplice robbed the Merchant's National Bank in South Bend, Indiana, where Van Meter shot dead an alerted policeman. During the robbery Nelson was shot in the chest, but was saved thanks to the bulletproof vest he was wearing. Escaping with $28,000 and amid a shoot-out with the police, the gang managed to wound several bystanders – it was to be the group's last collective effort.

Their other accomplice had been the gang's newest member, Charles Arthur Floyd. Known as 'Pretty Boy', he was born in 1904 in Georgia. His first arrest came at age eighteen when the six-feet-two-inches Floyd stole valuable coins from a Post Office. Three years later, in 1925, he'd graduated to payroll robbery for which he was sentenced to five years in prison, serving three-and-a-half. In various partnerships around Kansas City, Floyd took part in a series of bank robberies, acquiring the nickname 'Pretty Boy' when a witness to one of his raids described him as 'a mere boy – a pretty boy with apple cheeks'. Although Baby Face Nelson and Pretty Boy Floyd, in keeping with many gangsters of the time, hated the nicknames given to them by the press, they were part of the gangster mystique and contributed to them being remembered today.

Floyd carried out various robberies in the 1930s and was repeatedly arrested for vagrancy. In November 1930, he was sentenced to twelve to fifteen years in Ohio State Penitentiary for bank robbery, but he managed to escape. He was suspected in the death of bootlegging brothers Wally and Boll Ash of Kansas City who were discovered in a burning car in March 1931, as well as the deaths of a US patrolman in Bowling Green, Ohio and a Treasury Department agent in Kansas City, Missouri. In April 1932, Floyd killed an Oklahoma Sheriff who tried to arrest him, before he and his gang killed four more police officers in a June 1933 gunfight that became known as the 'Kansas City Massacre' – Floyd denied his involvement in a postcard he sent to Kansas City police, claiming it was his lookalike Sol Weismann who took part. His reputation backfired on him, however, and the authorities were willing to believe he was involved, whether it was true or not.

When Dillinger met his fate at the Biograph Theater later that same month, Pretty Boy Floyd was promoted to Public Enemy Number One, a position he held until he was also killed in a shoot-out with Melvin Purvis. On 22 October 1934 Floyd was cornered in a cornfield near Clarkson, Ohio, where he was shot dead by pursuing FBI agents led by Purvis. Accounts differ as to who actually fired the fatal shot, but Purvis claimed the credit regardless.

FBI director J. Edgar Hoover then anointed Baby Face Nelson as the new Public Enemy Number One. In the wake of the South Bend bank raid, Nelson, his wife and gang member John Paul Chase had gone to California, then back to Chicago by July 1934, where he was caught up in yet another inconclusive shoot-out with Illinois State Troopers. By that August, when gang member Van Meter was killed by police in St Paul, Minnesota, Nelson was the last remaining member of the Dillinger gang still active. Still teamed with his wife and John Paul Chase, Nelson headed west once more, again hiding out in various public camping sites. By October 1934, the FBI had tracked Nelson to the Lake Como Inn at Lake Geneva, Wisconsin where they believed the gangster planned to hole up for the winter period. When Nelson finally arrived at the end of November, he took the FBI agents who were staking out the building by surprise.

On 27 November 1934 what became known as the 'Battle of Barrington' took place in the town just outside Chicago, Illinois. The furious gunfight that claimed the lives of Nelson and two FBI agents followed a car chase in which the FBI followed Nelson, his wife and Chase in a stolen V-8 Ford on State Highway 14 heading for Chicago. Nelson spotted the pursuing agents, and the two cars alternately chased each other along sections of the highway. At Barrington, Nelson and Chase took cover behind their car, while Nelson's wife Helen sought refuge in a ditch. More than thirty people witnessed the ensuing shoot-out that concluded with a mortally-wounded Nelson advancing on the FBI agents firing off his .351 rifle so quickly that witnesses thought he had a machine-gun. The FBI agents – Herman Hollis (who'd been present at the killing of Pretty Boy Floyd and may have inflicted the fatal shot) and Samuel Cowley (who'd been among the officers who'd gunned down Dillinger) – were both killed by Nelson. He then collapsed into the FBI agent's car, which Chase then drove away, picking up Helen en route. Nelson had been shot at least seventeen times, and declared to his wife 'I'm done for!' Chase headed for a safe house in nearby Wilmette, where Nelson died that evening at 7.35 p.m., with his wife by his side.

John Dillinger, Pretty Boy Floyd and Baby Face Nelson were all dead, bringing to an end one of the most remarkable gangster crime sprees of the mid-1930s. Helen Gillis, who'd wrapped her husband's body in a Native American patterned blanket and left it outside St Peter Catholic Cemetery in Skokie, surrendered herself on Thanksgiving Day 1934. She served a year in prison for harbouring Nelson. John Paul Chase was later also captured and sentenced to jail in Alcatraz, where Al Capone was still in reluctant residence. The exploits of these Midwestern gangsters may have been exaggerated and exploited by an over-excitable press, keen to make them into colourful characters fighting the powers-that-be during the economic downturn of the Depression, but they remained violent lawbreakers who between them brought to an end the lives of many innocent law officers who were charged with enforcing society's rules – rules that America's gangsters lived beyond.

8

BONNIE AND CLYDE – DUSTBOWL DESPERADOES

There are myths and legends surrounding many gangsters and their exploits in the American Depression of the 1930s, but perhaps some of the most romantic and most inaccurate are those about Bonnie and Clyde, the infamous lovers turned bank robbers. Between 1931 and 1934, the pair criss-crossed the central United States robbing banks, but also hitting Clyde Barrow's preferred 'safer' targets of rural gas stations and small stores. John Dillinger had something of the matinée idol about him and Pretty Boy Floyd didn't gain that nickname for no reason, but the winners hands down in the glamorous gangster stakes were Bonnie and Clyde, even if the truth was very different from their post-humous image. While they were evading the law, the press started building myths around the couple far removed from their real-life exploits, helped by a cache of photos full of 'gangster poses' they left behind after a raid. Their romantic legend was even further extended by the violent, iconic way they finally exited the stage, together in a hail of bullets.

The desperate flight of Bonnie and Clyde

Bonnie Elizabeth Parker was born in October 1910 in Texas, the middle child of three. Charles, her father, was a bricklayer who died when his daughter was aged just four. Her mother, Emma, then raised the children in Cement City, Dallas where Bonnie's grandparents lived. Unlike many of the male gangsters, Parker was good at school, literate, numerate and good at public speaking. She later expressed herself in adulthood through poetry she sent to newspapers.

It was romance that saw Bonnie Parker drop out of high school to marry Roy Thornton in 1926, just two weeks before she turned sixteen. It was a short-lived union, punctuated with Roy's tangles with the law. Parker moved back in with her mother when Thornton abandoned her and she found work in Dallas as a waitress. Thornton was jailed for five years for robbery in 1929. Although never actually divorced, the pair didn't see each other again: however, she kept his wedding ring, and was wearing it on the day she died. Postal worker Ted Hinton was a regular customer in the café where Parker worked – he later joined the police and was part of the posse that would pursue Bonnie and Clyde across the country in 1934. For amusement, Parker often went to the movies and became quite a fan of 'talking pictures' and the glamorous stars who lit up the silver screen.

Bonnie Parker's eventual partner in life and death, Clyde Chestnut Barrow, was born into a Texan farming family in 1909, one of seven children of Henry and Cumie Barrow. By the early 1920s the impoverished family had left farming behind, relocating to Dallas and living in a district of urban slums. A poor student, Barrow quit school at the age of sixteen. He was arrested for the first time the following year: he'd failed to return a rental car. His next arrest, along with his older brother, Ivan 'Buck' Barrow, was for possession of stolen goods – the 'goods' in question were turkeys.

Barrow worked legitimate jobs in 1927 and 1928, but at the same time pursued the easy money of a career in crime by cracking safes, robbing small stores and stealing cars. By April 1930, Clyde Barrow was serving time in Eastham Prison Farm. During this period, Barrow was repeatedly sexually assaulted by fellow prisoner Ed Crowder, who he later beat to death (although another prisoner, 'lifer' Aubrey Scalley, took the blame). Barrow was paroled in February 1932, but the man who left prison was very different to the one who'd gone in two years before. Barrow was now an embittered and hardened man – fellow inmate and later Barrow gang member Ralph Fults said of Clyde, 'He changed from a school boy to a rattlesnake'.

Determined not to return to prison – he claimed he'd die first, and was true to his word – Barrow set out to focus on smaller, less risky jobs than robbing banks. He'd hold up grocery stores and gas stations, using his favoured weapon, the Browning automatic rifle, to threaten the clerks. Most didn't want to risk their lives and simply handed over whatever money they had in their tills – the amounts were small, so to keep eating, Barrow had to hit many stores.

There are conflicting accounts of where and when exactly Bonnie Parker first met Clyde Barrow. The most widely accepted version suggests they first encountered one another in January 1930 at the house of one of Parker's friends, even before Barrow served his initial prison time. It seems the pair were taken with one another almost immediately. For Parker, Barrow was representative of escape from her boring life: she wanted to have an exciting time just like she'd seen in the movies, and this fast-moving petty criminal seemed like the man who could offer her what she was after. However, he would be back in jail before they could get very far in realizing their dreams. He escaped briefly when she smuggled a .38 Colt pistol in to him strapped to her thigh, but he was quickly recaptured, so it wasn't until after Barrow's February 1932 release that the pair got together and began building the outlaw legend of Bonnie and Clyde.

Once out of prison, Barrow hooked up with old jail mate Ralph Fults and quickly recruited a gang. Fults started his career in crime at the age of fourteen when he was jailed for holding stolen goods, only to lead a mass jailbreak a week later after creating a key from an old tobacco tin. In and out of reformatories and prisons over the years, Fults had ended up in Eastham Prison Farm beside Barrow, from which he also briefly escaped in 1930.

Barrow intended for Fults to become his lead lieutenant in the gang he was assembling. Fults then recruited Ray Hamilton, an ex-jailbird and a friend of Barrow's from their youth, who would become an occasional member of the Barrow gang. Bonnie Parker became attached to the growing group, determined to follow Barrow wherever he was heading in life. Posthumous stories suggested she would happily share her bed with both Barrow and Hamilton, sometimes together, but that can't be substantiated. The three men and Parker then robbed a hardware store in Kaufman, Texas, intent on stealing a cache of weapons – the first known job pulled by the Barrow gang. A watchman sounded the alarm, causing Barrow and Hamilton to flee. Fults and Parker were apprehended, and Fults was sentenced to ten years in prison in 1932. While she was held, Bonnie wrote bad poetry, including the notoriously prophetic 'Suicide Sal' which told of a gangster and his moll shot down in a hail of bullets.

There was a rationale to Barrow's series of small criminal raids: he wanted to gather enough cash and weapons to mount an attack on Eastham Prison Farm, where he'd been abused, freeing the inmates in revenge for his treatment. However, the arrests of Fults and Parker set back the timetable. Without Parker, Barrow and new gang members Ted Rogers and Johnny Russell pulled off a series of jobs, but their activities quickly led to murder. During the hold-up of a jewellery store in Hillsboro, Texas, either Rogers or Russell – Barrow claimed he was just the driver and stayed outside the store, although he was the one identified from police mug shots – killed the store's proprietor, John Bucher. That July, Barrow temporarily reunited with Ray Hamilton. The pair opened fire on a sheriff, killing him and wounding his deputy, outside an Oklahoma barn dance.

Parker was released that June as the grand jury could not agree on an indictment. After visiting her mother, she quickly rejoined Barrow, but Fults never would – both Barrow and Parker would be dead by the time he was pardoned and released in 1935.

In the summer of 1932, Bonnie and Clyde were together again and with Hamilton in tow they set out to visit Bonnie's aunt in Carlsbad, New Mexico. Their brand new stolen car caught the attention of Eddy County Deputy Sheriff Joe Johns, who the gang promptly abducted, locking him up with his own handcuffs. After driving around with their captive for a while, they let him go in San Antonio, unharmed but with a message for the media: 'We ain't a bunch of nutty killers, just down home people trying to get through this damned Depression with a few bones.' Kidnapping and releasing people with messages for the newspapers would become a habit for Bonnie and Clyde. That October, the gang raided a bank and the National Guard Armoury in Abilene, Texas and Clyde killed again when during a robbery he shot dead the proprietor of a grocery store in Sherman, Texas (however, there is some dispute among historians over Clyde's responsibility for this killing). There was now a $250 bounty (a large amount of money at that time) on Clyde Barrow's head.

In the fall of 1932, Ray Hamilton finally departed the Barrow Gang, deciding to visit his father in Michigan. Feeling relaxed and at home, Hamilton got drunk and began telling stories of his exploits with the notorious Bonnie and Clyde. Word soon got around town, and Hamilton was quickly arrested and extradited to Texas, where he was sentenced to an outlandish 263 years in the penitentiary at Barrow's dreaded Eastham Prison Farm, north of Huntsville, Texas.

Barrow gained a young protégé in December 1932 when sixteen-year-old William Daniel Jones – known as W. D. – joined the pair of outlaws. A Barrow family friend since childhood, he was keen to join the older man in his criminal endeavours. Later reports would claim that Bonnie wanted a younger man around who could meet her sexual desires in a way Barrow often failed to, but this too has been disputed. Also questionable were Jones' later claims to have been subjected to Barrow's own sexual whims: in a 1968 article in *Playboy* magazine, Jones claimed, 'I've heard stories since that Clyde was homosexual, or, as they say in the pen, a "punk", but they ain't true.' Within days of joining up, Barrow and Jones had killed a man with a young family while stealing his car in Temple, Texas. Two weeks after that, on 6 January 1933, Barrow killed Tarrant County Deputy Sheriff Malcolm Davis, when he, Parker and Jones had the misfortune to stumble into a law-enforcement trap. In just under a year, the Barrow gang had killed five people.

In March 1933, Barrow's older brother Ivan, known as Buck, was granted a full pardon and released from prison. He hooked up with his wife Blanche and the pair joined Bonnie and Clyde, as well as Jones, in their hideout at a garage apartment in Oak Ridge Drive, Joplin, Missouri. Although supposedly laying low after their recent activities, the two couples and Jones stayed up all night taking part in alcohol-fuelled card games, in what was generally otherwise a rather quiet neighbourhood. Prohibition ended during their brief stay, so the opportunity to legally buy and drink beer was too good for the outlaws to miss. During the two weeks of their stay, the behaviour of the strangers was noted locally, and drew the attention of law enforcement.

On 13 April 1933, Joplin Sheriff's Department put together a five-man task force and set out to raid what they believed to be the headquarters of a gang of bootleggers at Oak Ridge Drive. Initially caught off-guard, Barrow and his gang soon fought back, and a fierce gun battle ensued. During the shooting, two detectives, McGinnis and Harryman, were killed. The gang escaped their hideout while (according to some breathless newspaper accounts of the event) Bonnie Parker kept the police isolated with covering machine-gun fire, an unlikely occurrence as there is no evidence she ever shot anyone. A Highway Patrol sergeant was pinned down behind a tree trunk into which the outlaw's volley of bullets impacted, sending wood splinters into the policeman's face. Parker joined the others in the getaway car, Barrow's 1932 V-8 Ford (the latest in a series of stolen V-8s; he wrote a letter to Henry Ford praising the vehicle), and sped away, after crashing past the police patrol car that blocked the road. Jones had been wounded in his side, Buck had been grazed by a bullet, and another had ricocheted off Barrow's coat button, so he'd narrowly escaped a potentially fatal injury.

Such had been the disorganized nature of their departure, the Barrow Gang left behind a haul of material in their Joplin hideaway that was taken by the police, but soon came into the possession of the press. Buck and Blanche's marriage licence identified them, allowing the police to deduce who the others had been. Buck's three-week-old parole papers were also abandoned in Joplin, along with a cache of weapons, a bunch of poems written by Parker and – most notoriously of all – several rolls of undeveloped film.

The pictures revealed when the film was developed would become some of the most iconic images of 1930s gangsters. The photos, most seemingly taken by Jones, depicted Bonnie Parker and Clyde Barrow in a series of menacing poses, with Tommy guns and pistols, around their car. In the most famous of all, Bonnie is the classic gangster's moll, a pistol in her hand (stolen from a police motorbike patrolman), leaning upon the car's huge head-light, her foot resting on the front fender of the V-8 Ford, with a defiantly unfeminine cigar, or 'stogie', in her mouth (the cigar was from Jones). In another photo, Bonnie is on one side of the car, while Clyde sits on the fender cradling a shotgun in his arms. One more image had Bonnie pointing a shotgun at a passive Clyde, as if holding him up.

Bonnie and Clyde appear to be the first gangsters to photographically chronicle their own criminal exploits. There's a picture of them standing proudly by a Route 66 US Highway sign somewhere in Missouri, appearing for all the world to be a honeymooning couple. There's a playful-ness to many of the images, despite their weaponry. For all their relative lack of education, they may have been the first image-conscious gangsters, determined to make a major contribution to the way they would be seen and perceived not only by contemporary newspapers, but also perhaps by history. Combined with Bonnie's self-mythologizing poetry, such as 'The Story of Suicide Sal' and 'The Story of Bonnie and Clyde', the gangsters wanted to communi-cate their own history, and to provide the newspapers with something else to use other than 'unappealing' mug shots. The only other photo that would come to be as famous as these was that of their bullet-ridden 'death car'.

The nationwide press and newsreel (would-be movie star Bonnie Parker made it to cinema screens, after all) coverage turned 'cigar-chomping gun moll' Bonnie and 'Tommy-gun toting gangster' Clyde into bona fide celebri-ties, just like the movie stars that Bonnie Parker so adored.

Now their exploits were covered in ever greater detail by the newspapers and true crime magazines, eager to serve a public determined to find any distraction from the rigours of the Depression. Everything was given exaggerated significance, and the presence of Bonnie allowed the newspapers and magazines to play up the illicit sex angle for all it was worth. The stories often bore more relation to the Depression-era movies of James Cagney and Edward G. Robinson [see chapter 22] than they did to the real events. However, the Barrow gang were now official Public Enemies, and the thrill-hungry public lapped it all up.

As well as robbery, kidnapping increasingly became a key part of the Barrow gang's M.O. They roamed far and wide, from Texas to as far north as Minnesota, robbing small stores along the way. Later in the same month as their dramatic escape from Joplin, they attempted to steal a car in Ruston, Louisiana, kidnapping the car's owner Dillard Darby and his friend Sophia Stone. Darby was an undertaker, and his Chevrolet was a brand new car, so he attempted to prevent its theft. The Barrow gang took him and his friend for a long drive at gun point, arriving after several hours in Arkansas. Learning of Darby's occupation, Bonnie Parker was reported to have said to him: 'When they catch us, you can fix us up'. This was just one of a series of premeditated, seemingly prophetic, quotes that Parker gave to kidnap victims to pass on to a press hungry for sensation, especially when it concerned the Barrow gang. She'd also taken to sending further examples of her poetry directly to the newspapers after they'd published verses from 'Suicide Sal'. During May the gang hit banks in Lucerne, Indiana and Okabena, Minnesota, but didn't get away with large sums.

Bonnie and Clyde's crime spree might have been no more than an innocent media spectacle had they not been responsible for so many deaths along the way. Barrow was never shy about firing his gun, whatever the circumstances, and ever since his experience in Eastham Prison Farm he had absolutely no compunction about killing people, especially if it meant the difference between him being captured and returned to prison and his continuing freedom.

The town marshal of Alma, Texas was one of the unfortunate victims of the Barrow gang, although – as with so many of their on-the-lam escapades – it was difficult to tell who exactly pulled the trigger: Barrow, Buck or W. D., or even Parker. The marshal had pursued the gang following the robbery of a local bank. Anyone who got in the gang's way was now fair game, lawman or civilian. Each of the gang members was suspected of murder. It would be the readiness of the Barrow gang to let fly indiscriminately with bullets that eventually turned an initially amused public off the gang's violent final run.

Now notorious outlaws, and easily recognized thanks to the wide distribution of those infamous photos, Bonnie Parker and Clyde Barrow found life on the road increasingly difficult. They had to continually evade discovery, avoiding public places, restaurants and motels as they weren't safe. The gang took to camping in the countryside, cooking on camp fires and bathing in streams. This wasn't the glamorous movie star life that Bonnie Parker had anticipated when she first hooked up with young 'outlaw' Clyde Barrow, and which she'd hoped might come her way with nationwide fame – or infamy. Relationships between the five members of the gang deteriorated. The two couples – Bonnie and Clyde, Buck and Blanche – often argued, with W. D. Jones isolated. It got so bad that he fled the gang, tired of the emotional abuse, taking the Chevrolet they'd stolen from the undertaker. He vanished for a while, and was not seen again by the gang until early June.

Adding to their troubles, on 10 June 1933, Bonnie sustained third-degree burns in a car crash caused by Clyde when he failed to see detour signs near Wellington, Texas, indicating that a bridge up ahead was still under construction. Acid from the car battery splashed Parker's right leg causing serious burn injuries from her hip to her ankle, while Clyde and Jones were shaken up. From then on, Parker had difficulty walking unaided and relied on Barrow – and occasional travelling companion Billie Jean Parker, her younger sister – to help her move around. Often, after this, the outlaws regularly returned to visit their families in West Dallas, and whenever they had a big haul of cash from a robbery it would be distributed among family members.

Two local lawmen, who pursued the gang after they'd obtained assistance from the inhabitants of a nearby farm, were taken hostage. County Sheriff George Corry and local Chief of Police Paul Hardy would provide vital information that would lead to the eventual downfall of Bonnie and Clyde. Taking the officers' Chevrolet, Barrow boasted of their identities, revealing to the police that 'notorious gangster's moll' Bonnie Parker had been hurt in the crash. This need for recognition and validation was shared just as much by Clyde as it was by Bonnie. Upon their release, the captive officers were able to advise law enforcement organizations and drug stores to look out for people buying burn medication or specific medical supplies.

Having released their hostages, the trio reconnected with Blanche and Buck Barrow. The five wanted outlaws hid out in a tourist park near Fort Smith in Arkansas. Parker needed to stay in one place for a while to recover from her injuries, but when Buck and Jones shot and killed town marshal Henry D. Humphrey during an attempted bank robbery in Alma, they were once more actively pursued by the law and had to make a break for it, regardless of Parker's deteriorating physical condition.

The Barrow gang checked in to the Red Crown Tourist Court, a combined tavern and motel located south of Platte City in Missouri, on 18 July 1933, hoping they'd get the rest they needed. The building was made up of two brick cabins connected by two garages, with the gang renting the whole property. Failing to learn from their experience in Joplin, they didn't keep the low profile that might have been expected from a group on the run from the law. Signing in to the Tourist Court as a party of three, they didn't make much effort to hide from the manager that there were actually five of them. They parked their car with the front pointing in the direction of the exit, a method that enabled a quick getaway but had become known as 'gangster style' parking. Having raided a gumball and other coin-operated machines at various gas stations, the gang had a lot of loose coins, and that's how they paid for everything, including the $4 per night rent. It certainly stood out as unusual to the Red Court owner/manager Neal Houser. Perhaps most recklessly of all, the gang taped newspaper pages over the windows so they couldn't be observed from outside. Another of Houser's properties – the nearby Red Crown Tavern – was a popular watering hole for Missouri Highway Patrolmen. So disturbed was Houser by his new tenants' odd behaviour that he took a note of their car licence plate and then mentioned them to Captain William Baxter of the Highway Patrol when he popped into the restaurant that evening.

Several of the Barrow party took a trip into town for vital supplies, consisting of not only crackers and cheese, but also bandages and atropine sulphate, used to treat burns. Alert to the purchase, and aware of the alerts that had come in regarding suspicious characters buying just such medical supplies, the druggist contacted local sheriff Holt Coffey who put the Red Crown cabins under immediate surveillance.

Captain Baxter recruited reinforcements from Kansas City and commandeered the use of an armoured car. This came just weeks after the 'Kansas City Massacre' in mid-June 1933 that had resulted in the deaths of several officers and convict Frank Nash, so the Kansas police were already on high alert. On the evening of 19 July at 11 p.m., Baxter and a group of officers armed with Thompson sub-machine guns set out for the Red Court cabins. Hoping to subdue the occupants without getting too close to the building, the posse nonetheless carelessly alerted the gang to their presence. In the gunfight that followed the sub-machine guns proved to be ineffective when used at a distance, whereas Clyde Barrow's preferred weapon, the Browning automatic rifle, was good for firing accurately over the same range. He was able to hold the sheriff and his men at bay, while the others prepared to flee in their car. One bullet set off the horn on one of the cars, and the lawmen seemingly interpreted this as a signal to cease firing, and their momentary halt allowed the Barrow gang to escape into the night.

Coffey, Baxter and their men did not pursue the outlaws any further that evening, but the gang were aware that the law was closing in on them, seemingly no matter where they went. Both Blanche and Buck Barrow had been wounded in the escape; she due to glass fragments in her eyes (Blanche's vision would be permanently damaged as a result), and he with a serious bullet wound to the head. The outlaws' chances of evading capture and continuing their on-the-road existence were decreasing with every encounter with the law.

Just a few days later the gang were camping out in an abandoned amusement park near Dexter, Iowa, called Dexfield Park. Believing Buck was near death as a result of his head wound, Barrow and Jones dug a grave. The bloody bandages used to cover their wounds made the gang stand out in the locality, and their presence was quickly reported to the authorities. Identifying them as the notorious Barrow gang, law enforcement officers and around a hundred locals surrounded the amusement park, with armed police eventually opening fire. Barrow, Parker and Jones managed to get out on foot, but Blanche and Buck were in no condition to effect yet another escape. Shot once again, this time in the back, Buck was captured by the posse, who also nabbed Blanche as she attempted to evade them. Blanche was taken into custody (she'd later be questioned by J. Edgar Hoover and serve ten years in prison), while Buck died in hospital five days later from pneumonia following surgery.

The Barrow gang now consisted of just three members: Bonnie and Clyde, and their sidekick, W. D. Jones. Traumatized by their recent experiences, the trio managed to avoid notice for the next six weeks, genuinely lying low and only robbing out-of-the-way stores for supplies they deemed immediately necessary to their survival. During this period they travelled away from their usual haunts, ranging from Colorado in the west, Minnesota in the north, and Mississippi in the southeast. To acquire new firepower, Barrow and Jones raided an armoury in Plattville, Illinois on 20 August 1933, escaping with three rifles, several handguns and a cache of ammunition.

In the final months of 1933, the exhausted gang split up, with Jones travelling to Houston to see his mother, while Barrow and Parker visited their respective families in Dallas. While they took time out for their various wounds and medical needs to be seen to, Barrow also continued to stage a series of small-time robberies through October and November, hooking up with local accomplices whom he then paid off, buying their silence. A rendezvous with family members on 22 November almost saw Barrow and Parker captured, as a Dallas sheriff had been wise enough to track their family members. Gunfire was exchanged, but no family members or police were injured. Both Barrow and Parker sustained leg wounds while making their escape. Bonnie and Clyde wouldn't see their sidekick W. D. Jones ever again – he was arrested in Houston on 16 December and taken into custody in Dallas (he'd spend fifteen years in jail).

Running out of options seemed only to embolden Clyde Barrow. A murder indictment against the pair had been issued by a Dallas grand jury on 28 November for the January 1933 killing of a Tarrant County Deputy, the first such notice to include Parker. With no more accomplices, and suffering as a result of the wounds they'd sustained over the months, Barrow returned to his original purpose and staged a daring raid on Eastham Prison Farm. On 16 January 1934, he took part in a break-out of former Barrow gang member Ray Hamilton and Henry Methvin, along with some lucky others, from the hated prison. The plan had actually been Hamilton's (he'd arranged for guns to be smuggled in; Barrow was only the getaway driver), but Barrow got the credit in the press, suggesting he was a 'criminal mastermind' rather than an incompetent stick-up artist at best.

Prison Chief Lee Simmons declared that the escapees would be hunted down and killed, especially as a prison officer had been wounded during the escape (shot by escapee Joe Palmer, not any of the Barrow gang). The Federal Government and the proto-FBI (then known as the Division of Investigation, part of the US Justice Department) stepped up their efforts to capture Bonnie and Clyde, while the Texas Department of Corrections tasked retired former Texas Ranger Captain Frank A. Hamer with hunting down the Barrow Gang – he had a good track record, and looked a likely candidate to pull out all the stops to bring the crime spree of Bonnie and Clyde to an end once and for all.

Early in 1934, Hamer was on the trail of the outlaws, seemingly always just one step behind them. He took to living out of his car, so he would be able to hit the road at a moment's notice if there were any reports of their activities or any sightings. Prison escapee Ray Hamilton had once more split from the Barrow gang and was soon captured: he was executed in May 1935 for the murder of a prison guard.

On Easter Sunday, 1 April, 1934, Barrow and Methvin killed two Highway Patrolmen near Grapevine, Texas, although the killings were initially attributed to Barrow and Parker by an overenthusiastic press who played up her status thanks to those infamous photos. The Dallas newspapers went to town on the Grapevine killings, and public opinion soon turned against the romanticized outlaws. Bonnie and Clyde went from on-the-run lovers to cold-blooded killers, especially when the papers had (inaccurately) reported Bonnie as gleefully firing the final, fatal shots that killed the two young law officers, leaving behind her cigar butt. In reality, Methvin had been the first to fire when the Highway Patrol officers approached, with Barrow joining in as Parker most likely slept in the back of their car. The funeral of one of the officers was attended by his bride-to-be in her full wedding dress, and the photos ran in countless newspapers, further souring the public's relationship with the outlaw couple – one editorial cartoon depicted an electric chair with a sign noting it was 'reserved' for Bonnie and Clyde.

Driven by the media outcry and the public backlash, the police were forced into ever more drastic action in their pursuit of Bonnie and Clyde. An increased $1,000 reward was offered by the Highway Patrol for 'the dead bodies of the Grapevine slayers' – not their capture, their execution. Texas Governor Miriam A. Ferguson put an additional $500 bounty on each of the outlaw's heads. Things were made worse for the gang when only five days after the Grapevine incident, Barrow and Methvin killed again, this time shooting a sixty-year-old widower single father near Commerce, Oklahoma. Once again, the gang resorted to kidnapping, taking Commerce police chief Percy Boyd prisoner, only to release him hours later with an important message for the media: Bonnie Parker did not smoke cigars! Although she had bigger issues to worry about, Parker was most concerned with this aspect of her public image, ignoring the fact that although she'd killed no one, she was now regarded by the law and the public alike as a ruthless 'gun moll'. If captured, her opportunities for clemency had been severely reduced.

The road runs out . . .

The end of the road for Bonnie and Clyde came on 23 May 1934 in Bienville Parish, Louisiana. Texas Ranger Frank Hamer studied Barrow's track history, plotting his routes across the central United States. He figured out that Barrow was a creature of habit, repeatedly running through the same places in roughly the same order, consciously or not. Often, their movements were predicated upon pre-arranged family visits. Hamer reckoned that the Barrow gang were next most likely to resurface in Louisiana, on a visit with Methvin to see his family. They were aided by Methvin's father, Ivy, who arranged a pardon for his son if he would lure the outlaws into a pre-arranged ambush.

Hamer armed his posse with Barrow's own favourite weapon, Browning automatic rifles, and they set out for Shreveport, arriving on 21 May. Methvin's parents' home in Bienville Parish was designated as a gang rendezvous point if they ever got separated. That's exactly what happened, with Methvin deliberately separating himself from the outlaw pair, forcing them to return to his parent's home. Hamer's six-man posse established an ambush point on Louisiana State Highway 154, where they waited overnight until the morning of 23 May, when Bonnie and Clyde were expected at the Methvin's place. Barrow's latest stolen Ford V-8 appeared, approaching the posse's position slowly, as Clyde spotted Ivy Methvin's disabled truck on the road (a ruse arranged by the posse to lure in Barrow) and a logging truck approaching from the opposite direction on the single-track road.

Determined that the criminal gang would not evade the law this time, Hamer ordered his team to open fire; Parish

Deputy Sheriff Prentiss Oakley was the first to fire, before Hamer could give the outlaws a chance to surrender, as the posse had agreed on. After that, all of them took shots at the car containing Bonnie and Clyde, unleashing an estimated 150 rounds of ammunition. Clyde Barrow was killed instantly due to a fatal head shot by Oakley, while one member of the posse reported hearing Bonnie Parker loudly screaming when she realized Barrow was dead and the shots from the others began to hit her. The law officers nonetheless emptied their guns, firing at the car, with Hamer especially wanting to be certain Bonnie Parker had been killed.

Posse members Dallas County Sheriffs Deputies Ted Hinton (who knew Bonnie Parker from her waitressing days) and Bob Alcorn recalled their attack on the vehicle in their statements to the press: 'Each of us six officers had a shotgun and an automatic rifle and pistols. We opened fire with the automatic rifles. They were emptied before the car got even with us. Then we used shotguns . . . There was smoke coming from the car, and it looked like it was on fire. After shooting the shotguns, we emptied the pistols at the car, which had passed us and ran into a ditch about fifty yards on down the road. It almost turned over. We kept shooting at the car even after it stopped. We weren't taking any chances.' Hinton shot the 8mm film footage of the aftermath of the shooting, featuring the dead bodies of Bonnie and Clyde in the car, that has featured on newsreels and documentaries ever since (and is available on YouTube).

Press accounts differed as to the wounds suffered by Bonnie and Clyde in their 'death car' ranging from twenty-five bullet wounds each (so fifty overall) to over fifty hits to each of them. Any of the shots that hit was likely to prove fatal – the rest was just overkill by officers determined to stop the car in its tracks and end the criminal career of a pair of determined outlaws who'd made a laughing stock of the police and the Justice Department. The parish coroner's official report listed seventeen wounds for Barrow (one had snapped his spinal column) and twenty-six for Parker, each including several fatal head shots. Supposedly, legend has it that the assigned undertaker's assistant – who was Dillard Darby, their earlier kidnap victim – had trouble embalming their bodies due to the number of bullet holes.

In the immediate aftermath of the shooting, several of the posse went to the nearest town to call in their reports, thus alerting locals to what had happened. A curious crowd soon gathered at the isolated site, where the remaining posse members standing guard failed to prevent access to the corpses. Members of the public reportedly cut off locks of Bonnie Parker's hair and pieces from her bloodied dress – later sold as ghoulish souvenirs. It was said that one overzealous man had to be prevented from cutting off Clyde Barrow's trigger finger as a keepsake. A circus-like atmosphere pervaded the crowd around the 'death car', which contained an arsenal of weaponry, including sawn-off semi-automatic shotguns and pistols. When he arrived at the scene, coroner J. L. Wade claimed: ' . . . nearly everyone had begun collecting souvenirs, such as shell casings, slivers of glass from the shattered car windows, and bloody pieces of clothing from the garments of Bonnie and Clyde. One eager man had opened his pocket knife, and was reaching into the car to cut off Clyde's left ear . . .' Ear or trigger finger, the bloodthirsty crowd was out to get what they could from the infamous Bonnie and Clyde.

Print the legend

Although Bonnie and Clyde had wanted to be buried together, side by side in death as they had been in life, Bonnie Parker's family would not allow it. Around 20,000 sightseers attended Bonnie Parker's Dallas funeral on 26 May 1934, with floral tributes and cards supposedly sent by the likes of Pretty Boy Floyd and John Dillinger, as well as a huge floral arrangement from the Dallas city newspaper delivery boys, grateful for the half-million sales the out-law's violent end had brought them. Parker was buried in Fishtrap Cemetery, but her body was moved in 1945 to the Crown Hill Cemetery in Dallas, where her grave can be seen today.

Barrow's funeral, held the previous day, was a quieter affair, demonstrating that he didn't attract quite the public following that had become attached to 'gun moll' Bonnie Parker in life and death. He was buried next to his brother Buck (whose proper first name of 'Marvin' appears in the grave marker) in Western Heights Cemetery in Dallas: his granite gravestone notes that the gangster was 'Gone but not forgotten'.

Neither Bonnie nor Clyde would ever be forgotten. They outshone rival rural American gangsters such as Alvin Karpis, Ma Baker and her five hoodlum sons, and George 'Machine Gun' Kelly, who all had their moment in the spotlight. Changes in the law made bank robbery a federal rather than state crime, while the use of machine-guns was criminalized. This allowed for a more aggressive pursuit of the notorious names covered extensively by a fascinated press. During 1934 most of the 'celebrity' outlaw gangsters met their various ends. Dillinger was killed two months later in July, Pretty Boy Floyd in October, Baby Face Nelson in November, and Ma Barker and her son, Eric, in January 1935. J. Edgar Hoover's policy of going after the 'big names' of crime had paid off.

Bonnie and Clyde would not be forgotten by the rela-tives of all those killed during their two-year reign of terror across the central United States, when no lawman was seemingly safe. They would not be forgotten by the public, either, ever eager to lap up 'true life' crime stories. The pair would soon be the subject of cheap dime novels and questionable 'factual' accounts of their exploits, and they'd feature in many movies, most notably in Arthur Penn's explosive, romanticized and heavily fictionalized

1967 account starring Faye Dunaway and Warren Beatty, simply titled *Bonnie and Clyde*. Even their 'death car' is now no more than a tourist attraction, in a casino near Las Vegas. The ride had been short for Bonnie and Clyde, but their legend would be long-lasting.

9

MICKEY COHEN'S HOLLYWOOD TAKEOVER

Increasingly, American gangsters had transformed from the taciturn likes of Lucky Luciano and Meyer Lansky, who preferred to keep themselves and their business out of the limelight, to Al Capone, John Dillinger and Bonnie and Clyde who all – to varying degrees – used the press to further their fame and notoriety. There was only one mobster who loved Hollywood, and all that it offered, more than Bugsy Siegel and that was Mickey Cohen.

Born in Brooklyn, New York as Meyer Harris Cohen in September 1913, the self-styled 'Mickey' Cohen began his criminal career in New York just when a lot of the original gangsters of the 1920s were making their exits, either voluntarily or in pine boxes. He sold newspapers on Brooklyn's street corners from the age of six, many of them recounting the exploits of the first graduates of the Five Points Gang. Widowed in 1914 when her husband Max died, Cohen's mother Fanny relocated with him and his two brothers, Louie and Harry, to Los Angeles in the early 1920s, where she opened a grocery store.

In common with many gangsters-to-be, Cohen was never a good student and hated school, especially religious education (despite his Jewish heritage). Petty crime occupied him, and he ended up doing time in reform school in 1922. His prime occupation as a teenager was boxing, an activity that saw him take part in some illegal prize-fights. Aged fifteen, in 1929, Cohen fled Los Angeles so he wouldn't have to attend school any more. He turned up in Cleveland, where he became a professional prize-fighter taking part in matches there and in Chicago from 1930. In 1931, Cohen lost a bout with World Featherweight Champion Tommy Paul, and his last professional fight was in May 1933 against 'Baby' Arizmendi in Tijuana, Mexico. He later claimed – before a Senate committee – to have fought his way to victory in thirty-two different professional fights, although one reporter referred to Cohen as 'a second rate [fighter] with a glass chin . . . [who was] knocked out in most of his fights'.

It was during his boxing years that Mickey Cohen fell in with gangsters in Cleveland, especially Lou Rothkop, one of mobster Moe Dalitz's major-domos. Rothkop – himself connected to Meyer Lansky and to Bugsy Siegel's Las Vegas developments – ran gambling interests in Cleveland from the 1930s through to the 1950s. Like Al Capone he was convicted on income tax evasion charges and spent four years in jail. Dalitz was a bootlegger who made the most of his family's laundry trucks in the early days of Prohibition. He ran the Cleveland Syndicate covering alcohol distribution in Cleveland, Detroit, and Ann Arbor, Michigan, sourcing his liquor from Canada and Mexico. In the 1940s and 1950s he was a 'silent partner' with heavy investments in Las Vegas casinos and hotels, eventually selling the Desert Inn to entrepreneur Howard

Hughes in 1967. He lived until the age of ninety and died in 1989.

With the patronage of Rothkop and Dalitz, Cohen moved between the mob in New York and Chicago, building connections and making alliances. He then settled in Chicago, running gambling operations for Al Capone's Chicago Outfit.

Although he boasted of a personal connection to Capone, it is unlikely the pair met on more than a few, superficial occasions. Instead, Cohen was working with Capone's 'accountant' Jack 'Greasy Thumb' Guzik, for whom he functioned as an enforcer collecting debts and banging heads. After one particular high-stakes card game went wrong, Cohen was arrested on suspicion of involvement in the deaths of several Chicago mobsters. Back in action after a brief prison spell, he was once again running card games and other illegal gambling in Chicago. However, keen to escape, he was happy when Rothkop sent him to Los Angeles in 1939 to work directly with Bugsy Siegel.

The Los Angeles crime family
There was little more than a small ranch town to Los Angeles until 1820, by which time the population had increased to 650. 'New Spain', as the area was then known, separated from the Spanish Empire in 1821 and became part of Mexico, with Los Angeles as the area's capital. It switched to be part of America, following the Mexico–America war, in 1847. The arrival of the railroad in 1876 brought new prosperity and expansion to Los Angeles, and with it came organized crime. The discovery of oil in 1892 only accelerated the process. In 1910, Los Angeles annexed the nearby settlement of Hollywood, rapidly becoming the home of the movie industry, another nexus for criminal activity throughout the years to come [see chapters 10 and 11].

Mickey Cohen would have an automatic 'in' with the

Los Angeles 'Crime Family', the west coast wing of the Italian-American Mafia. As in the East and in New York, it had become established at the turn of the century through immigration, but it was bootlegging in the 1920s that really saw the growth of organized crime on the West coast, with gangster Jack Dragna's Commission running things – at least until Cohen set about putting him out of business.

The earliest elements of organized crime in Los Angeles were off-shoots of the New Orleans-based Matranga family. Charles Matranga, along with his brother Tony, had established one of the earliest Mafia organizations in New Orleans at the end of the nineteenth century. The Matrangas arrived in the United States around 1870, and quickly opened saloons and brothels as the beginnings of a criminal empire. Extortion and labour racketeering quickly followed. During a gang war in New Orleans between rival groups from Sicily, New Orleans police chief David Hennessy was assassinated. Charles Matranga was tried and cleared of the crime in 1891, but he was determined to expand his operation beyond New Orleans – especially when an angry mob killed eleven members of his gang who were awaiting trial following his acquittal in the Hennessy affair.

Charles Matranga had things tightly sewn up in the 'Big Easy', hiding his criminal activities behind a legitimate fruit-selling business. If any other members of his family or wider organization wanted to make it big, they'd have to go elsewhere, so Matranga 'sponsored' the establishment of an off-shoot in Los Angeles. Based around the Plaza area, where the immigrant Italian-American community was concentrated, the kingpin was Orsario 'Sam' Matranga, leader of the family business from 1905, with his family members Salvatore, Pietro (known as Peter) and Charles's brother, Tony. The earliest organized criminal activity in Los Angeles was perpetrated by the Black Hand gangs, mainly Italian street gangs organized and co-ordinated by the Matranga family. They maintained their criminal enterprises through violence, killing their competitors. Rival crime boss and Black Hand gang leader Joseph Ardizzone, known as 'Iron Man', had – as with many of the earliest Mafia leaders in the United States – been born in Palermo, Sicily. Although the Matrangas were his distant cousins, that didn't stop Ardizzone battling them for control of the lucrative proceeds from criminal activity in early Los Angeles.

Ardizzone got into a dispute with Matranga gang member George Maisano (the exact details of the dispute have been forgotten), but the pair agreed to an arbitration process run by translator Joseph Cuccia – who was a relative of Ardizzone's and active in his crime family. As might be expected, Cuccia ruled in Ardizzone's favour causing the Matrangas to threaten his life. On 2 July 1906, Ardizzone shot and killed Maisano (claiming self-defence), bringing the wrath of the Matranga family down upon him.

As a result, Ardizzone fled Los Angeles, leaving the Matrangas to consolidate their position of control. Tony Matranga shot and killed Cuccia in September 1906, securing the family's dominant position in the Los Angeles underworld. The Matrangas were also happy to turn over their enemies to the legitimate forces of law and order, while the police would in turn go easy on the Matranga family's own illegal activities. Despite having the police on their side, both Sam and Peter Matranga were 'taken out' in 1917 by a vengeful Ardizzone (who'd secretly returned to Los Angeles by 1914), provoking a new gang war. Matranga cousin Tony Buccola took over the gang and gained revenge by having Ardizzone's gunman Mike Marino (aka Mike Rizzo) bumped off in 1919.

The Matranga–Ardizzone conflict allowed a new player from New Orleans to build a substantial presence in the Los Angeles criminal underworld. Vito Di Giorgio had also been born in Sicily and had come to New Orleans via family connections in New York. Arriving in 1920, along with his 'underboss' Rosario DeSimone (who would later replace him), Di Giorgio was able to take advantage of the ongoing feud between two of the city's most prominent gangs to organize the remaining groups into something resembling a traditional Mafia 'family'. His reign was to be short-lived, however. After surviving a pair of assassination attempts, he was finally killed in 1922 when he was at the barbers having a haircut (just like 'Little Pete' in San Francisco and Albert Anastasia in New York). The arrival of Prohibition in 1920 and the rise of the bootlegger gangsters saw the Matranga clan's power recede, and Tony Buccola himself had disappeared, fate unknown, by 1930. Almost the last man standing from the early years of organized crime in Los Angeles was, ironically, Joseph Ardizzone. He took over from Rosario DeSimone as the head of the organization, and faced the challenges and opportunities of Prohibition.

Joseph Ardizzone's chief lieutenant was Jack Dragna – who'd been born Ignazio Dragna in Sicily in 1891 – running the bootlegging operations across southern California. Dragna became president of the Italian Protective League, set up by Ardizzone as a cover for their illegal activities – it was chaired by California State Senator Joseph Pedrotti. As an organization, it had both political and social benefits for members, but it also served as a recruitment arm for the group's protection rackets. When Ardizzone mysteriously vanished in 1931 – it was believed he'd been 'taken out' by the East coast Mafia Syndicate, with whom he'd been in conflict – Dragna stepped up to become top man of the American Mafia in California. He quickly settled things with The Commission bosses back East, leading to speculation that Dragna played a part in Ardizzone's downfall in order to give the East coast Mafia a foothold in LA.

Along with Girolamo 'Momo' Adamo and John Rosselli (from the Chicago Outfit, see chapters 10 and 11), Dragna

masterminded off-shore gambling ships (run on behalf of
Dragna by Anthony Cornero) and a lucrative heroin trade,
as well as the more usual protection rackets and gambling
dens. Dragna's New York contact was Tommy Lucchese,
who told him he had to work in co-operation with newly
arrived East coast operatives Bugsy Siegel and Mickey
Cohen.

The rise of Mickey

There's no doubt Mickey Cohen started out in Los Angeles
low in the mobster pecking order: some suggest he was
little more than an errand boy for Siegel, at least to begin
with. Early on, Cohen ran a 'floating' craps game based
around a portable fold-out table he took to wherever he
could get a game going. His association with Siegel grew
to the point where he became more fully involved in his
operations in gambling and bookmaking on America's
West coast. According to Cohen's own account, he was
in charge of all local gambling operations in southern
California when Siegel's interests turned to Las Vegas. Part
of his job involved setting up and maintaining the 'race
wire' operation that was vital to getting the information
on horse-racing winners through to the betting syndicates
as quickly as possible. He was also involved with Siegel in
establishing the Flamingo Hotel.

Along with Siegel, Cohen helped reinstate the Syndicate's
control over Jack Dragna's 'Mickey Mouse Mafia' – so
called by the police department because it was badly
organized and ineffective – in Los Angeles. With the death
of Siegel in 1947 [see chapter 5], Mickey Cohen stood to
inherit virtually all his operations, as long as he played
by the rules established by the gangsters back East who'd
conspired to bring down Siegel, including Meyer Lansky.
The remainder of Dragna's gang saw Cohen as ripe for a
targeted hit and they made several attempts on the gangster's life, which only provoked Cohen to hit back at them,

harder. Meanwhile, through his lawyer Murray Chotiner, Cohen invested in the future by financing the campaign of a rising politician named Richard Nixon.

During his time in Los Angeles in the aftermath of World War Two, Mickey Cohen wanted some of the fame and respect accorded Hollywood's silver screen stars for himself. He hobnobbed with well-known actors and actresses throughout Hollywood 'café society', and built relationships with newspaper editors, reporters and columnists who would ensure Cohen, his associates and his activities were reflected in the best possible light. One of Cohen's 'pet' reporters was the *Los Angeles Herald*'s James Richardson, who would blow up items of minor interest concerning Cohen into big-headline stories. In return, Richardson benefited from underworld tips from Cohen and his pals, which ensured he was always the first to report on major incidents in Los Angeles.

Cohen made great copy for the newspapers. Despite his violent temper and criminal involvements, he was presented largely as a harmless James Cagney-style movie mobster, a 'businessman' who perhaps went a little too far on occasion with his negotiating techniques (which sometimes involved Tommy guns). He spent plenty of money in the nightclubs of Los Angeles and was often photographed arriving or departing with a glamorous buxom blonde on each arm, in reality often strippers like Liz Renay and Candy Barr, or prostitutes, rather than aspiring movie starlets. He enjoyed the lifestyle of the rich and famous, and wasn't afraid to brag about it, inviting reporters into his home on Moreno Avenue in Brentwood to show off his 500 pairs of socks, sixty pairs of shoes and 200 suits. Stored near the clothes was his well-equipped armoury, something few Hollywood stars had.

All this publicity attracted the attention of the Los Angeles Police Department (LAPD). In 1946, under Chief of Police Clemence B. Horral, a specialized eight-man team (known colloquially as the 'gangster squad', and featured in the 2013 movie of the same name, as well as 1996's *Mulholland Falls*) was established to keep the East coast Mafia out of Los Angeles. Their prime target was Cohen, but they also carried out surveillance on Dragna and Siegel, among others. There was a tacit understanding that the squad might use methods that, strictly speaking, would be considered illegal to achieve their aims but would be tolerated for the right outcomes, whether it was bringing down Cohen or rounding up the city's many corrupt cops.

For a gangster, Mickey Cohen seems to have killed relatively few people himself. In 1945 he shot and killed a fellow gambler, Maxie Sherman, but was cleared by the courts on the grounds of self-defence. More often, it was Cohen's life that was threatened, usually in retaliation for the actions of one of his many henchmen. One occasion saw his home bombed, resulting in it being refurbished with fortress-style defences, including floodlights, with dedicated alarm systems and firearms secreted in every room in case of unexpected attack. In 1948, his office was attacked by gunmen killing one of his bodyguards, but Cohen escaped injury or death as he was in the bathroom at the time. He was targeted again in 1949 outside a Sunset Strip nightclub, with the attackers missing Cohen and hitting instead another of his henchmen. One of his more unlucky bodyguards was Johnny Stompanato [see chapter 10].

By 1949, William Worton had taken over as head of the LAPD and he renamed the 'gangster squad' the 'Intelligence Section', adding extra manpower and a clear mandate: Get Cohen! 'There was a no holds barred policy,' said squad member Jack O'Mara. 'You did what you had to do.' To Cohen, the gangster squad were 'the stupidity squad'. For the police, it was sometimes necessary to use a gangster in an attempt to entrap a gangster, as they did with mobster Jack Whalen. It didn't do the Siegel-linked Whalen much good: he was killed in a restaurant in Sherman Oaks in 1959 while out with Mickey Cohen and three other gangsters. Cohen would eventually be acquitted of Whalen's murder.

Cohen remained the criminal kingpin of Los Angeles until Federal authorities began to take a close interest in him and his activities in the 1950s. Along with several other underworld figures, Cohen was investigated by the Kefauver Commission. Established by Democrat US Senator Estes Kefauver, the United States Senate Special Committee to Investigate Crime in Interstate Commerce ran from 1950–1 and focused on cross-border interstate organized crime.

The Kefauver Commission conducted hearings in fourteen US cities taking testimony from over 600 witnesses, many of them big crime bosses such as Frank Costello, Joe Adonis, Meyer Lansky and Willie Moretti. Costello [see chapter 12] made himself notorious by refusing to have his face filmed, and then by staging a dramatic walkout. Broadcast on television, the Commission revealed many of the corrupt links between politicians and organized crime, bringing to an end several careers, including those of former New Jersey Governor Harold G. Hoffman and New York City mayor William O'Dwyer. The existence of the criminal organization known as 'the Mafia' became popularly known for the first time as a result of the Commission's deliberations.

Mickey Cohen was among those questioned, and his exposure led to a conviction for income tax evasion in June 1951. Given a four-year prison sentence, Cohen served three-and-a-half years in McNeil Island Federal Prison. Released in October 1955, Mickey Cohen was a wiser 'Wise Guy' than previously, emerging to discover he'd become an even greater celebrity than before. He made a significant appearance on the new medium of television, interviewed by newscaster Mike Wallace in May 1957, claiming 'I have killed no men that didn't deserve killing', and attacked Los Angeles Police Chief William Parker as 'a known degenerate' (Parker sued for slander). Cohen later claimed to be running legitimate businesses, including the more mundane floral shops and paint stores, alongside more lucrative casinos and nightclubs. It was even claimed that mobster Mickey Cohen spent time in the 1950s driving an ice-cream van in Brentwood. Also in 1957, Cohen claimed to have become a Christian who was 'high on the Christian way of life'.

Although he said he had left crime behind and was now an ex-gangster, the law had not finished with Mickey Cohen. He was convicted once again in 1961 of income tax evasion, and this time was sent to Alcatraz, the one-time home of Al Capone, where he was attacked by another prisoner with an iron bar in an attempt to kill him. Cohen sued the Federal Government over the attack, and won a payment of $110,000 in compensation that was then seized by the Internal Revenue Service as payment for his outstanding tax bill. When Alcatraz was closed in 1963, Cohen was moved to the Federal Penitentiary in Atlanta, where he remained until 1972. Upon release, he began a campaign against abuse of inmates in the United States prison system.

Mickey Cohen lived his final few years in relative obscurity, preferring his newfound privacy to his old Hollywood lifestyle. A misdiagnosed ulcer turned out to be stomach cancer, limiting his mobility. After surgery, though, he reappeared in public, taking part in media interviews once again, including one with civil rights activist Ramsey Clark. One of his last public acts was to become involved in the 1974 search for kidnapped heiress Patty Hearst – who had been taken by members of the Symbionese Liberation Army – offering to use his former underworld connections to track her down. Mickey Cohen died in his sleep in 1976, aged sixty-two, with the *Los Angeles Times* summing up his gangster career as that of someone 'striving for the title of Public Enemy Number One, [but reaching] no higher than the leading public nuisance'.

10

THE MOB IN HOLLYWOOD

While many Italian immigrants to America became embroiled in organized crime and rose to the top of the gangster roster, many Jewish immigrants to America went West and became bosses of the Hollywood movie studios. The movie moguls and the gangsters of the 1930s and 1940s had much in common: they dressed alike, talked alike and employed similar strong-arm methods in their business. The connections between the Mob and Hollywood were more than superficial, though, as the American Mafia at various times had direct links with the movie studios and movie stars. Hollywood was soon seen as a post-Prohibition opportunity by America's top gangsters.

Johnny Rosselli: the Mob's man in Hollywood
The initial representative of the East Coast Mob in Hollywood was Johnny Rosselli (also sometimes spelled Roselli), a former driver for Al Capone who'd been born

Filippo Sacco in 1905 in Italy. Having fled New York in the early 1920s when he was wanted on a murder rap, Rosselli quickly found a place for himself as part of the Chicago Outfit. Despite that, he was on the move once more in 1924, this time to Los Angeles, where he was directed to hook up with Jack Dragna, the local mobster that the bosses back East didn't fully trust. Before Mickey Cohen's arrival, Rosselli was their man on the spot in Hollywood.

Rosselli took his Hollywood responsibilities a bit too seriously – some thought he'd gone native. He started with bit parts in Hollywood movies as an extra, before connecting with Chicago-born film producer and director Bryan Foy who would later become head of the B-picture unit at Warner Bros. studios.

When Capone briefly visited Hollywood in 1927, it was down to Rosselli to negotiate with the local gangster bosses who tried to run the Chicago capo out of town. He functioned as a 'labour consultant' during the 1933 strike in Hollywood, connecting the mob-run unions with the studio moguls. Rosselli dated actress Lana Turner, long before Johnny Stompanato got to her, suggesting her unfortunate attraction to gangsters was long standing. By 1934, it was to Johnny Rosselli, not Jack Dragna, that the Chicago Outfit would turn when they wanted to establish a more serious foothold in Hollywood's underworld. He was also possibly one of the key gunmen in the biggest Mafia-connected hit of them all [see chapter 11].

The Kennedy case

Another key name involved with Hollywood and gangsters in the later 1930s was Joseph P. Kennedy, patriarch of the political Kennedy clan that included President John F. Kennedy and his brother Robert, just two of his nine children. During Prohibition, the Irish Catholic Kennedy was a prominent society bootlegger, providing alcohol brought in from Canada for parties attended by stars and

hangers-on from Hollywood, including those held in San
Simeon by newspaper publisher William Randolph Heart's
mistress, Marion Davies.

Joseph P. Kennedy was reputed to have used Al Capone's
men to ship his alcohol across the country to California.
A contract was briefly taken out on Kennedy's life when
he tried to muscle in on the bootlegging trade in Detroit,
run by the Purple Gang. Gangster Frank Costello made
the claims of Kennedy's history in bootlegging shortly
after the entrepreneur's death in 1969, but biographers
have disputed them. It is certainly true that with the end
of Prohibition in 1933, Joseph Kennedy was one of the first
to legitimize his alcohol interests by doing deals to import
Scotch Whisky from Scotland and spirits from Canada
into the newly 'wet' United States.

The other mob connection in Kennedy's early career
was the suggestion that Capone's Chicago Outfit fronted
Kennedy the cash he needed to pull off the amalgamation
of several smaller studios and theatre chains into RKO
Studios in 1928. RKO would produce *King Kong* (1933) and
Citizen Kane (1941), whose story was loosely modelled on
that of William Randolph Hearst. Kennedy used frontman
David Sarnoff, the head of RCA, to pull off the lucrative
deal, but the entire operation was reputedly funded by Mob
money. These early Mob connections would come back to
haunt the Kennedy clan, especially eventual United States
President, John F. Kennedy [see chapter 11].

Starlets and gangsters

Kennedy's RKO wasn't the only Hollywood studio
supposedly established with the help of Mob funding.
Columbia Pictures had been founded in 1918 by brothers
Jack and Harry Cohn and Joe Brandt as Cohn–Brandt–
Cohn Film Sales. They released their first film in 1922 and
renamed the studio Columbia Pictures in 1924. The studio
was partly funded in the 1930s by New Jersey bootlegger

Abner 'Longy' Zwillman who dated *The Public Enemy* (1931) actress Jean Harlow and secured a two-picture deal for her at Columbia by 'lending' Harry Cohn $500,000 to buy out his partners. Zwillman also bought Harlow a jewelled bracelet and a bright red Cadillac. Fellow mobster Johnny Rosselli was attached to Columbia as a 'producer', although he did no actual film work, simply keeping an eye on the Syndicate's 'assets', including Harlow. The actress strengthened her Mob connections by becoming god-mother to Bugsy Siegel's daughter, Millicent.

Harlow had come to Hollywood as a teenager in 1923, with her mother Jean Carpenter and minor mobster Marino Bello, who married her mother in 1927. By all accounts, Carpenter, known as 'Mama Jean' to Harlow's 'Baby', was the archetypal 'stage mother' keen to push her daughter in show business. Harlow quickly won a contract with Hal Roach and appeared in a trio of Laurel and Hardy comedy shorts in 1929. She featured in Howard Hughes's sound version of *Hell's Angels* (1930) and then as gangster James Cagney's moll in *The Public Enemy* (1931). During the 1931 nationwide publicity tour for her starring role in *Platinum Blonde*, Harlow met mobster Longy Zwillman, and the pair soon embarked upon an affair. Zwillman put the screws on Hughes to release Harlow from her contract and got her regular gigs in Mob-run nightclubs. The pair would often meet up in the Hollywood hotel complex The Garden of Allah, a regular Mob hangout, and Zwillman was said to have distributed lockets containing cuttings of Harlow's pubic hair to his gangster buddies.

By 1932 Harlow was signed to a seven-year contract with MGM, one of the 'big six' studios in Hollywood, appearing in films like *Red Dust* (1932) with Clark Gable and *Bombshell* (1933). She dumped Zwillman to take up with studio executive Paul Bern. They were married in July 1932, but Bern was dead by that September, his body found in their shared home. MGM studio fixer and publicity man Howard Strickling re-arranged the death scene to suggest suicide – in league with studio head Louis B. Mayer and MGM security man Whitney Hendry – before the police were even called in. Engaging in a Mafia-like cover-up, studio mogul Mayer showed that the people who ran Hollywood were not all that different from the gangsters who extorted money from the moguls. An eventual inquest confirmed that it had been suicide, but there were persistent rumours that mobster Longy Zwillman had killed Bern, either on his own behalf after being dumped by Harlow, or on behalf of Harlow's stepfather Marino Bello, who had lost control over his stepdaughter. In 1960, *Scarface* (1932) scriptwriter Ben Hecht would popularize the murder theory in an article in *Esquire* magazine.

Jean Harlow wasn't the only prominent Hollywood starlet to be involved with gangsters. Thelma Todd was arguably just as popular, and her Mob connections made her sudden death at the age of twenty-nine in 1935 all the more suspicious. Todd was best known for her roles in comedy films, such as the Marx Brothers' *Monkey Business* (1931) and *Horse Feathers* (1932), as well as several Laurel and Hardy movies. In 1932 she married Pat DiCicco, who was by-then Lucky Luciano's man in Hollywood looking after the lucrative drug trade. Todd was reputed to have confided in her comedy partner Patsy Kelly that when Luciano was in Los Angeles, the pair of them would also get together.

By 1934, Todd had divorced DiCicco and opened 'Thelma Todd's Sidewalk Café' at Pacific Pallisades on the Pacific Coast Highway overlooking the ocean, which became a popular 'in joint' with Hollywood names, gangsters and tourists alike. Her partners in the café were Hollywood producer and director Roland West (with whom Todd was also having an on-off affair) and his wife, Jewel Carmen. The trio lived on one floor of the three-storey property, with the restaurant on the ground floor. The empty floor was used for after-hours gambling sessions, hosted by West and patronized by Hollywood stars like Clark Gable and Spencer Tracy.

Thelma Todd was found dead on the morning of 16 December 1935, sitting in a car in Jewel Carmen's garage, a block from the restaurant. An accidental death was ruled, with the story being that upon returning home late at night after a party, Todd had been unable to gain access to her restaurant apartment and so had gone to the garage, turned on the car ignition to keep herself warm, and accidentally died of carbon monoxide poisoning. Her autopsy noted that there were 'no marks anywhere upon or within the body', but this was not true. Todd's face and clothes had blood on them, she had two broken ribs, one of her teeth was missing and her nose was broken – her bruising was blamed on post-mortem lividity by the coroner, but he ignored the rest of the apparent injuries.

Foul play by gangsters was suspected in the death of Thelma Todd, but nothing could be proven. There were several suspects, from her ex-husband DiCicco who was extorting West over illegal alcohol supplies to the café, to West himself or Carmen, driven to it by the café's financial troubles and Todd's affairs, to Lucky Luciano, who was said to have been pressuring Todd to use her café as a front for his Hollywood drugs, gambling and prostitution interests. His ultimate plan was said to be to lure the studio moguls into his debt, thereby engineering the Mob's final takeover of Hollywood. Luciano had been seen with Todd on her last day, and he flew from Los Angeles to New York on the day her body was found. Even Todd's mother, Alice, was a suspect as she'd told friends shortly before her daughter's death that she expected soon to receive enough money to build herself a new mansion. Hollywood starlet and gangsters' moll Thelma Todd's death was explained away by an establishment that didn't want to rock the boat, but it remains to this day one of Hollywood's great unsolved mysteries.

Virginia Hill, Bugsy Siegel's girlfriend, was also a rising Hollywood starlet as well as a courier for the Mob. Dark-haired Hill featured in several movies, but mostly in bit parts, and she didn't seriously pursue an acting career – she was much more interested in becoming a traditional gangster's moll. She started on that route by hooking up with Genovese crime family boss and Luciano henchman Joe Adonis, running messages between him and other gangsters with nothing written down thanks to her prodigious memory. Moving to Los Angeles, Hill rented Rudolph Valentino's one-time home, the Falcon's Lair, and signed up with the Columbia Pictures' drama school, taking acting and elocution lessons. A seven-year contract with Universal saw her appear in a handful of movies, including playing an heiress (a fake role she'd adopt off-screen, too) in *Ball of Fire* (1942) opposite Gary Cooper.

Movies weren't her thing, however; mobsters were. She soon began an affair with Bugsy Siegel, then the New York Mob's main man in Hollywood. The affair brought about Siegel's divorce from his wife Estelle. Four days before Siegel's assassination, Hill flew to Paris, France on an unscheduled flight. She was subpoenaed in 1951 to testify before the Kefauver hearings into organized crime, something she professed to know nothing about. That didn't stop *Time* magazine crowning Virginia Hill the 'queen of the gangster's molls'. Indicted for tax evasion – the favourite tool of the government against gangsters – she fled to Europe, and died in Austria in 1966 aged forty-nine as a result of an overdose of sleeping pills. Her apparent suicide was suspicious to some who worried she knew the ins and outs of Mob business in the 1930s and 1940s. The FBI eventually concluded that Hill had been an intelligence 'clearing house' for Chicago and Los Angeles gangsters, acting as an untraceable messenger for

many in the American Mafia, and may have taken many
secrets to her grave.

When Johnny met Lana

One of Mickey Cohen's most prominent Los Angeles
lieutenants was Johnny Stompanato, an ex-United States
Marine who served as Cohen's 'muscle' both as a personal
bodyguard and as a general all-round enforcer. Stompanato
had been born in Illinois in 1925, the youngest of four children in a family whose parents had come to America from
Italy. Stompanato's mother died just six days after he was
born due to peritonitis.

Having attended military school, it was no surprise when
Stompanato joined the US Marines in 1943. He served in
the South Pacific, including being stationed in Okinawa,
Japan and in China, where he was discharged from the
service in 1946. He married his first wife, Sarah Utish,
while in China – she was Turkish, and Stompanato converted to Islam for the sake of the marriage. He returned to
Woodstock, Illinois, where he'd grown up, and the couple
had a son, also named John. For a while, Stompanato worked
as a salesman for a bakery, before moving to Hollywood.
Divorced from Utish, he sent his son to stay with his parents in Illinois. Moving to Hollywood, Stompanato set
up a gift shop selling trinkets in Westwood, Los Angeles.
Then he met Lana Turner.

The story of the blonde movie star's 'discovery' was the
stuff of Hollywood legend. Julia Jean Turner had been
born in Idaho in 1921, and was allegedly signed up by a
Hollywood agent who saw her in Schwab's Pharmacy on
Sunset Boulevard, aged just sixteen. In fact, Turner was
skipping a typing class at Hollywood High School and
had stopped at the Top Hat Malt Shop (opposite Schwab's),
where she was spotted by *Hollywood Reporter* publisher
William R. Wilkerson. He recognized the young woman's
film potential, hooking her up with agent Zeppo Marx

(the non-performing Marx Brother). Marx brought her to director Mervyn LeRoy who promptly cast Turner in *They Won't Forget* (1937).

The film brought Lana Turner a certain amount of notoriety as 'The Sweater Girl', due to the tight-fitting clothes she wore that emphasized her physicality. Like the gangsters variously known as 'Scarface', 'Pretty Boy' and 'Baby Face', Turner also hated the media nickname that nonetheless stuck with her. Signed to MGM Studios, she was groomed by movie mogul Louis B. Mayer as the 'next Jean Harlow', the actress who'd died young just six months previously. Turner played a precocious teen in a series of light late-1930s movies.

Johnny Stompanato came into Lana Turner's life in 1957, just after she'd divorced her fourth husband (of an eventual eight), Tarzan actor Lex Barker. By then Turner had made a name for herself in a variety of movies, including the film noir thriller *The Postman Always Rings Twice* (1946) and the film business melodrama *The Bad and the Beautiful* (1952). In 1957, when she hooked up with Stompanato, she'd just revived her career by starring in the movie *Peyton Place*, although her MGM contract had come to an end. Aged thirty-seven, she didn't know the well-built gangster was almost five years her junior: he claimed to be forty-three. Since arriving in Hollywood and falling in with Mickey Cohen, it had been Stompanato's habit to briefly associate himself with well-off women, living on their dime for a while (in return for sexual favours) before moving on – George Raft had allegedly subsisted in a similar fashion in the late 1920s.

Stompanato originally called himself 'John Steele' when he first called up Lana Turner. Spurned initially, the would-be gangster then arrived on her doorstep unannounced, bearing gifts and flowers. Soon they were involved in a full-blown romance, but Turner remained unaware of Stompanato's underworld connections. He used Turner's young daughter, Cheryl, as a way into her affections, offering the girl regular horse-riding lessons.

The relationship hit the rocks, however, when Turner discovered Steele's real name and real-life role as a Mob enforcer. Newly rehabilitated in the eyes of Hollywood, Turner was worried what the news that she was dating a gangster might do to her improving reputation in the movie town. She poured cold water on her relationship with Stompanato and began seeing other men. He didn't let up, however, and asked Turner to help him become a movie producer – perhaps he'd seen her as a way into the world of movies the whole time? The relationship allegedly became abusive, but she was too frightened to involve the law, fearing retaliation from Stompanato and his violent underworld friends.

The chance to make a movie in London gave Turner an escape. She flew off to film *Another Time, Another Place* (1958), co-starring with Sean Connery, but Stompanato followed her to the UK. For the sake of appearances and to keep Stompanato calm, she humoured him. Banned from visiting her on the movie set, as she didn't want people to know of their connection, the jealous Stompanato fantasized it was because she was having an affair with Connery. Threatened with deportation from Britain, the gangster arrived on set with a gun and threatened Connery, according to Turner's later autobiography. Long before he became James Bond, Connery proved he had the chops for the role by swiftly disarming the bulkier Stompanato and chasing him from the set.

In March 1958, Lana Turner attended the annual prize-giving Academy Award ceremony (known as the Oscars), leaving Johnny Stompanato behind and taking daughter Cheryl with her. She'd been nominated for Best Actress for her role in *Peyton Place* (she lost to Joanne Woodward), and certainly didn't want a known gangster to accompany her. A few weeks later on Good Friday, 4 April 4 1958, a heated argument broke out between Turner and Stompanato in her Beverly Hills home – Turner claimed she attempted to end the relationship once and for all. According to the official story, fearing that Stompanato was going to kill her mother, the then fourteen-year-old Cheryl Turner stabbed the mobster to death (it has been suggested this was a cover story, and that Turner actually held the knife but knew her daughter, being a juvenile, would never be convicted). Naturally, given the mix of elements, the story became a media sensation. At the later coroner's inquest, at which Turner testified, her daughter Cheryl was deemed responsible for a justifiable homicide, acting in self-defence. For all his Mob connections and tough guy posturing, nothing – not even Hollywood gangster Mickey Cohen (who had identified the mobster's body) – could save Johnny Stompanato from the assault of an aggrieved, knife-wielding teenager.

Corrupting the unions

Perhaps the most powerful, and least known, gangster in Hollywood was Willie Bioff, whose power came through the corruption of Tinseltown's craft unions. William Morris Bioff was born in 1900, but unlike most of the other prominent gangsters of this period, Bioff wasn't Italian or Jewish. He was from Russia and had immigrated to the United States with his family at the age of five. Otherwise, his story was much the same as Al Capone's or Lucky Luciano's. He grew up in Chicago, where he got involved on the fringes of the Outfit's criminal activities. He started in protection rackets, before graduating to pimping in Chicago's notorious Levee district. He worked as muscle for Mob accountant Jake Guzik and was used to settle outstanding accounts by breaking bones and knocking heads together. Bioff moved in the same circles as Al Capone and Frank Nitti, but was never a key figure in the Chicago Outfit. His chance to star came in 1935 when he was sent to Los Angeles by Frank Nitti to take up a role as the Mob enforcer for corrupt union boss George Browne. While New York and Chicago organized crime bosses fought over who would control vice, gambling and drugs in Hollywood, Bioff would be Chicago's secret weapon, taking over the unions.

The plan was for Bioff and Browne to take over IATSE, the International Alliance of Theatrical Stage Employees, which represented technicians and craftsmen in the entertainment business: in Hollywood, that meant movies. Nothing could happen on a film set without the co-operation of IATSE members, meaning their union organizers held a powerful hand should they decide to pull their members out on strike. Under Bioff and Browne the union became a near-legitimate vehicle for extortion, not only of the movie studios but of their connected theatrical exhibitors in cities like Chicago and New York as well. Between skimming money from members' obligatory fees (increased every year under Bioff and Browne) and blackmail payments from studio moguls to prevent strikes, the Mob were said to be bringing in $1.5 million each year from Hollywood studios in 'protection' money. IATSE membership had been less than 200 in 1934, but by 1937 the figure was nearer 12,000, all paying fees, a large proportion of which went straight into mobster's pockets. Both Capone and Luciano thought the ultimate end game of their presence in Hollywood would be ownership of the studios themselves, but despite occasional 'investments' such as that by Longy Zwillman in Columbia, this didn't happen. They did institute other scams, though, such as extorting celluloid film manufacturer Eastman for an amount that was equivalent to a 7 per cent levy on all Eastman film stock sold to the Hollywood studios. Breakaway unions would be intimidated into disbanding, strikes were called or prevented – depending on what the gangsters needed, and who they wanted to influence – and workers' wage cuts were enforced as the Mob took their slice of the available money.

No studio escaped the attention of gangsters, who were happy to live up to the roles depicted on screen by Edward G. Robinson and James Cagney. Larger studios, such as Warner Bros. (home of many of the popular gangster movies of the 1930s; see chapter 22), MGM (where Jean Harlow mostly plied her slinky trade), Paramount and Fox each paid $50,000 every year, while smaller outfits such as Universal, Columbia and the Joseph Kennedy-created RKO (along with at least twelve others) paid up $25,000 each year. Several of the studio heads claimed that Bioff personally threatened them with violence if they failed to comply with his bosses' demands.

The first attempted fight-back came in 1937, when a California state government committee was persuaded by a Los Angeles lawyer to look into the leadership of the IATSE union after member complaints. The Mob's own lawyer Colonel William Neblett managed to have the investigation sidelined, as he worked for the same law firm that employed California assembly speaker William Mosley Jones. By 1939, Willie Bioff overreached in an attempt to take over the Screen Actors Guild (SAG). The SAG leadership refused to be intimidated by the gangsters of Hollywood, despite physical assaults and death threats. The result was a no-holds-barred investigation of Bioff by SAG president Robert Montgomery (star of 1930 prison drama *The Big House*), newspaper columnist Westbrook Pegler and *Variety* (Hollywood's trade paper) editor Arthur Ungar.

In 1939 Bioff was investigated over income tax evasion, but it was 20th Century Fox chairman Joe Schenck (who'd paid off Bioff with a $100,000 studio cheque) who went to jail for perjury and tax fraud in 1941. Sentenced to three years in prison and possible deportation upon release, Schenck agreed to testify against the gangsters who'd corrupted the unions and extorted Hollywood. He was eventually granted a full pardon by President Truman and released in late 1945.

Schenck's testimony resulted in Bioff, Browne and other mobsters, including the ubiquitous Hollywood mobster Johnny Rosselli, being indicted for tax evasion, racketeering and extortion in 1943. As with Schenck, Bioff decided to testify against the others – including Rosselli and Frank Nitti – rather than face a full jail term himself. Bioff blew the lid off the Chicago Outfit's activities in Hollywood, taking down most of the top men with him. Faced with returning to jail himself, one-time Outfit capo Nitti committed suicide soon after Bioff's testimony, blowing his own brains out on an Illinois railroad track, while Bioff got ten years in prison and Browne just eight. The pair were out after only three years as a reward for their testimony that put most of the others, including Rosselli, away for a decade.

While Browne retreated into private life, Bioff adopted the name 'Bill Nelson' and moved to the suburbs of Phoenix, Arizona. The change of name – he used his wife's maiden name – didn't fool the Mob enforcers out for revenge for long, especially when Bioff unwittingly took a job with a Chicago Outfit-controlled casino in Las Vegas. In November 1955, Bioff turned the key in the ignition of his Ford pick-up truck and was blown sky-high. Organized crime had once again found Bioff and the Mob had their revenge.

11

THE MOB AND THE PRESIDENT

While Hollywood entertainers like Marilyn Monroe and Frank Sinatra had well-documented Mob connections, it would be the links between them and the 'first family' of American politics, the Kennedys, that led some to believe that the Mob played a role in the assassination of President John F. Kennedy in November 1963. While there are many theories about the Kennedy assassination – and fifty years on it remains unsolved – there is a strong case put forward by certain researchers for the involvement of the Mob in what may have been their ultimate 'hit'. The House Select Committee on Assassinations of 1976 would eventually conclude: 'The committee believes, on the basis of the evidence available to it, that the national syndicate of organized crime, as a group, was not involved in the assassination of President Kennedy, but that the available evidence does not preclude the possibility that individual members may have been involved'. Those 'individual members' accused in the slaying of the President were the Mob's original man in Hollywood, Johnny Rosselli; Chicago mob boss Sam Giancana; and Florida criminal kingpin Santo Trafficante Jr, among others.

The Mafia–JFK connection

The Kennedy family connections with organized crime dated back to the dynasty's founding figure, Joseph P. Kennedy, and his days as bootlegger to high society. His business dealings over importing alcohol from Scotland and Canada inevitably involved him with the likes of Al Capone and Frank Costello; in particular, Costello claimed to have had a significant hand in making Kennedy rich. After the repeal of Prohibition, Kennedy quickly went 'legitimate', establishing a bona fide alcohol import business. However, he had other, far more ambitious plans for his family.

Joseph P. Kennedy groomed his children for high office from their earliest days. He used the connections built up through many years in business – legitimate and illegitimate – to achieve his aims. The large Irish-American communities in cities such as Boston, New York and Chicago would play an important part, and Kennedy cultivated their support – not coincidentally, each of these cities were Mob strongholds. He also used the media, especially highly placed sympathetic editors and reporters, such as *The New York Times'* political columnist Arthur Krock, to position his children in readiness for their opportunities to climb the greasy pole of politics to the very top.

Kennedy was close to the Democratic Party, where much of the Irish-American influence was felt, but he was not tied to any one party. He happily told Richard Nixon, Mickey Cohen's favoured candidate, that if none of his own children were to make a bid for the Presidency, then Nixon would have his support. Similarly, in hedging his bets, Kennedy was a strong supporter of Senator Joseph McCarthy, who drove the American 'anti-Reds' witch-hunts of the 1950s. In placing his son John F. Kennedy in the Senate, the older Kennedy made a deal with McCarthy whereby neither one would make speeches against the other. His other son, Robert Kennedy, even worked with McCarthy on a Senate sub-committee. Kennedy was clearly willing to make any deals necessary with whomever could help him in order to advance his aim of getting one of his children behind the desk in the White House.

In the late 1950s, both Jack and Robert Kennedy had become defined in the public mind for their anti-organized crime crusade. In 1960, the year of his brother's election to the White House, Robert Kennedy wrote: 'If we do not on a national scale attack organized crime with weapons and techniques as effective as their own, they will destroy us.' Whether through shame over their father's past, or in an attempt to make amends, the Kennedy brothers had set their sights on the American Mafia. The senior Kennedy violently objected to his sons' crusade, warning them of the potential dangers of tangling with the Mob. Regardless, the pair ploughed on, with Robert Kennedy using his first speech as Attorney General to re-state what he was fighting against: 'Organized crime,' he said, 'has become big business.'

Joseph Kennedy's initial plan had been for his oldest son, Joe Jr, to be the first in the family to try for the Presidency, but his death in August 1944 while serving in the American military necessitated a rapid change of plan. Kennedy Sr's ambition was then put upon the next eldest son, John – known widely as Jack. Since Joseph's spell as American Ambassador to the United Kingdom in the late 1930s, when he'd appeared to give tacit support to Hitler's Nazi regime in Germany when he declared that 'Democracy is finished' in the West, the older Kennedy's political ambitions had been thwarted. Now he saw a way to succeed through his children, Jack and Robert, but he knew he'd need some unorthodox help if he was to pull off his planned political coup.

The Kennedy patriarch wisely kept out of the limelight during Jack Kennedy's 1960 campaign for the Presidency, but he played a key role in formulating the strategy of the campaign, and was especially responsible for raising the necessary funding and in guaranteeing a certain section of the vote for his son's candidacy. To achieve this, the Kennedy patriarch had to call upon some old 'friends' for help. Prime among them was his occasional golf partner Johnny Rosselli and mobster Sam Giancana.

Giancana had been born on Chicago's West Side in 1908 as Salvatore Giangana. As a youngster he'd quickly joined the Forty-Two Gang, a street mini-Mob who worked as muscle for Joseph Esposito, the Republican political boss of the area who was into bootlegging, prostitution, extortion and labour racketeering in an alliance with the notorious Genna brothers. The six Genna brothers ruled Chicago's Little Italy ruthlessly throughout the early 1920s. Giancana gained a reputation for being equally as violent as his sponsors, as well as for being an excellent getaway driver. He was much in demand.

The would-be mobster quickly rose through the ranks, becoming well liked among his crew, earning huge amounts of money, and more than willing to get his hands dirty when it came to killing. When Esposito was bumped off in a drive-by shooting in March 1928, it was believed that Giancana had played a role in the hit as part of his own plan for ruthless advancement through the hierarchy of the Chicago Outfit. Giancana had served his time as a gunman for Al Capone, gaining the nickname 'Mooney', because he was as crazy as under a full Moon and for the joy he seemed to take in killing. Giancana was sometimes reckless, but he was organized enough to properly plan out each and every hit he was involved in, down to the finest detail.

When Capone left the Chicago scene in the early 1930s,

his second-in-command, Frank 'The Enforcer' Nitti, took over the Outfit. Nitti had taken a shine to Giancana, despite his wild side, and brought him onto the Outfit's 'management' team that included Paul Ricca and Tony Accardo. Married to a singer in 1933, Giancana would have three daughters, although family life was never a major focus for him. In the 1940s, Giancana told his children he was going 'away to college', but he was in fact locked up in the Federal Correctional Complex at Terre Haute, Indiana. When he was released, he convinced Accardo, who'd succeeded Nitti as head of the Outfit, to move in on the African-American 'policy' (lottery) racket in the city, as a way of expanding the Mob's influence. The takeover produced a lucrative new income stream for the Outfit, one they'd use to fund later political campaigns.

Sam Giancana made his ultimate power play in 1957 when he 'persuaded' Accardo to step down from being the 'boss' of the Outfit to a new role of 'consigliere' (literally 'wise advisor', but in many ways the power behind the throne), letting Giancana step in as the new capo of the Chicago wing of the American Mafia. His first major appearance as Chicago's new boss was at the ill-fated 1957 Apalachin meeting in up-state New York [see chapter 13].

Giancana was recruited by Joseph Kennedy to play a major role in the 1960 election of his son Jack to the White House. The older, more experienced Kennedy knew that every vote would count and that Jack had several obstacles to overcome in his battle with the Republican candidate, Richard Nixon, including his youth and relative inexperience, as well as his Catholicism. Kennedy relied on Giancana to ensure that the large Irish-American vote turned out nationwide for Jack Kennedy, a role Giancana was only too happy to accept, knowing that in the way these things worked between such 'friends' the Kennedy clan would be in his and the Mob's debt and therefore owe them some 'obligations' once they were in office. The

Kennedy campaign also needed quick and easy funding, and was only too happy to rely on Mob money syphoned to them through Joseph Kennedy's connections.

After a tense campaign, Kennedy won the election very narrowly, by just over 100,000 votes (just 0.1 per cent of the overall vote, although the Electoral College system counts states not individual votes). Later, voter fraud (something the Mob had excelled at since the 1920s) was suspected in two key states: Kennedy's running mate Lyndon B. Johnson's state of Texas and Illinois, where the Chicago Mob ran things. If these states had gone to the Republican side, the White House would have been Nixon's. Both in Dallas, Texas and Chicago, Illinois, the Mob under Giancana's overall direction was alleged to have 'fixed' the vote to ensure a Kennedy victory. A series of recounts and legal challenges followed, but the result was ratified.

With his son in the White House, Joseph Kennedy had achieved his lifetime ambition, but he'd had to rely on Mob muscle and Mob money to do it. Later analysis would suggest that whatever fraud may have taken place, it possibly was not enough to materially affect the outcome. At the time, however, the deal was clear, at least as far as Giancana was concerned. Not only had Kennedy got his son into the highest office in the world, the Mob now had 'their man' in the White House and they were prepared to take advantage of that fact. They had 'leverage' over JFK (as the new President rapidly became popularly known), and were not afraid to use it. Despite warnings from other mobsters, both Giancana and Rosselli believed that the Kennedy brothers' high profile anti-Mob campaign was for public consumption only, and not real. Their in-house entertainer, Frank Sinatra (connected to the Kennedy clan when his 'rat pack' entourage pal Peter Lawford married into the family in 1954), had assured them that the Mob had nothing to fear from the Kennedys. By the time they realized the campaign was all too real, it would be too late.

The Cuba conspiracy

The Mafia were said to have been involved with the Kennedy administration in plots to assassinate Cuban leader Fidel Castro – who had taken control of Cuba in a 1959 revolution, closing down the Mafia-controlled casinos – after several Central Intelligence Agency-sponsored attempts failed. Kennedy saw Communist Cuba, just under 500 miles off the coast of Florida, as a growing threat to American interests. It just so happened that legitimate American political interests and illegitimate Mob interests in Cuba coincided nicely under the new Kennedy administration. The Cuba connection also tied JFK directly to one of the original mobsters of the 1920s, Meyer Lansky, who had lost huge revenues from his Cuban interests following the ascent of Castro, and he wanted revenge.

Official CIA documents released in 2007 confirm that in the summer of 1960 the Agency, through ex-agent Robert Maheu (then employed by eccentric millionaire Howard Hughes), approached the West coast representative of the Mob, Johnny Rosselli, with an offer of $150,000 if the Mob would kill Castro. Unaware the approach was from the CIA on behalf of Kennedy, but believing he'd been recruited by an advocate for disgruntled international corporations, Rosselli declined payment, claiming his 'associates' would gladly do the job of 'rubbing out' Castro for nothing. Rosselli then brought the task to Chicago Outfit head Sam Giancana and Florida mobster Santo Trafficante Jr. Trafficante, along with many in the Mob, had direct interests in Cuba. Several Mafia families had investments in Cuban casinos that they wanted to protect, and they had strong ties with anti-Castro Cubans.

The Senate Church Committee hearings of 1975 into government intelligence activities revealed that the CIA had if not directly recruited, certainly developed links with a variety of Mafia figures, including Rosselli, Giancana and Trafficante in the hope of using them to benefit American foreign policy in Cuba. Whether the Mob were scamming the US government and simply pocketing the 'fees' they were being paid for the hit on Castro (as was Sam Giancana's cynical attitude), or if they ever actively planned anything in relation to carrying out the job (which Johnny Rosselli supposedly did) is unconfirmed. There were allegations of an aborted 'poisoned pill' plot, and the CIA became a laughing stock after they sent 'exploding' cigars to take down Castro. These attempts, whether by the Mob or the CIA and which would continue throughout 1962 and into early 1963, failed entirely.

In April 1961, the CIA led the American military in the disastrous so-called 'Bay of Pigs' invasion by Cuban counter-revolutionaries into Cuba, a move that backfired politically on Kennedy. The President came to believe the poorly exe-cuted plan was a deliberate set-up to make him look bad, but he never revealed who he thought was behind it: the CIA, the American military, the Mob or some other party.

By the end of 1961, Joseph Kennedy had suffered a mas-sive stroke, which weakened his influence over both the President and his Mafia allies. He'd been able to keep both on the leash, but now he was in no position to keep the two groups under control. No one among the conspirators had expected Kennedy's brother Robert, the Attorney General, to significantly step up his long-running campaign against organized crime in the United States. However, he made it his ambition in office to clean up the unions, many of which had been corrupted by the influence of the Mob, particularly focusing on the Teamsters labour union and its leader, Jimmy Hoffa. The battle was seen by Hoffa as a 'blood feud' between him and Kennedy. The Attorney General's crusade succeeded in increasing to the power of twelve the number of successful Mob convictions in the United States, but it is unclear if his zeal was driven by knowledge, or ignorance, of his father's past dealings with organized crime.

There were stronger, more intimate links between President Kennedy and mobster Sam Giancana. Phyllis McGuire, a member of a successful singing trio, had a long-standing relationship with Giancana (he'd used CIA assets to spy on her in 1960), and was also said to have had an affair with Kennedy. If so, the mobster and the President had more than one woman in common, with Judith Campbell (later Exner) and even Marilyn Monroe (also connected to Rosselli) claiming to have had affairs with both – Monroe's death in August 1962 may have been connected. The man who introduced both women to Giancana and Kennedy was (once again) Mob-connected entertainer Frank Sinatra. Campbell was also connected to LA Mob man Johnny Rosselli, who may have solicited her to pander to Kennedy in the first place. By early 1962, it appears that the head of the FBI J. Edgar Hoover was all too aware of these multiple connections between the Kennedys, the CIA, the mobsters and Judith Campbell, adding yet another layer of intrigue to these events. Hoover had a habit of collecting information on friends and enemies alike and filing it away for future use.

In a 1988 interview with *People* magazine, Campbell claimed to have been the 'go-between' for Kennedy and Giancana during the 1960 election campaign – shuttling envelopes of cash to the campaign offices – as well as during the planning for action against Castro. Campbell, who died in 1999, has been described by many as an 'unreliable witness', although FBI, Secret Service and White House phone logs itemizing seventy calls to the President in an eighteen-month period seem to support her claims of a long-running affair with Kennedy. This network of personal relationships may have been deliberately constructed by members of the Mob in order to reinforce their ability to blackmail JFK in order that he'd pull his brother, Robert, away from his pursuit of the American Mafia.

The assassination plot

One of the many theories about the unsolved assassination of John F. Kennedy is that organized crime, in the form of the Mob, had a central role to play. In reaction to what was seen by the Mob as Kennedy's 'appeasement' policy towards Communist Cuba, the plot against Castro instead became a plot against Kennedy. The Mafia believed their 'investment' in the President had not paid off in the way they expected, and had – in the actions of Attorney General Robert Kennedy – actually turned out to their disadvantage. The 'honey trap' tangle of relationships between the President, the Mob and several women did not seem to be having the desired effect of clipping Kennedy's wings either. In 1962, during a meeting with Cuban exile Jose Aleman, Jr (who reported his conversation to the FBI), Santo Trafficante suggested that Kennedy would 'not make it to the election. He is going to be hit' – meaning assassinated, Mob-style.

The Mafia, upset over Robert Kennedy's actions against them, rogue CIA agents opposed to Kennedy's foreign policies, and anti-Castro Cubans angered by the failure of his administration to support their efforts, were alleged to have colluded in a plan to assassinate Kennedy. The Mob would, as they had so often in the past in so many different contexts, provide the 'muscle' to carry out the hit in the form of various trigger-happy gunmen willing to do the job.

Assassination historian Anthony Summers saw no contradiction in these various parties uniting against a common 'enemy': 'Sometimes people glaze over about the notion that the Mafia and US intelligence and the anti-Castro activists were involved together in the assassination of President Kennedy. In fact, there's no contradiction there. Those three groups were all in bed together at the time and had been for several years in the fight to topple Fidel Castro.' Prime among the Mob men involved in the plan was Carlos Marcello.

Known as 'The Little Man', Carlos Marcello had been born in Tunisia in 1910 to Sicilian parents and had come to America with them a year later. He was soon pursuing a life of petty crime, graduating to carrying out armed robberies with a teenage gang around New Orleans, Louisiana. He served several prison sentences, then became connected with New York's Mob capo-to-be Frank Costello. It was Marcello who supplied the muscle in the South to look after Costello's slot machine interests after his business had been driven out of New York. By the end of the 1940s, Marcello was New Orleans' Mafia crime boss, who not only had links to Costello but also to Meyer Lansky in Miami.

In 1959 Marcello was summoned by the Senate McClellan Committee (1957–60) investigating organized crime: the committee's chief legal counsel was Robert Kennedy, while then-Senator John F. Kennedy was a key member of the inquisition. The Kennedys gave Marcello a particularly hard time, pointing out he was an illegal immigrant and potentially subject to deportation. Marcello invoked the Fifth Amendment of the United States Constitution in order to avoid answering any questions that might serve to incriminate himself. In 1960, he supposedly helped finance Richard Nixon's election campaign to the tune of $500,000 via the Teamster's Jimmy Hoffa – perhaps the Mob were hedging their bets in case Kennedy lost the Presidential election?

In 1961, Marcello was grabbed by federal agents who deported him to Guatemala (listed falsely as his place of birth on his 'official' papers): his arduous trek through the jungle to re-enter the United States further increased the mobster's personal enmity towards the Kennedy brothers. He was alleged by New Orleans private investigator Ed Becker to have once predicted the President's demise, claiming the Mob could 'set up some nut to take the fall for the job, just like they do in Sicily'. Marcello's New

Orleans-based crime family had links to both Cuban-sympathizer and pro-Cuba activist Lee Harvey Oswald and would-be mobster Jack Ruby (Marcello controlled the rackets in Dallas, where Ruby was based in his notorious Carousel Club). According to conclusions reached in their report by the House Select Committee on Assassinations of 1976: 'The committee found that Marcello had the motive, means, and opportunity to have President John F. Kennedy assassinated, though it was unable to establish direct evidence of Marcello's complicity.'

According to the theory that 'the Mob did it', Lee Harvey Oswald, the 'lone gunman' – as the official Warren Commission had it, having been extensively lied to by almost all interested parties, including the FBI, the CIA and the Dallas Police Department – who killed President Kennedy in Dallas on 22 November 1963, was in fact a patsy (he said exactly that himself), set-up to take the rap for the killing. Mob-connected hitman and gangster Jack Ruby's assassination of Oswald a day later had all the hall-marks of a Mafia hit – Chicago-born Ruby had once been an errand boy for Al Capone. The claim is that the Mafia both carried out the job and then cleaned up after itself in the most public way possible, content with the idea that no one would ever believe such a conspiracy was even possible, never mind had actually been successfully carried out. Oddly, they could rely on the unwitting collusion of the FBI and the American Government, then led by Lyndon B. Johnson, who supposedly covered up the plot as it was believed that its revelation to the public would destroy confidence in America and reveal past government collusion over Cuba with Mafia bosses. G. Robert Blakey, a former federal prosecutor and chief counsel to the House Assassinations Committee bluntly declared: 'I am now firmly of the opinion that the Mob did it. It is a historical truth.'

Later it was revealed that the FBI had monitored two

meetings between Jack Ruby and Johnny Rosselli in Miami motels in October 1963. Throughout summer and autumn 1963, Ruby had criss-crossed the United States meeting with various Mob figures, including Santo Trafficante-connected mobster Lewis J. McWillie, a Dallas gambler and former manager of Meyer Lansky's Tropicana Hotel in Havana, and the Jimmy Hoffa-connected Irwin Weiner in Chicago who the *Daily News* called 'the Mob's favoured front man' and who'd lost a packet in Castro's takeover of Cuba. These contacts appear to put Jack Ruby in the middle of the planning of a Mob conspiracy to bring down the President.

The FBI investigated Carlos Marcello, who'd predicted there'd be a 'hit' on the President, shortly after the assassination of JFK, and concluded he was simply 'a tomato salesman and real estate investor' and not a Mob boss after all. Indicted on conspiracy, racketeering, mail and wire fraud charges connected to a multi-million dollar insurance scam, 'tomato salesman' Marcello was imprisoned in 1983. In December 1985, according to a fellow inmate who was also an informant for the FBI, Marcello allegedly confessed to having organized the 'hit' on JFK: 'Yeah, I had the son-of-a-bitch killed. I'm glad I did. I'm only sorry I couldn't have done it myself.' The informant's information was confirmed in an FBI memo released in 2006. Carlos Marcello died in 1993, aged eighty-three, after having suffered a series of strokes over the previous four years.

In 1992, tabloid newspaper *The New York Post* claimed the conspiracy against the President had involved Marcello, Trafficante Jr and Mob messenger Jimmy Hoffa. After the event, Hoffa was quoted by Mob lawyer Frank Ragano as having said: 'I told you that they could do it. I'll never forget what Carlos and Santo did for me. This means Bobby is out as Attorney General.' Hoffa was finally convicted in 1964 for jury tampering, locked up in 1967, and then vanished in 1975 when intending to meet with two Mafia leaders, Anthony Giacalone and Anthony Provenzano. Declared legally dead in 1982, Hoffa's fate remains unknown. Robert Kennedy, preparing his own run at the Presidency, was himself assassinated in 1968 in Los Angeles, with blame falling variously upon 'lone gunman' and Manchurian Candidate 'brainwashed' assassin Sirhan Sirhan, Kennedy's own bodyguards (as some have claimed is revealed in audio evidence), or another CIA plot. Despite their obvious motives, no Mob connection has ever been seriously considered in the Robert Kennedy case.

The 'Mob hit' idea as a solution to the Kennedy Assassination is simply one of many competing JFK conspiracy theories. At the heart of it is the supposition that there was more than one gunman in Dealey Plaza on 22 November 1963, and that all the gunmen were mobster operatives. Bill Bonanno, son of Mafia boss Joe Bonanno, claimed in his 1999 memoir that there were three gunmen involved. Oswald was one, set to take the fall, while according to Corsican Mafia member Christian David another was Lucien Sarti, a French killer-for-hire who'd also been involved in the so-called French Connection heroin smuggling network (although later a French newspaper claimed he was in Marseilles' Baumettes Prison at the time of the assassination). The third gunman, reputedly the primary Mob hitman disguised as a police officer and who fired the fatal head shot from the Elm Street storm drain, was the New York Mafia's one time Hollywood operative, Johnny Rosselli. The FBI had been keeping Rosselli under close surveillance, but mysteriously lost his whereabouts between 19 and 27 November 1963.

In 1975, before the Senate's Church Committee inquiry into the activities of the intelligence agencies, Johnny Rosselli spilled the beans about the anti-Castro plot that involved the CIA and the Mob. With 'Operation Mongoose', as Rosselli claimed the plan had been called, now public knowledge, many connected people across the

United States got very nervous. Days before Sam Giancana, who'd had a falling out with the Chicago Outfit, was due to testify to the same committee, he was shot and killed in his own home after his protective police detail was mysteriously ordered to stand down. Among the suspects in the killing were Mob bosses Tony Accardo and Santo Trafficante Jr, as well as agents of the CIA who wanted to prevent him from talking, especially about the Mob hit on JFK.

The death of Giancana caused long-time Los Angeles and Las Vegas resident Johnny Rosselli to flee to Miami, perhaps intending to escape to Cuba. In April 1976, Rosselli was called to testify before the Senate committee investigating an alleged conspiracy to kill President Kennedy. However, the mobster was nowhere to be found. He'd vanished that summer, destination unknown. The FBI were tasked with investigating Rosselli's disappearing act.

On 9 August 1976, the body of the supposed Mob triggerman on the JFK hit was found stuffed into a 55-gallon steel fuel drum floating miles out in Dumfoundling Bay near Miami. His legs and head had been cut off so his torso would fit in the oil drum, and they had then been stuffed in beside the body. Perhaps Johnny Rosselli had already said too much about the assassination, or perhaps the Mob lived in fear that he was about to blow the whole deal. Either way, the Mob credo of omertà had been enforced, and Johnny Rosselli had finally been silenced forever.

PART THREE: THE POST-WAR AMERICAN MOB

12

PRIME MINISTER OF THE UNDERWORLD

Since the end of Prohibition, the attention of America's gangsters had turned away from bootlegging and elsewhere. One of the country's most respectable (and secretive) bootleggers, Joseph Kennedy, went legitimate after 1933, formalizing his relationship with Canada's Bronfman family. By 1946, he'd sold his booze business, called Somerset Importers, to other former bootleggers, Longy Zwillman and Joe Renfield. There were other areas of power that Joseph Kennedy wanted to explore [see chapter 11].

As the 1950s loomed, the gangsters who'd been the big names in the 1930s were exiting the stage. Many were dead, killed by law enforcement as a result of their activities, or by fellow gangsters in seemingly endless turf wars. A few were sitting in jail, while others had done their time and were in exile or retirement. Just as the younger men of the 1930s had replaced the 'Mustache Petes' from the 'old country', so another new breed of 'young Turk' gangster was rising to the top of the American Mafia. These men would dominate organized crime in the US through to the early twenty-first century. Prime among them was the so-called 'Prime Minister of the Underworld', Frank Costello.

Slow rise to the top
Born Francesco Castiglia in Calabria, Italy in 1891, Frank Costello arrived in the United States as a young boy of four: his father ran a successful grocery store. As a teenager Costello joined a street gang in East Harlem, Americanizing his name along the way. From these small beginnings he'd go on to dominate the underworld of organized crime, becoming one of the most influential and – despite the dangers inherent in his business – one of the most long-lived of all the Mob bosses. He would work with and then supplant Lucky Luciano as head of the Luciano/Genovese crime family.

Petty crime was Costello's focus when he was starting out, despite his aptitude at school, but he was careless. Repeatedly caught and punished, he was jailed for assault and robbery three times, in 1908, 1912 and 1917. Building up a reputation as a tough young hoodlum, soon enough Costello had fought his way to the top of the mainly Italian 104th Street gang in New York. He also found the time, in 1918, to get married to Lauretta Giegerman, the sister of one of his friends. The marriage had barely begun, though, when Costello was jailed for ten months after he was caught carrying a concealed weapon during an attempted robbery. Finally, the lessons sunk in – upon his release, Costello decided not to rely on his fists or weapons to advance his criminal activities, but to use his intelligence instead. He gave up on the street rackets that had been his forte up to this point, vowing never again to carry a gun. His focus would be on building legitimate businesses that would act as public fronts for his ongoing crime interests. Costello also began to cultivate the political connections that would serve him well in the future. It would be over three decades before he once more saw the inside of a jail cell.

While in the Morello gang, Costello met Lucky Luciano who'd take over the organization following the Castellammarese–Maranzano war. Siding with Luciano, he would emerge from the 1930–1 fraternal fracas as first lieutenant of the Luciano crime family. Luciano's partnership with Costello was disapproved of by older mafiosi, who called Costello 'the dirty Calabrian' as he was not from Sicily. However, as part of the rising younger generation Luciano was keen to expand the group's membership to take in Italians from other areas and even Jews. Costello was more than happy to go along with Luciano in ignoring the traditional ethnic divisions within the underworld, joining in with the criminal activities of Italians, Jews and Irish gangsters alike.

While mixing freely with Luciano, Arnold Rothstein and Meyer Lansky, Costello's main partner in the early years of Prohibition was William 'Big Bill' Dwyer, an Irish rum-runner who dominated Manhattan's Hell's Kitchen area. Dwyer was eight years older than Costello, and American-born. He'd worked the New York docks in the days before the Volstead Act made the manufacture, transportation or sale of alcohol illegal. His access to trucks, drivers and garages meant he had all the necessary resources to become one of Manhattan's biggest bootleggers. He imported his booze directly from Europe, and after a brief partnership with UK-born Cotton Club owner Owney Madden (who hired a young George Raft as his driver), Dwyer and Costello teamed up. They were mentored by Arnold Rothstein. Dwyer's long-cultivated links with Tammany Hall politicians afforded them a degree of protection from the law, especially the New York Police Department and the Coast Guard, who allowed their shipments to reach shore unmolested.

For the first five years of Prohibition, Frank Costello prospered. Despite splitting the proceeds with other mobsters, he rapidly became a millionaire. The party came to an end in 1926 when Dwyer was arrested as he engaged in his customary business of bribing the Coast Guard to let his shipments through. The Prohibition Unit of the US Treasury (later the Bureau of Prohibition from 1927) was determined to score a high-profile success in curbing the power of New York's gangsters. An extensive undercover operation was staged in the docks and Coast Guard, eventually entrapping Dwyer. Indicted for bribery and rum-running, Dwyer was sentenced to two years' jail time. He was released after just thirteen months, left crime behind and reinvented himself as a legitimate businessman moving into the sporting field.

Costello took the opportunity of Dwyer's misfortune to take over the 'combine', managing bootlegging in New York's docklands. He teamed up with Dwyer's old partner, Owney Madden, sidelining Dwyer's former cohorts, especially Charles Higgins. As Dwyer's second-in-command, Higgins wanted to take over, but was beaten to the punch by the quietly ambitious Costello. Resentful of the Italian muscling in on Irish gang territory, Higgins launched a crusade that became known as the 'Manhattan beer wars' in which he attempted to frustrate the bootlegging activities of Costello, Madden and Dutch Schultz. For two years, from 1928, the rival gangs battled for control of the local bootlegging trade, with Costello's outfit eventually coming out on top. Although the Atlantic City conference of 1929 had laid the framework for co-operation between the various East coast gangsters, it took the resolution of the Castellammarese–Maranzano war of the early 1930s before the dust really settled. By then, Costello – with one eye on the future and the expected forthcoming repeal of Prohibition – was branching out into more legitimate business activities.

Unlike many of his contemporaries, Frank Costello had chosen to keep a low profile as a gangster. The extensive media coverage afforded Al Capone was not for him, nor the living-it-large social life of Bugsy Siegel in Los Angeles. In 1931 Costello bought up the New York area rights for slot machine operations from the Mills Novelty Company of Chicago. He went into business with former Rothstein associate 'Big Phil' Kastel and set up the Triangle Mint Company, installing over 5,000 slot machines around the city and reaping a profit in excess of $20 million during the first year of operation. This form of gambling was almost as profitable as the then still-illegal alcohol business, and a lot less dangerous. Within a few years, Costello had increased the number of installed machines to around 25,000, with a proportionate increase in profits.

Despite Costello's political connections, his activity drew the attention of anti-corruption crusading New York mayor Fiorello La Guardia. In 1934, La Guardia moved against Costello's primary business, arranging for thousands of his gambling machines to be ripped from their premises, loaded onto a barge and dumped into the river. The dramatic gesture – a staged photo opportunity rather than a real policy – made La Guardia's point, so Costello switched his slot machine operations to New Orleans where Louisiana governor Huey Long was happy to have the gambling machines installed in his state, as long as he was paid 10 per cent of the total take. Long was someone Costello could do business with. Kastel was installed as overseer of the New Orleans operation, syphoning millions of dollars from the 'one-armed bandit' racket to Costello, who in turn sent a proportion of the funds on to the Luciano crime family.

Top of the world
By 1936, Luciano's luck had finally run out. Convicted of running a prostitution ring, he was locked up, but made

attempts to continue to run his criminal empire from jail. Costello and Meyer Lansky attempted to make the system work, but it proved unwieldy. Luciano then put Vito Genovese in charge, but when he was indicted in 1937 for an old murder rap from 1934 and fled to Italy, the role of top man in the organization fell to Costello. He ruled the Luciano crime family with the help of his lieutenants Joe Adonis, Anthony Carfano and Michael Coppola, ensuring the profitable gambling interests ran smoothly. As well as the New Orleans slot machine operation, Costello had interests in illegal gambling in Florida and Cuba, supervised by Lansky in Miami, and ran the racing wires with Bugsy Siegel in Los Angeles. He continued to build his political connections, but steered clear of any involvement in drugs. Costello kept his underlings on board by ensuring there was an equal sharing of profits, so giving them no excuse to make a move on him. His legal fronts included a New York meat-packing firm and a chain of meat retailers.

For much of this period in charge, Costello seemed to be biding his time, anticipating bigger things. Genovese returned from exile in 1945, after a run-in with the US Army. He was free of the outstanding murder charge against him due to the suspicious sudden deaths of two of the key witnesses, and was determined to recover his American power base. Despite attempts to maintain his low profile, wider notice had been taken of Costello's activities and he had featured on the covers of both *Time* and *Newsweek* magazines in 1949, emerging with the nickname the 'Prime Minister of the Underworld'. Despite being uncomfortable with this increase in his public profile, Costello was still not willing to cede power to Genovese. However, after Genovese knocked off his deputy Willie Moretti in 1951, Costello had little choice but to make Genovese the 'underboss' of the Luciano family.

The ambitious Genovese was no doubt happy to see Costello's higher profile result in him being one of several gangsters called before the Kefauver Committee in 1951. The televised investigation into organized crime was a fourteen-city roadshow that garnered extensive media coverage, but achieved little else. Mickey Cohen and Meyer Lansky were two of the bigger names who were questioned in public, but the most secretive was Frank Costello. Whether it was a power play performance or a sign of genuine anxiety, Costello negotiated his appearance very carefully. He won agreement that his face would not be seen, so the live television cameras only focused on his constantly fidgeting hands as he nervously tackled the questions put to him. Newsreel documentary film footage of the sessions, however, showed Costello's full appearance and was often used in the television nightly news reports. Unlike many other Mob bosses, Costello refused to hide behind the Fifth Amendment that protected his right against self-incrimination. He seemingly saw the showdown with Senator Kefauver as like one between the sheriff and the outlaw in a Western movie. Costello's raspy voice (the result of a botched throat operation as a child) became connected to the popular image of the gangster, especially when Marlon Brando freely appropriated it for his role in *The Godfather* (1972).

Costello had been built up by his inquisitors as 'American's Number One gangster' and the controller of political corruption at Tammany Hall. Asked what he had ever done for his country, Costello rasped back: 'Paid my taxes!' He had learned from the downfall of other gangsters, such as Al Capone, not to be caught out in such a mundane fashion. Instead, his mix of legitimate and illegitimate business served to raise a cloud of confusion around his affairs, making them all but impenetrable to the forces of law and order. The mystery created around Costello during the hearings seemed only to increase his profile as an untouchable crime kingpin, pulling the strings of his minions and the investigators alike, while he remained hidden in the shadows. Costello upped the dramatic stakes by walking out on the committee claiming he was suffering a sore throat, only to later return and continue testifying. Kefauver may have thought he was running the committee, but Costello was determined to show his inquisitor otherwise.

It was all to no avail, however. Congress didn't get Costello on income tax evasion, as he feared might be their aim. Instead, the technicalities of his temporary walkout saw him imprisoned for contempt, serving fourteen months of an eighteen-month term between 1952 and 1953. Then in 1954 came the long-awaited charge on tax evasion that again saw him imprisoned, serving eleven months of a potential five-year sentence before it was overturned on appeal and he was freed. By 1957, all these political and legal troubles were behind Costello, but he'd found the decade of the 1950s to be a troubling time with his near-continual harassment by law enforcement and his heightened public profile both playing havoc with his legitimate and illegitimate 'business' interests alike.

Keep your friends close, but your enemies closer

Costello's troubles had given his rival Vito Genovese the opportunity he needed to build up allies among the Luciano family mobsters. When Joe Adonis, who had never taken American citizenship, accepted voluntary deportation to Italy in 1956 instead of a long prison sentence as a result of the Kefauver hearings, Costello lost a senior loyal ally. Genovese's position was strengthened, but there was one more key Mafia figure standing in his way of deposing Costello. Albert Anastasia was a big name and Costello ally on the Mob Commission, still the crime group's overall organizing committee. The Mangano crime family boss had avoided answering questions at the Kefauver hearings by pleading the Fifth. During 1951 the Mangano brothers, Vincent and Philip, were both killed – no one was ever caught for the killings, but responsibility was widely attributed to Anastasia who had consolidated his power following their deaths. Genovese knew he had to get rid of Anastasia if he were to ever depose Costello. He won the support of Anastasia's lieutenant Carlo Gambino by promising him control of the Mangano family. Genovese argued for the hit on Anastasia by depicting him as an unstable killer (in the wake of the Mangano killings), who was up to his eyes in gambling debts and therefore susceptible to blackmail or control by law enforcement investigators. Anastasia's demands for a larger share of the casino gambling profits in Cuba brought Meyer Lansky, who ran the Cuban operations, on board the conspiracy. However, the law got to Anastasia first, locking him up for tax evasion in 1955, putting the mobster beyond the gangsters' reach.

Impatient to gain further power, Genovese moved on Frank Costello anyway, authorizing a hit on his boss in May 1957. Genovese's driver and Mafia gunman Vincent Gigante was tasked with the job, but his marksmanship let him down. He shot and wounded Costello outside his apartment building, The Majestic in Manhattan. The wound to Costello's head was superficial, and Gigante fled the scene before he could verify Costello's 'death', but the shock of being attacked in this way after all this time caused 'America's Number One gangster' to reconsider his position as head of the Luciano crime organization.

Costello decided to retire, for the sake of his health. However, account sheets detailing illegal profits from Las Vegas casinos that had been found in his pockets in the aftermath of the assassination attempt saw Costello serving another prison term. Vito Genovese stepped up to the 'Number One' spot he'd long coveted, changing the name of the crime family from Luciano to Genovese. He then completed the job on Anastasia, having him assassinated in the barber shop of the Park Sheraton hotel in New York in October 1957. The high-profile police investigation that followed failed to find any suspects, and Genovese further tightened his hold on the New York Mob – it had taken him over a decade to achieve, but Vito Genovese was now the 'capo di tutti capi' of Lucky Luciano's former organization.

Frank Costello was released in 1961 after serving forty-two months of a five-year sentence and accepted his move into early retirement from running the Mob. He spent several years fighting the Immigration and Naturalisation Service, which put major effort into attempts to have him deported to Italy. However, Costello still exerted great influence as a retired 'Don' of the Mafia. He maintained various gambling interests, and stayed in touch with his friendly former associates. Taking a penthouse apartment in the Waldorf Astoria, Frank Costello, one time Prime Minister of the Underworld, found that newer, still-active Mafia men would visit to pay homage to him, bringing gifts and keeping him up-to-date on Mob goings on. Although he supposedly took up gardening and cultivating flowers, Costello had in fact been cultivating an altogether more ambitious plan: revenge on Vito Genovese.

In a plot hatched with old associates Lucky Luciano and Meyer Lansky during his jail time, Costello achieved a successful frame-up that sent Vito Genovese and several of his allies straight to jail. In mid-1958, Genovese was indicted on charges of conspiring to import and sell narcotics in the United States, the kind of business that Costello himself had always steered clear of. The star witness was a Puerto Rican drug dealer, Nelson Cantellops, who claimed he'd met with Genovese personally to set up the deal. This was enough for the authorities to convict the mobster of selling a huge quantity of heroin, sentencing him to fifteen years in the Atlanta Federal Penitentiary. Whether he was, strictly speaking, guilty or not of this particular charge didn't matter much to the agencies of law enforcement – they were simply happy to take down Genovese for anything.

Many observers were troubled by Cantellops' testimony

– it was unlikely that a Mafia boss of Genovese's standing would personally get involved in such a transaction. The Costello revenge theory posits that he was responsible for Cantellops testimony, as a way to bring down Genovese. In an attempt to maintain his control from prison, Genovese appointed a three-man 'ruling panel' to look after business in his absence, consisting of Anthony Strollo, Gerardo Catena and Mike Miranda. It would do Vito Genovese little good, however: he died of a heart attack in 1969, while still imprisoned.

Frank Costello enjoyed his influential retirement as a Mafia Don. He also died of a heart attack in New York in February 1973 at the age of 82 – a long life for some-one so prominent in the violent world of organized crime. Costello was the bridging figure between the 'old guard' of the 1930s mobsters like Lucky Luciano (who himself had died in 1962) and Meyer Lansky (similarly long-lived, dying in 1983, aged 80) and the up-and-comers who domi-nated the modern American Mafia in the 1960s, 1970s and 1980s, such as Sam Giancana, Carlo Gambino and the so-called 'Teflon Don', John Gotti.

13

CAPO DI TUTTI CAPI: INSIDE THE AMERICAN MAFIA

The American Mafia was a very distinct operation from the Sicilian original, and it developed its own traditions and divisions, especially as the American-raised gangsters began to replace those who'd grown to adulthood in the 'old country' before coming to the United States. It was the Kefauver Committee of the early 1950s that brought the concept of organized crime and 'the Mafia' to the attention of the American public. The notion that Prohibition-era crime had been run by a single 'boss of the bosses' caught on, even if it was never really strictly true. As far as the excitable press went, the 'capo di tutti capi' became any well-known gangster who seemed to have been in charge. While every major American city had their own Mafia variants, the big two were Chicago and New York, with important off-shoots in New Orleans and Los Angeles. The best illustrative example of how the system worked is provided by the history of the leaders of the Five Families that largely made up the New York Mafia.

The idea of a 'capo' or boss first gained currency at the turn of the century with the activities of Giuseppe Morello, the first American boss of the oldest of the Five Families of New York. His successors Joe Masseria and Salvatore Maranzano both claimed the title for themselves, until their mutual destruction following the Castellammarese War. Maranzano had declared himself the capo following that gangland conflict, and demanded the other families pay him homage. Charles 'Lucky' Luciano ultimately supported neither Masseria nor Maranzano, and was instrumental in their removal, with himself becoming replacement capo.

With his creation of The Commission – the committee that controlled organized crime made up of representatives from each of the Five Families and other minor Mob groups – Luciano had become the self-created first genuine capo di tutti capi of the American Mafia. The five original American-Italian crime families recognized by Luciano were his own (later Genovese), Bonanno, Profaci (later Colombo), Gambino and Lucchese. While each family had its own leadership and structure, Luciano's creation of The Commission saw him become the first 'equal among equals'. Others would follow him in the position: although there was no overall 'boss', some were the most powerful among their peers during any given period.

From 1931 to his imprisonment and exile following 1946, Luciano ran things. His successor was Frank Costello, the mobster who'd learned from the examples of others to at least attempt to keep a low personal profile. He dominated until his own downfall and replacement in 1957. Vito Genovese had long sought the title of capo, but when it finally came his way it was short-lived, just two years, until 1959. By the 1960s, most of the original American gangsters of the 1930s and 1940s were dead, locked up or in retirement. The new blood was now in charge, and a new set of capi di tutti capi would see the American Mafia through the next five decades, with mixed results.

Going Bananas

Probably the longest lived of all the prominent gangsters (he was 97 when he died in 2002), Joseph Bonanno – known by the nickname Joe or Joey Bananas – was the capo who took over from Vito Genovese in 1959. He would run things for just three years, but he prepared the way for one of the longest-running capi, Carlo Gambino. He would also be responsible for his family being the first to be expelled from The Commission, leading to a loss of power for three decades.

Bonanno was born in Castellammare del Golfo in Sicily, Italy as Giuseppe Bonanno in 1905, arriving in the United States at the age of three when his family moved to Brooklyn where he grew up over the next decade. A return to Italy was short-lived, with Bonanno stowing away on a Cuban fishing boat that brought him back to Tampa, Florida. Like several key Sicilian Mafia figures in the mid-1920s, the nineteen-year-old Bonanno was fleeing Benito Mussolini who was attempting to suppress the old-style Mafia in Italy as part of the Fascists' rise to power.

When he eventually got back to New York City, Bonanno quickly allied himself with fellow Castellammarian Salvatore Maranzano and got involved in bootlegging. Bonanno became one of the key figures in the strife that followed, functioning as an 'underboss' or chief lieutenant to Maranzano who was up against Joe Masseria's squad that included the likes of Luciano, Genovese, Costello and Gambino (all of whom would at one point take the capo position). When Luciano took out both Masseria and Maranzano and reorganized things in 1931, Bonanno inherited Maranzano's old interests at the age of twenty-six. He was one of the youngest ever bosses of any of the Five Families. Sensing which way things were going, Bonanno was happy to serve under Luciano and his successors until it came his turn to take the 'big chair' on The Commission.

Following the repeal of Prohibition in 1933, Bonanno and his associates were into all the usual criminal activities in their territory: bookmaking, loan sharking, running the numbers racket, and prostitution. In 1938, he left the United States in order to re-enter legally through Detroit so he would be able to apply for legitimate citizenship, perhaps anticipating a future move into a more legal business. Real estate investments and strong interests in the garment and trucking industries alongside his criminal activities kept Bonanno flush with cash. His Brooklyn funeral parlour proved useful when the Mafia had inconvenient bodies they had to dispose of.

Joseph Bonanno kept things ticking over nice and quietly, until the disastrous Apalachin Conference of November 1957. The meeting had been called by then-capo Vito Genovese in an attempt to assert his authority over The Commission, which had expanded with the addition of members from Detroit and Philadelphia. A series of shifting alliances had put Genovese on the defensive by the time he took control in 1957. Around a hundred Mafia top men were said to have been present at the Apalachin meeting, at which the late Albert Anastasia's criminal interests were to be divided following his assassination. The small, quiet town was overrun by flash cars and even flashier Mob bosses, inevitably attracting the attention of law enforcement. The meeting broke up as the gangsters fled the arrival of 'the heat', but around sixty, embarrassingly including Genovese himself and Bonanno, were caught up in local police roadblocks and detained. Of those, around twenty were charged by January 1959 with 'conspiring to obstruct justice by lying' about the nature of the underworld meeting, and were fined up to $10,000 each, facing prison sentences of between three and five years. However, all the resulting convictions had been overturned on appeals by 1960. The absence of key figures like Luciano, Lansky and Costello at the meeting led to whispered suggestions that the whole thing had been a set-up designed to undermine Genovese as capo.

By the time the convictions were overturned, Bonanno had succeeded the hapless Genovese as the capo of The Commission, during a period of shifting alliances and political positioning by many of the individual family heads. He kept the lid on some of the simmering resentments that threatened to return the Mob to the pre-Commission situation where gunfights and assassination settled disputes. Bonanno was suspected of being behind a plot to wipe out several other Mob leaders, including Gambino and Tommy Lucchese – as a result he and his family were dismissed from The Commission. Bonanno was then kidnapped in 1964, supposedly on The Commission's orders. After being locked up for six weeks, Bonanno was persuaded to 'retire', a decision aided by a looming grand jury investigation during which some in The Commission worried that 'Joey Bananas' might spill the beans. Bonanno spent time in Haiti, but when there was an attempt on his son's life, he returned to the US in 1965–6 and attempted to regain control of his criminal clan. Finally, a heart attack in 1968 brought about his permanent withdrawal from active involvement with any faction of the New York Mafia. He moved to Arizona, while immediate family members muscled in on his used-car business in California, which had been a vehicle for laundering money. An FBI operation brought the then seventy-five-year-old Joseph Bonanno his first criminal indictment. Sentenced to five years, he only served one, and was released in November 1986. His autobiography *A Man of Honour* revealed much about his gangster life and involvement with The Commission, much to the horror of his fellow mobsters. Despite that, Joseph

Bonanno – who'd fled Fascism and survived the gang wars of the 1930s – lived on into the twenty-first century, dying of heart failure in 2002, at the grand old age of 97.

The real Godfather

Succeeding Joseph Bonanno as head of The Commission in 1962 was Carlo Gambino, who remained in position until his death at the age of seventy-four in 1976. Gambino, born in Palermo, Sicily in 1902, was another who fled Mussolini's clampdown on the Italian Mafia. His family belonged to 'The Honoured Society', a local Sicilian variation, also known as the Cosa Nostra. Gambino began to carry out 'hits', targeted assassinations, in his teens, becoming a 'made man', meaning an 'honoured member', of the Sicilian Mafia. He claimed political asylum upon arrival in the United States, but rapidly set about involving himself with the New York variation of the Cosa Nostra, the American Mafia. He became a driver and hitman for Vincent Mangano and the brother-in-law through marriage of crime boss Paul Castellano, who would eventually replace him as the capo on The Commission.

Gambino was on the fringes of much that went on in organized crime in the 1920s and 1930s, including the Castellammarse War, the rise and fall of Lucky Luciano and the creation of The Commission. With Mangano representing the family on The Commission, Gambino concentrated on building up his criminal enterprises in protection, loan sharking and illegal gambling. His low profile served him well. When Mangano vanished in 1951, believed killed, Albert Anastasia took over, with Gambino as his 'underboss'. Gambino would eventually join Vito Genovese as part of the faction that opposed Anastasia and conspired to kill him. When Genovese was the capo of The Commission, Gambino switched sides once more, aligning with Luciano, Costello and Lansky against Genovese. After the disastrous Apalachin meeting and the fall of Genovese, and the forced retirement of Joey Bananas (which Gambino had been instrumental in bringing about), Carlo Gambino himself ascended to the Mob throne.

As Bonanno had caused his family to divide into two fighting factions, humorously dubbed the 'Banana Split', Gambino – as boss – first wanted to kill Bonanno, but then settled upon the kidnap-and-forced-retirement gambit instead. His reasoning was that Bonanno 'took up too much space and air', Sicilian Mafia code for arrogance. With Bonanno firmly out of the way – but only after an on-and-off shooting war that lasted until 1968 – Gambino was finally firmly in control. Gambino's supposed 'mercy' in the Bonanno affair sat well with the other family heads.

A period of relative peace followed, and Gambino ensured this continued by employing his relatives. The Gambino family tentacles spread far and wide through the New York Mob, protecting the capo from any overt plots. It wasn't until the early-1970s and the death of rival family boss Joe Colombo Sr that action was again required by Gambino to maintain his power over The Commission. He refused to be slighted – when Tommy Eboli either could not or would not repay a loan of $4 million, Gambino had him rubbed out as a warning to others. He ruled The Commission with a rod of iron: in 1974 when insulted on the street by minor Mob man Carmine Scialo (who was connected to the Colombos), it wasn't long until Scialo's body was found encased in concrete, the origin of the slang Mob phrase 'concrete overcoat'. From 1972, Gambino was under more-or-less constant surveillance by the FBI, which was attempting to link him to organized crime. No secret was made of the organization's attempts to catch him involved in something illegal, which only made it easy for Gambino to conduct his business in such a way that he was never incriminated.

In his final years, Gambino cultivated several possible replacements as head of the family and ultimately The

Commission: Aniello Dellacroce (whom he did not rate particularly highly); Dellacroce's own ambitious understudy, John Gotti; and Gambino's preferred successor, Paul Castellano. When Carlo Gambino died from a heart attack (while at home watching the New York Yankees game on television) in October 1976 at the age of seventy-four, it was indeed Castellano who stepped into his shoes, but Gotti would be waiting in the wings, gun loaded, ready for his chance at the top job.

King of the castle

Following his ascension in 1976, Paul Castellano made sure to keep Dellacroce happy, giving his 'underboss' control of traditional Mafia activities while Castellano himself expanded into new areas of 'white collar' crime such as stock embezzlement and other high finance scams. Costantino Paul Castellano had been born in Brooklyn, New York in 1915 – at over six feet two inches tall, he used his height and heft to physically intimidate other mobsters. Castellano dropped out of school early to become a runner for the mob, collecting and delivering gambling receipts. First arrested at nineteen for a raid on a haberdashery, Castellano served a three-month prison sentence – he refused to name his accomplices, so enhancing his reputation as a 'stand up guy' among his Mafia associates. By the 1940s, he'd risen to the position of 'underboss' in the Mangano crime family, serving under Anastasia and Gambino and becoming one of those arrested during the Apalachin round-up. Again, he refused to talk and was jailed for a year on contempt charges, and for a further five years for 'conspiracy to withhold information', a jail term dropped on appeal in 1960.

A year before the death of Gambino, Castellano ordered the killing of his daughter's boyfriend, Vito Borelli, supposedly for insulting him. Joseph Massimo, the last – to date – capo of The Commission, was the triggerman on that hit. As Gambino's health declined, Castellano was effectively the acting boss of The Commission, until he fully took over with Gambino's death. For the better part of a decade, he'd be in charge, but with a revival in the old way of settling things with bullets, Castellano would be the first capo in decades to be assassinated while in office.

At the time Castellano took over, Dellacroce had been jailed on tax evasion charges, so couldn't mount a direct challenge. He waited, keeping his powder dry, pursuing opportunities in loan sharking, extortion and robbery. Fearing an attempt on his life, Castellano had built up a private army, largely made up of the so-called 'Westies', an Irish gang based in Hell's Kitchen in Manhattan, and the Cherry Hill branch of the Gambino family. Feeling protected, Castellano didn't hesitate to drop the hammer on threats and rivals, such as Nicholas Scibetta, James Eppolito and his son, James Eppolito Jr, and Frank Amato – all Mafia operatives who'd cross Castellano one way or another.

In the early 1980s, paranoid about his associates, Castellano became ever more reclusive, retreating behind the walls of his Staten Island mansion, from where he ran his business, rarely changing out of a succession of silk dressing gowns. Resentment of Castellano grew within Dellacroce and his supporters, who included John Gotti. Although Castellano banned drug dealing (like former capo, Frank Costello, he was against dealing in dope), this was a lucrative area that Gotti began to explore ever more deeply. Gotti fancied himself a future boss, but he pledged to take no action against Castellano as long as his own mentor, Dellacroce, was still around.

Things began to unravel for Paul Castellano from 1983, when he ordered a hit on Roy DeMeo, a Gambino family member who ran a particularly violent and vicious crew that had killed over 100 people. Following DeMeo's death, the FBI bugged Castellano's house while he was on vacation in Florida. The resulting tapes revealed much about

Mafia activity, as well as Castellano's sexual impotence, resulting in the capo being indicted in 1984 on federal racketeering charges and several murders, including the Eppolito killings. He was also charged with extortion, theft, prostitution and narcotics trafficking for good measure, but was released on $2 million bail.

The 1985 death of Aniello Dellacroce from lung cancer gave John Gotti his cue. Castellano failed to attend Dellacroce's wake, a calculated insult, and named his own bodyguard Thomas Bilotti, rather than Gotti, as the replacement underboss. He also threatened to dissolve Gotti's crew for drug dealing, with the possibility of also killing Gotti heavily hinted at. Convincing other family members that Castellano was preparing to talk to the authorities as part of the Mafia Commission Trial of the mid-1980s, they conspired to assassinate him on 16 December 1985 at a dinner meeting at the Sparks Steak House in Midtown Manhattan. They took out Bilotti, too, for good measure. A 'hit team' of Gambino mobsters carried out the job on Gotti's orders, with the result that Gotti himself became capo before the year was out – despite the objections of long-standing gangster Vincent Gigante, who lamented Gotti's lack of permission for the hit on Castellano. Gigante would, in turn, simply bide his time . . .

The Teflon Don
Born in New York in 1940, John Gotti Jr was one of five brothers, all of whom pursued careers in the criminal underworld of the city, largely as a way out of the poverty in which they grew up. As had been the pattern half a century before, the teenage Gotti joined street gangs, a tried-and-tested route into the lower levels of organized crime. At fourteen, he attempted to steal a cement mixer from a construction site, injuring his foot in the process, an accident that left him with a permanent limp.

Married in 1962 and quickly starting a family, Gotti

attempted to 'go straight' taking up jobs in the garment industry and in trucking, both Mob-related areas. The easy money from major crime was too tempting, however, and Gotti spent time in jail twice before 1966. Connecting with Mafia figures once more, he hijacked trucks at Idlewild (now JFK) airport, working closely with future capo Joseph Massino. Making a name for himself, Gotti was taken under the wing of Aniello Dellacroce, who mentored the young would-be gangster. Then the late 1960s saw a series of hijacking charges catch up with Gotti, and he went to jail for three years.

Paroled in 1972, Gotti returned to the Mob as an enforcer, collecting gambling debts, before graduating to the hitman team tasked with taking out Irish gangster James McBratney, who was suspected of killing Carlo Gambino's nephew. Gotti was also the triggerman in the killing of Vito Borelli, capo Paul Castellano's daughter's boyfriend. Charged in the McBratney killing, Gotti was back in the slammer for manslaughter in the mid-1970s, serving two years of a four-year term. By 1977, Gotti was third in line behind both Dellacroce and Castellano for the top Mafia position. In 1980, Gotti's twelve-year-old son Frank was killed in a mini-bike accident by Gotti's neighbour, John Favara – within two months, Favara himself had mysteriously disappeared.

Growing in confidence, Gotti took his crew into drug dealing, an area prohibited by Castellano, who was weakening in his authority as the capo di tutti capi. Gathering enough support among the other senior mafiosi, Gotti finally dropped the hammer on Castellano in 1985, stepping into the dead man's shoes. The smartly dressed, publicly-visible John Gotti became known in the press as the 'Teflon Don' to whom no charges would ever stick. He was the most well-known, high-profile public mobster since Al Capone – a fact that would lead to his downfall and seriously damage the Mafia in the process.

A 1986 assassination attempt on Gotti, led by Castellano loyalist Vincent Gigante, failed, leading to an uneasy truce between the Gotti and Gigante factions. The FBI were determined to bring Gotti down and convened a special anti-Gotti task force – a replay of the 'Get Capone' drive of the late 1920s – that used near-constant surveillance to try and get the goods on the capo. Gotti took to conducting his business outdoors, the only place where he could be sure he wasn't being bugged. Gotti was repeatedly in and out of court, but nothing could be conclusively pinned on him.

In the style of Dons in days past, Gotti insisted that lesser mafiosi 'pay homage' to him weekly at the Ravenite Social Club, thereby allowing the FBI to match names to faces and figure out the membership and hierarchy of the Gambino crime family in the late 1980s. They finally managed to catch him on tape discussing killings and attacking family 'underboss' Salvatore Gravano. The FBI brought Gravano in and played him the tapes. Fearing he was being targeted by Gotti for assassination, Gravano decided to become a witness for the state. Gotti was arrested in 1990, charged with several murders – including those of Castellano and Bilotti – as well as conspiracy, loan sharking, illegal gambling, obstruction of justice, bribery and the old law enforcement favourite of tax evasion. Gotti's usual Mafia-connected attorneys who'd been so successful at getting him off were denied the right to act on his behalf as they might have been called as witnesses, thus removing his legal support structure. The 'Dapper Don' did, however, win backing from some notable Hollywood names during his trial, including Anthony Quinn and Mickey Rourke. Despite that, John Gotti was convicted in June 1992, receiving a life sentence.

The remainder of his life – just a decade – was lived under harsh conditions in the United States Penitentiary at Marion, Illinois. He was held in solitary confinement, supposedly for his own protection, only leaving his cramped cell for one hour each day. Despite that, he held onto his position as capo, relaying his orders through his brother, Peter, and his son, John A. Gotti Jr. Gotti's lifetime cigarette habit saw him succumb to terminal throat cancer, and he died in June 2002 aged just sixty-one. Gotti's daughter and grandchildren would later feature in a 2004–5 television reality show called *Growing Up Gotti*.

John Gotti's public profile, failure to hide his Mob connections, and self-serving reign as capo all brought the Mafia into further disrepute in the eyes of the public. His killing of Castellano had upset the other bosses, especially Gigante who was aligned with the Lucchese family faction. It would be Gigante who, having failed to kill Gotti, would replace him after his death in prison as head of The Commission.

The enigma in the bathrobe

Born in 1928, Vincent Gigante had once been a boxer and always seemed ready for a fight. As an enforcer, he rose up the ranks of the then-Luciano crime family before it became the Genovese family. The 'Chin' – as Gigante was known, after his most prominent feature – was the triggerman in the failed 1957 assassination attempt on 'Prime Minster' Frank Costello, so he had form in trying to bump off bosses. Ironically, he secured his position in the family when he shared a jail cell with Vito Genovese in the 1960s, and by the 1980s, had risen to become head of the Genovese family and sat on The Commission, directly under Paul Castellano and John Gotti.

Where Gotti escaped prosecution through crooked lawyers and jury fixing and tampering, Gigante decided to feign madness, wandering the streets of New York's Greenwich Village in a bathrobe muttering to himself. He became known as 'The Oddfather' or 'The Enigma in the Bathrobe', but it was enough to prevent him standing trial in 1990 on federal racketeering charges when he was declared mentally unfit. There were questions as to whether Gigante had been masquerading as mentally ill for two decades, or whether he was genuinely suffering from the conditions that various experts diagnosed, including schizophrenia, dementia and psychosis.

Regardless, he had enough wits about him to succeed Gotti in the capo role on The Commission, even if it was during a period when the Mafia's power was in sharp decline, thanks in part to stronger law enforcement due to the Racketeer Influenced and Corrupt Organizations (RICO) act, changes in technology and the rise of new forces in American crime fighting. The Genovese family connection was enough to keep Gigante in place during attempts to lock him up from 1990 onwards. Salvatore Gravano, the informer who'd brought down Gotti, proved instrumental in bringing Gigante to justice. He testified against the mobster, claiming he had been consistently perfectly lucid when conducting Mafia business and that the 'craziness' was just an act, albeit one that had kept him out of jail for over twenty years. Former Lucchese family members backed Gravano's testimony, claiming Gigante's role as capo on The Commission proved he was sane, as the other families wouldn't have put up with him otherwise.

In 1997, Vincent Gigante was finally convicted on a variety of racketeering and conspiracy charges, and handed a twelve-year sentence, followed by additional charges of obstructing justice in 2002. In April 2003, the seventy-five-year-old Gigante pleaded guilty to the charges and finally admitted to faking his mental illness across many decades. His health went into a severe and rapid decline in jail, and Vincent Gigante died in December 2005, aged seventy-seven.

The Last Don?

Three years before Gigante's death, the title and role of capo of The Commission, which had lain vacant since Gigante's 1997 conviction, had been filled by former Gotti associate and member of the Bonanno (of previous capo Joey Bananas fame) family, Joseph Massino. He would be the final capo of The Commission to date, gaining the inevitable nickname of 'The Last Don'.

Born in 1943, Massino had become a truck hijacker like Gotti, who subsequently secured power by assassinating rivals. A racketeering conviction resulted in Massino being sentenced to ten years, but he was cleared due to a statute-of-limitations expiry in 1987. The late 1980s saw the heads chopped off many of the Five Families thanks to the RICO act and other tougher law enforcement actions. Massino believed that Gotti had caused a huge amount of trouble for the American Mafia due to his high-profile and reckless conduct, so he decided to adopt a lower profile himself. When Gigante was finally banged up in 1997, Massino stepped into the role of capo after a gap of several years where there was no single overall leader of The Commission.

Massino himself was brought down in 2003 on a racketeering charge thanks to testimony from former Bonanno 'underboss' Salvatore Vitale, who also happened to be Massino's best friend and brother-in-law. Vitale worked in conjunction with undercover FBI agent Joseph Pistone who'd infiltrated the mob between 1976 and 1981 (and was code-named Donnie Brasco, as played by Johnny Depp in the 1997 movie). Massino faced seven charges of murder, as well as money laundering, illegal gambling, extortion, conspiracy and arson. A key alleged murder victim was 'Sonny Black' Napolitano (played by Al Pacino in the movie), who had first connected Massino and Pistone.

New laws meant that Massino faced the death penalty if convicted – which he was in July 2004. Sentencing was on hold, however, thanks to the discovery by the FBI of a 'Mafia graveyard' in Queens, known as 'The Hole'. Supposedly, a 'reliable informant' had put the agents on the trail of the burial site, from which several corpses were exhumed. It turned out that, in order to save his life and secure a lesser sentence, Joseph Massimo himself had turned state's evidence – the only ever sitting capo of The Commission to do so – and led the FBI to 'The Hole'. In turning informer, Massimo had broken the Mafia 'blood oath' of omertá or silence. He was given a life sentence, and his position on The Commission has apparently remained vacant ever since.

Joseph Massino went on to provide evidence and testimony in a variety of Mob trials, often giving background information on the structure, operation and principles of the modern American Mafia. His revelations essentially brought to an end the successful organizing principles of the Mob put in place by Lucky Luciano back in 1931. In 2013, as a result of his co-operation and in recognition of his failing health, Joseph Massimo – truly The Last Don – was freed on a 'supervised release' at the age of seventy. As of spring 2014, no Mafia operative has yet taken revenge against him for his actions as an informer, but Massimo must know it is only a matter of time before the Mob or his age brings his reign as the last American gangster to an end.

14

THE CHANGING FACE OF AMERICAN GANGSTERS

The nature of organized crime has changed dramatically since the earliest days of the American Mafia in Chicago and New York, when Al Capone and Lucky Luciano were kings in their respective cities. Gangsters like them might not recognize the tools of the trade these days (weapons more sophisticated than Tommy guns, and – increasingly – computers), but the basic crimes being committed would still be familiar. The methods and tools may have changed, but the aim remains the same: to enrich yourself and your associates at the expense of someone else. Between the 1940s and the twenty-first century, the nature of crime has changed, as have gangs and gangsters. Several broad movements characterize the era, from the rise of the biker gangs of the 1940s through the 1960s, to the increasing dominance of American street gangs by African-American groups, like the Crips and the Bloods, to The Council

– actively modelled on Luciano's Commission – to the modern-day terrors of cybercrime. No longer do gangsters need a Tommy gun to rob a bank: a computer, the right software and a broadband connection is all it takes in the twenty-first century.

The biker gangs

A different kind of 'gang' and gangster bridges the 1940s and the 1970s: the 'outlaw' biker gangs. The oldest biker gang, known as The Outlaw Motorcycle Club, dates back to 1935, expanding from its base in Joliet, Illinois to take in much of the United States and Canada, across Europe to Asia and Australia. Just as the automobile helped crime spread from the centre of cities to the suburbs in the 1920s and 1930s, so the easy mobility offered by the motorcycle allowed criminal gangs to stage 'hit and run' raids on small towns across America. One 'president' of the organization, Harry Bowman, even made it onto the FBI's Ten Most Wanted list before he was eventually caught and convicted on a triple murder charge in 1999.

The idea of freedom and non-conformity is central to biker gang culture, but it is also often a crime-based enterprise, although not all motorcycle clubs or biker gangs are necessarily criminal. Law enforcement has identified biker gangs as unique among organized crime in that they maintain published rules and regulations and are easily identified through patches, unlike the days of Lucky Luciano when membership of crime gangs was kept secret.

Four specific biker gangs have been identified by the FBI and the Criminal Intelligence Service of Canada as largely criminal: the Outlaws, the Hells Angels, the Pagans, and the Bandidos. These 'Big Four' were considered large enough (with around $1 billion annually in estimated illegal income) and organized enough to qualify for prosecution under the RICO statutes used against older forms of organized crime. For a decade between 1974 and 1984 the Outlaws and the Hells Angels were engaged in a bloody gang war across Florida and North Carolina that is said to have taken around ninety-five lives, reminiscent of the gangster turf wars of old. One Outlaw-specific biker patch reads 'A.H.M.D.', standing for 'All Hells Angels Must Die'. Among the gangs, the Outlaws had a reputation for being widely engaged in criminal enterprises including the usual drug trafficking and prostitution, but also extending into mail fraud, gun smuggling, armed robbery and even murder-for-hire.

The Hells Angels originated in the post-war period, starting in Fontana, California around 1948, and were named after a 1930 Howard Hughes movie, but they dropped the apostrophe in 'Hell's'. The original members were young war veterans who began their motorcycle club as a social organization, but it wasn't long until a significant number of its members turned to criminality. The US Department of Justice considers the Hells Angels to be an organized crime syndicate. Developing beyond the usual criminal enterprises, the gang became particularly known for the manufacture and sale of particular drugs, especially methamphetamine. Their battles with other biker gangs were usually over distribution territories for their illegal drug trade. The Hells Angels gathered particular cultural credibility in the 1960s, thanks to the rise of the counter-culture (especially in the Haight-Ashbury district of San Francisco, where Hells Angels provided 'security' for events), biker films like *The Wild Angels* (1966) and *Easy Rider* (1969), and the writing of 'gonzo' journalist Hunter S. Thompson.

As with the Italian Mafia gangs of the 1930s and 1940s, the Hells Angels had no compunction about killing each other if their 'rules' had been broken. An entire 'dissident chapter' of the gang was killed off in the 1980s in Montreal, Canada. At the 1969 Altamont concert (as seen in the 1970 documentary film *Gimme Shelter*), tensions between the

crowd watching bands like Jefferson Airplane and The
Rolling Stones and the Hells Angels members providing 'security' rose all day, culminating in the murder of a
member of the audience, Meredith Hunter, by an Angels
member. Alan Passaro was later acquitted of stabbing
Hunter to death on grounds of self-defence, claiming that
Hunter had pulled a gun – he died in 1985.

Many other Hells Angels members were caught up in
illegal actions, ranging from bar fights to outright murder.
One leader, Ralph 'Sonny' Barger (who was at Altamont),
was jailed for four years in 1988 on conspiracy charges
relating to a plan to blow up the rival Outlaws' clubhouse,
only to later write an autobiography and have a beer named
after him. He also featured in episodes of Hells Angels television drama *Sons of Anarchy* (airing from 2008). The 2002
'River Run Riot' at a casino in Nevada saw gangs of Hells
Angels battle rivals from the Mongols biker gang, resulting in three deaths. Two Angels were jailed, while charges
against another thirty-six were thrown out.

The Pagans were formed in 1959 in Maryland by Lou
Dobkin, a highly-educated biochemist. Members were
identified by their preference for denim jackets and
Triumph motorcycles (and later Harley-Davidsons).
Largely non-violent until the mid-1960s, the Pagans joined
other biker gangs by getting involved in the lucrative
drugs trade. By 1970 there were 900 members split across
forty-four chapters, while leader John 'Satan' Marron led
the gang into other illegal activities and battles with other
motorcycle clubs, most often the Hells Angels. A gang war
during 1974–5 between the Pagans and the Warlocks in
Pennsylvania saw fifteen people lose their lives. The Pagans
became well known for using smaller affiliated motorcycle gangs (dubbed 'puppet clubs') to distribute their drugs,
including PCP, cocaine and heroin, at street level. Arson
and extortion were favourite tools of the Pagans, with
members of the gang in the 1970s associated with several

underworld bombings and the actions of a serial killer who claimed the lives of at least six women.

Forming in 1966, the Bandidos were a Texas motorcycle club whose motto was 'We are the people your parents warned you about'. Drugs, dealing in weapons and murder-for-hire contracts were central to the activities of the Bandidos. Five of the club's past presidents served jail time for various charges, while reports linked the gang to the 1979 murder of Texas Judge John Wood Jr – the first federal judge killed in the twentieth century. Charles Harrelson, the estranged father of *Cheers* and *The Hunger Games* actor Woody Harrelson, was convicted of the crime, and died in jail in 2007 aged sixty-eight. Some researchers also implicated Harrelson in the Mob-arranged assassination of JFK, claiming he had connections to organized crime, Jack Ruby and the CIA, and may have been present, possibly as a gunman, on the 'grassy knoll' during the assassination in 1963 [see chapter 11].

Many of the motorcycle gangs maintained that 99 per cent of their members were law-abiding citizens, while just 1 per cent were outlaws. However, for some the reach of their criminality was international. In 2006, three Bandidos were jailed in Thailand on charges of extortion and money laundering, with allegations they'd 'cleaned' just under $80 million through Thailand tourist operations in four cities between 2004 and 2006. While not all bikers or members of motorcycle clubs are criminal, there have been enough of them to convince the FBI and other law enforcement agencies to put some still very active biker gangs firmly into the category of gangster.

African-American gangsters

There is no greater example of the changing face of American gangsterism through the 1970s than the African-American outfit known as The Council, a New York area combine that dealt in hard drugs, especially raw heroin.

The members of The Council consciously modelled both themselves and their organization after the infamous mobs of the 1930s (it was, after all, loosely connected to the Lucchese family, one of the original Five Families), but it differed from the 'classic' gangsters in several important ways.

The Council was built around Leroy 'Nicky' Barnes, born in Harlem in 1933. There had always been black gangsters, but back in the 1920s through to the 1940s, they'd largely kept to their own areas (primarily Harlem) or existed on the periphery of the organizations run by the 'big name' gangsters like Luciano and Lansky. The numbers racket in Harlem in the 1920s was controlled by Casper Holstein, while his rival, Stephanie St Clair, supervised the running of a lottery scam known as 'policy' – her operation was taken over by Dutch Shultz in the 1930s.

Holstein had served in the US Navy during the First World War, moving into the numbers racket upon his return to Manhattan, expanding into nightclubs and other legitimate businesses. St Clair was unusual in being both a female gang leader and in successfully resisting being taken over by the white Italian Mafia. Born in Martinique and known as 'Queenie', she arrived in the US in 1912. Self-funded but associated with the Forty Thieves gang of Irish immigrants, she fought against police corruption when they took her bribes but still persecuted her. Ellsworth 'Bumpy' Johnson served as her enforcer and liaison between the black gangs and the Italians, like Luciano. With Mafia backing, Johnson would eventually supplant St Clair, who retired from gangsterism a rich woman.

It was to these figures that Leroy Barnes looked for inspiration. A good student, Barnes nevertheless fell into crime as a way to escape his abusive father. A heroin addict himself in his twenties, it took a jail spell in the middle-1960s to break his addiction. He was, however, happy to feed the addictions of others if it brought him a profit. In prison Barnes had hooked up with Lucchese family heroin dealer Matthew Madonna, and Gambino crime family member 'Crazy' Joe Gallo. It was Gallo who wanted to succeed where his 1930s forebears had failed and break into the Harlem drug market. Barnes was the man to help him achieve it.

When a Mob lawyer got Barnes's drugs conviction overturned on a technicality, he became beholden to them. He put together a gang, and began selling cut heroin that was supplied raw by Madonna. He created The Council, a clearing house for black gangsters to settle disputes, divide up territories or co-operate to exploit new opportunities. Other members of The Council included Joseph 'Jazz' Hayden, Wallace Rice, Guy Fisher, Ishmael Muhammed and Thomas 'Gaps' Foreman.

By the middle of the 1970s, Leroy Barnes was a bona fide 'drug lord' known as Mister Untouchable, dubbed by *The New York Times* Harlem's biggest drug dealer. His business spread across all of New York state, stretched into Pennsylvania, and even reached Canada. His band of seven lieutenants controlled designated areas, while lower-level distributors handled the actual drugs, reaching down to over forty street-level dealers. The money all flowed back to Barnes, who developed a taste for the finer things in life, including fancy cars like Mercedes-Benz or Bentleys, Italian suits and shoes, and an excess of jewellery.

His nickname of 'Mister Untouchable' was a reversal of the 1930s 'Untouchables', the incorruptible police officers associated with Eliot Ness and his anti-gangster squad. Instead, Barnes came by the name due to his habit of 'beating the rap' by constantly evading charges or escaping jail time. Under surveillance by the law, Barnes would relish complicating his day with pointless stop-offs and detours, and even car chases to nowhere, simply to confuse and frustrate those trying to catch him.

Barnes smug appearance in 1977 on the cover of *The*

New York Times Magazine (the magazine said they'd use a police mug shot to illustrate their feature unless they could take a new photograph), so infuriated then-President Jimmy Carter, that – in yet another echo of the 'Get Capone' drive – he instructed the US Attorney General to bring down Barnes, no matter the cost. The Justice Department launched all it had at the mobster, finally pulling him in on a drugs charge and succeeding, under chief prosecutor Robert B. Fiske, in getting him sent down for a life sentence in January 1978.

The remaining members of The Council abandoned Barnes when he was jailed – something the Italian gangsters of the 1930s would never have done. Guy Fisher, who took over Harlem's Apollo Theatre in 1977, began an affair with Barnes's wife. He was convicted in 1984 on a series of RICO violations, including drug trafficking, murder and conspiracy and joined Barnes in serving a life sentence without parole. Fisher's conviction was aided by testimony from Barnes, who co-operated with prosecutor Rudolph Giuliani (later the mayor of New York). Infuriated by Fisher's affair with his wife (a contravention of one of the 'rules' of The Council, as well as in wider gangland), and worried his criminal assets were not being suitably looked after in his absence, Barnes turned on his former Council members. He also gave law enforcement authorities a tip-off that Wallace Rice was transporting heroin, and the unlucky mobster was caught with over two kilos in his car. He joined Barnes and Fisher in serving a life sentence. Barnes offered the authorities over one hundred names of people involved in The Council's activities, helping to indict more than forty, resulting in sixteen convictions. As a result of his co-operative testimony, Leroy Barnes left jail early in 1998 and the now eighty-year-old is part of the Witness Protection Programme living under a new identity. He did, however, write a memoir and appear in a documentary, so he hasn't kept an especially low profile, despite the dangers from his former colleagues on The Council.

The Los Angeles gangs

From the late-1960s onwards, the focus of criminal gang culture, especially among African-Americans, had shifted from the East coast to the West, especially Los Angeles, one time stamping ground of Johnny Rosselli, Mickey Cohen and Bugsy Siegel. Their criminal descendants were members of very different gangs, such as the Crips and the Bloods.

The Crips grew out of a gang founded by fifteen-year-old Raymond Washington in Los Angeles around 1969. The origin of the gang name is obscure, with it having been both assigned to a mishearing of 'Cribs' for neighbourhood or houses, or a reference to gang members early penchant for carrying canes, so resulting in them being called 'Crips', a shortened insult for 'crippled'. The gang grew with the addition of a 'West Side' chapter set up in 1971 by Stanley 'Tookie' Williams.

Primarily, but not exclusively, African-American, the Crips grew far larger than any of the East coast Italian-American gangs ever did, encompassing between 30,000 and 35,000 active members, often made up of self-contained smaller gangs. These sub-divided Crips gangs would fight with others over territory, perceived insults, or to gain control over a particular criminal activity. Murder, robbery and drug dealing were central activities of the Crips in their 1970s and 1980s heyday. Gang members identified themselves to one another through the use of the colour blue in their clothing, although this was largely discontinued once LA law enforcement figured it out.

Growing out of LA ghetto neighbourhoods, the Crips founders initially wanted to echo the political motivations of 1960s gangs like the Black Panthers, who fought for black liberation, but the poor educational attainment of the majority of its members saw the gangs rapidly fall into basic non-political criminality. In the 1980s, the Crips and other LA gangs benefited from the flood of crack cocaine sweeping America (coming up from South America via gangsters like Pablo Escobar [see chapter 19]), a situation comparable to the benefits that Prohibition in the 1920s brought to the East coast Italian-American gangsters. Turf wars exploded across Los Angeles as young, largely uneducated black men (and some whites) saw an opportunity to escape poverty and perhaps score some wealth for themselves. Their style became to drive around town in luxury cars, draped in 'bling' or luxury jewellery and often sporting military-level firepower, a 'gangsta' image that would come to dominate black rap music.

In 1972, a rival gang – identified through the use of the colour red – grew in Los Angeles, dubbed the Bloods. Starting as a variety of smaller gangs opposed to the Crips, they got together for mutual protection, only to discover that there was strength in numbers. Violence between the Crips and the Bloods grew to such an extent that Los Angeles law enforcement often felt unable to cope. Certain places became no-go areas for police, so dominated were they by the gangs and their supporters. An entire criminal sub-economy grew up around Los Angeles, and the gangs even spawned an East coast off-shoot, dubbed the United Blood Nation, in 1993 – supposedly formed as a self-defence group against the Latin Kings, the biggest and best organized Latino and Hispanic gang in American that had originated in 1940s Chicago.

Made up largely of Puerto Ricans and Mexicans, the Latin Kings originally boasted the mission statement of 'overcoming racial prejudice', but its ultimate aim came to be the inclusion of all and any races in the criminal underworld equally, a philosophy that Lucky Luciano had once employed in building his network in 1920s New York. Divided into Tribes arranged under two umbrella labels

– the Motherland faction and the Bloodline faction – the Latin Kings' primary focus was, once more, drug distribution, although they attempted to maintain a legitimate front as a 'community organization'.

The 1990s wars between these gangs spread from Los Angeles to take in Chicago and New York, although the first of several failed attempts at a truce was called in the aftermath of the 1992 Los Angeles riots (sparked when four white LA police officers were acquitted of beating black suspect Rodney Brown, although the attack had been caught on videotape). Rivalry between the likes of the Crips and the Bloods, still bloody on occasion, switched in the 1990s and 2000s to expression through rap and hip hop music. Key figures aligned themselves with one side or the other, such as Snoop Dogg, Eazy-E and Tone Loc for the Crips, and Suge Knight (founder of Death Row Records), DJ Quik, and members of Damu Ridaz for the Bloods. Taunts and insults were traded through lyrics, or in dances such as the 'Crip-walk' (music broadcaster MTV would eventually ban videos featuring such activities).

The East/West rap music feud hit the headlines with the 1996 killing in Las Vegas, Nevada of rap star '2Pac', aka twenty-five-year-old Tupac Shakur – members of the Crips were suspected, but never charged. Shakur had a tattoo that read 'MOB', understood to mean 'Member of Bloods' (Suge Knight has the same tattoo). A year later, presumably in retaliation, Shakur's main rival and personal hate figure 'Notorious B.I.G.', aka twenty-four-year-old Christopher Wallace, was killed in a drive-by shooting carried out by unidentified gunmen in Los Angeles. The whole East/West gang-and-rap feud was chronicled in the 2002 documentary film *Biggie & Tupac*, made by British documentarian Nick Broomfield. Broomfield lays both murders at the door of Suge Knight, who supposedly acted in conjunction with Los Angeles Police, although their motives remain murky.

Like Al Capone and John Dillinger before them in the 1930s and 1940s, the Crips and Bloods became the subject of movies in the late 1980s, early 1990s. A number of the gangs appear to have genuinely moved on from crime in the twenty-first century, in a style some have dubbed as being 'Ghetto reformers'. This drive was spearheaded by Crips founder and ex-jailbird Tookie Williams, who re-entered the gang scene in 2004 in an attempt to further his prison reform agenda and anti-gang activism by arranging a lasting truce between the Crips and the Bloods. The 'Tookie Protocol for Peace' saw Williams nominated (whether genuinely or satirically is not clear) for the Nobel Peace Prize several times up to 2005. Facing a death sentence for several murders, Williams may have been motivated to attempt to achieve some form of absolution, although clemency was denied and Williams was executed in December 2005. Other gangs – the one he helped create and the one that developed in response – continue in their criminal activities today, although their mode of illegality looks more and more old-fashioned in the high-tech twenty-first century.

The changing nature of organized crime

While the nature of most organized criminal activities has remained the same since the days of Lucky Luciano and Al Capone in the 1920s and 1930s, from the 1980s to the twenty-first century there has arisen a new form of organized crime the likes of which Luciano and Capone could only have dreamt of: cybercrime. Since computers became commonplace in homes and offices from the 1980s onwards, high-tech gangsters have used them to conduct criminal activities, often as part of an organized group or endeavour.

There are many types of criminal activity in which computers are either the target or are used to facilitate criminal activity across a network. Computers can be targeted directly through the use of cyberviruses, through 'denial of service' attacks during which a website (often commercial or political) can be overwhelmed and fail to function, and the release of 'malware' or malicious software designed to hamper the effectiveness of specific computers. Many of these activities have become associated with terrorism, whether state or ideologically sponsored.

More straightforward are those more general crimes merely facilitated by computers and networks, such as financial fraud, 'phishing' scams, identity theft, cyberstalking or information warfare. Modern 'bank robbers' don't charge into a local branch brandishing Tommy guns in the Dillinger style: instead sophisticated computer hacking techniques are used to access bank accounts or financial assets resulting in the transfer of funds from legitimate accounts to criminal enterprises. In September 2013, eight men were arrested in connection with a £1.3 million fraud enabled when the gang remotely took control of a Barclay's Bank computer, transferring the funds from a Swiss Cottage, London branch into their own accounts. The gang were caught when they attempted to repeat the trick on a Santander bank.

At a lower level, there is ATM fraud, where an Automatic Teller Machine, or 'hole-in-the-wall' cash machine, is tampered with so that criminal gangs can obtain customers' PIN (personal identification numbers) pass codes and so access accounts or perpetrate identity theft. The easier, less sophisticated method of simply holding up a customer at an isolated cash machine late at night and forcing them to withdraw and hand over the maximum cash available under threat of violence is still practised – and would be something of which Al Capone would approve. Falsification and altering of data to someone's criminal benefit is also widely practised using computers.

Stalking and bullying online have become increasingly common, and can be used as a form of intimidation to provoke others into carrying out criminal activity: threats to friends or family made online have been used to coerce those in positions of power, at financial institutions or elsewhere, to participate in criminal activity that benefits a cybergang. Drug trafficking has increasingly become an online activity, with sites such as Silk Road involved in anonymous buying and selling of various drugs, from marijuana to cocaine and heroin, as well as weapons and other contraband. Other offline gangster activities are believed to be funded through copyright theft, starting with bootleg videotapes, through DVD and on to online downloading of pirated copyright material.

The scope of criminal activity facilitated by the internet and computers is as wide and varied as that practised offline, now and in the past. The biggest difference is that today's online gangsters can conduct their activities with less threat of being machine-gunned to death in an alley by rivals, or even members of their own gangs, often at the click of a mouse.

The nature of gangster activity may have changed in the new century, but the kind of criminal engaged in organized crime largely remains the same. The organizational skills of a Lucky Luciano, Arnold Rothstein or Johnny Torrio may well have come up with something like The Council in the 1970s. Someone who had a facility with numbers, like Meyer Lansky, may have been into computer crime if he'd been young and active in the twenty-first century. Whether styled as a 'gangster' or a 'gangsta' (as black rap music would have it), they are still very much around in modern day America and beyond.

PART FOUR: GANGSTERS WORLDWIDE

15

UNITED KINGDOM: THE KRAYS

When it came to gangsters in Britain, several key names dominated the organized crime scene. As with the United States, there were regional gang leaders in most of the major towns, but unlike the American Mafia, crime in the United Kingdom was never nationally organized and co-ordinated to the same extent. Those who made names for themselves – London's Kray twins, 'Mad' Frankie Fraser, 'Glasgow Godfather' Arthur Thompson – did so themselves, and largely on their own patch. However, as with America, organized crime had deep roots in history.

Before the Krays
As in the Old West of America, the past of the British Isles featured several criminal gangs of note. During the reign of Queen Anne, in the early 1700s, gangs known as the Hawkubites and the Mohocks (named after the American Indian tribe, the Mohawks) terrorized the inhabitants of

London with random attacks. One preacher claimed to have consulted with the ghost of a victim and revealed that the gang's activities were a harbinger of the 'end times' foretold in the Biblical Book of Revelations. The world didn't end, but the gangs had disbanded by around 1715.

The late-Victorian era brought about the rare spectacle of a gang of female criminals known as the Forty Thieves (not to be confused with the later American gang of the same name). They specialized in shoplifting and were led by key figures known as the 'Queens', including Alice Diamond and Maggie Hill. In 1906, the then-Queen Helen Sheen was jailed for 18 months for stealing £100 worth of jewellery. The gang – made up of no more than forty members at any one time – thrived into the 1960s, making them one of the longest lasting of all Britain's gangster organizations.

Other early UK gangsters included Billy Hill, brother of Forty Thieves Queen Maggie Hill, and Jack Comer. Hill, born in 1911, conducted a life of crime for over fifty years. Beginning as a basic housebreaker while still a teenager, he graduated to smash-and-grab store robbery in his twenties, enriched himself thanks to the black market during the Second World War, and then fled to South Africa in the late 1940s after being charged following a London warehouse robbery. He followed his criminal instincts for a while in Johannesburg, but was charged with assault and extradited back to the UK, where he was jailed before retiring in the 1950s – although he continued to launder money for other gangsters through his nightclubs. He died of natural causes in 1984.

Jack Comer was a contemporary of Hill, who was caught up in Jewish versus Irish gang fights in the neighbourhood where he grew up. He became leader of a street gang, then began running protection rackets like the young Meyer Lansky and Bugsy Siegel. Becoming a bookmaker, Comer was notable for his anti-Fascist actions between the wars when he opposed Blackshirt leader Oswald Mosley by taking part in the violent 'battle of Cable Street' in 1936. Comer and Hill battled one another for control of their territories in the early 1950s, before Hill 'retired', much in the way that Frank Costello stepped back from the American Mafia in the same period. Comer didn't last much longer, though, and he was violently replaced as a gangland figurehead by 'Mad' Frankie Fraser [see below]. Jack Comer died from natural causes in December 1996, aged eighty-four.

The Firm
While several American and British gangsters were siblings, perhaps the UK's best-known gangster brothers had the edge – they were identical twins. Reginald and Ronald Kray, known infamously as the Kray Twins, ruled the underworld of 1960s London. Born in Hoxton, in London's East End, on 24 October 1933, the twins had an older brother, Charlie, and a younger sister who died in infancy.

The Krays' father, also called Charlie, was an army deserter during the Second World War who'd been in hiding since 1939. Essentially growing up without a father, the twins came to resent authority following repeated visits from the military police hunting for their absent father. Lacking his influence, the boys – known as Ronnie and Reggie – were unnaturally close to their mother, Violet Lee, and to each other, forming an unshakeable bond that lasted their entire lives. Undiagnosed as a child, it appears likely that dominant twin Ronnie suffered from paranoid schizophrenia.

Although performing decently enough at school in Brick Lane, London, the young Kray boys soon entered the world of crime, attracting a gang of like-minded adolescents around them. They each clocked up several arrests for minor offences. Under the influence of their grandfather, Jimmy Lee, the Krays took up amateur boxing as teenagers, as had several young would-be gangsters in New York, including Paul Kelly and Vincent Gigante. Their biggest competitors were each other, with each twin out to achieve more than his brother. Ronnie almost died in 1942 following a fist-fight with his brother that resulted in a serious head injury, and Reggie seemed to always defer to him after that. Neither Kray ever lost a boxing bout, and the pair had turned professional by the age of nineteen.

In 1952, the Kray twins were 'called up' for National Service, the UK's mandatory two-year military service following the Second World War. Deciding the military life wasn't for them, as it hadn't suited their father, the twins left during the sign-up process, with Ronnie punching an army corporal in the face on his way out. Next morning the pair were arrested at home. They repeatedly deserted from the army, but unlike their father they were unable to stay hidden and were often recaptured by military police. They spent some time locked up in the Tower of London, being among the last ever prisoners to be held there. Following several assaults on military and civilian police officers, the Kray boys were finally dishonourably discharged from military service. Rather than go back to the legitimate world of boxing, the twins turned to crime full-time.

The Krays managed to obtain ownership of a run-down snooker club in Bethnal Green, London, which became their base of operations for a variety of protection rackets they operated across late 1950s London. Their criminal activities slowly stepped up a gear, moving from protection rackets and threats to vehicle hijacking and, eventually, straightforward armed robbery. They built up their club and property empire through threats and arson.

In 1960, Ronnie Kray was locked up for eighteen months, convicted in relation to the twins' extensive protection rackets. While in prison, Ronnie was examined by prison psychiatrists who came to the conclusion that his unprovoked violent and unpredictable behaviour that had caused the brothers so much trouble in the army was a symptom of paranoid schizophrenia. They declared Ronnie Kray to be clinically insane – despite this, he was released back into the community once he'd served his time.

While Ronnie was in prison, Reggie had continued to build up their criminal empire. Through corrupt and violent London slum landlord Peter Rachman, Reggie took over the ownership of the Knightsbridge nightclub Esmeralda's Barn. This gave the Krays access to the celebrity nightlife of London, a step above their Bethnal Green operations. The twins themselves became celebrity criminals, rubbing shoulders with the likes of movie star Diana Dors – the UK's nearest equivalent to Marilyn Monroe – and 'Carry On' star Barbara Windsor. They also associated with visiting American stars, especially the Mob-connected George Raft and Frank Sinatra, as well as *The Wizard of Oz* actress Judy Garland. The twins' club ownership gave them a level of cover for their criminal enterprises while also serving as an entrée into 'respectable society'. They were widely regarded as 'charming' hosts who had prospered in London despite their poor backgrounds. Celebrity photographer David Bailey, who'd produced famous images of Terence Stamp, The Beatles and Andy Warhol, snapped a moody portrait of the two Krays that was soon to become an infamous image of the London 'tough guys'. In his autobiography, Ronnie Kray classed the 'swinging sixties' as 'the best years of our lives . . . me and my brother ruled London . . . We were untouchable.'

Details of many of the Kray twins' activities did not fully emerge into the public domain until after their deaths. However, UK tabloid newspaper the *Sunday Mirror* attempted to expose their criminal pursuits, albeit without naming them, in the summer of 1964. The paper revealed that Scotland Yard, home of the London Metropolitan police force, had been investigating a homosexual relationship – illegal in the UK until 1967 – between a prominent peer and a leading figure in the London underworld. Even without the names (although they were published in Germany by *Stern* magazine), society and media gossip quickly settled on the twice-married Lord Robert Boothby, a former Conservative minister and aide to Winston Churchill, and Ronnie Kray. Threats of violence against the *Mirror* journalists from the Kray twins and legal threats to sue from Boothby saw the paper back down, sack the editor Reg Payne, issue an apology and pay $40,000 to Boothby as an out-of-court settlement. Although the story was true – Boothby had been introduced to Kray after he had an affair with London cat burglar Leslie Holt – the outcome prevented other papers from risking reporting on the Kray's growing criminal activities.

Although attempts were made by the police to investigate the Krays, intimidation and outright death threats made witnesses unwilling to speak up or come forward. There was also a political dimension to the Krays' seeming ability to evade the law. As well as his relationship with the Conservative Boothby, Ronnie Kray was also alleged to have had a similar relationship with controversial homosexual senior Labour MP Tom Driberg (a friend of Boothby and connected to occultist Aleister Crowley, MI5 and the KGB). The Kray's biographer John Pearson noted that such political contacts 'opened up an avenue of possibilities [for the twins]. Politicians had their uses which could be exploited; the twins were good at using human frailty to make men do as they were told. Quite suddenly, they saw what could be done with a discrete gangsters' lobby of carefully fixed members in either House.' The Krays were reputed to procure young working-class criminals for the sexual pleasure of both Boothby and Driberg, thereby giving them leverage over the politicians. Where American gangsters gained political influence through bribery and general corruption (vote rigging, labour bashing), the Krays seemingly settled on personal sexual blackmail as their route to power. Both Boothby and Driberg used their positions to lobby, privately and publicly, on behalf of the Krays.

As with some other gangsters of the past, a feeling of invincibility caused Ronnie and Reggie to overreach. In March 1966, Ronnie Kray shot and killed George Cornell in the Blind Beggar pub in Whitechapel, the notorious stomping ground of Victorian serial killer Jack the Ripper. Cornell was an associate of the Krays' rival gang, the Richardsons (another gang led by brothers, although not twins), and there had been a long-running feud between Ronnie Kray and Cornell. Ronnie's reason for killing Cornell was said to have been in retaliation for the Richardsons' killing of Kray associate Richard Hart. Then, having helped 'Mad Axeman' Frank Mitchell escape Dartmoor prison at the end of 1966, the Krays were implicated in his subsequent disappearance – but they were acquitted of his murder.

In October 1967 – just months after his wife's suicide, later alleged to have been a murder carried out by a jealous Ronnie – Reggie killed Jack 'The Hat' McVitie, a minor member of their own gang who had been paid for, but failed to carry out, a hit on another mobster. The killing took place in a basement flat in Stoke Newington, North London; Reggie first attempted to shoot McVitie, but the gun misfired, so he stabbed him to death instead – all in the presence of older brother, Ronnie. Other members of the Kray gang – known as The Firm – were convicted of the killing, so the Krays escaped justice once more.

Scotland Yard Inspector Leonard Read, nicknamed 'Nipper', tasked his 'murder squad' with bringing down the Krays once and for all. Read had been investigating the brothers for several years, but had failed to secure any use-able evidence, a process further sidelined by the fall-out from the Boothby affair. In 1967, he set out afresh, determined to convict the Krays, but ran up against the East End London gangster version of the Mafia's omertà, the

'wall of silence'. No one would talk, and Read had difficulty building up a case that would stand up in court.

Then in early 1968, Paul Elvey was arrested in Glasgow
attempting to buy explosives for the purpose of building
car bombs. He confessed to involvement in three murder
attempts, and claimed to be connected with the American
Treasury Department who were investigating links
between the American Mafia and the Krays. The 'botched
murders' were supposedly attempts to compromise the
Krays.

In May 1968, Ronnie and Reggie Kray, along with key
lieutenants, were finally arrested, which brought several
witnesses out of the woodwork, especially in relation to
the Cornell and McVitie killings. All but one of those
arrested were convicted. Both brothers were sentenced to
life imprisonment for the murders of Cornell and McVitie,
with no eligibility for parole for thirty years – the longest
sentence then passed at the Old Bailey, the London criminal courts. Their older brother, Charlie, was also sentenced
to ten years for his role in their crimes, but was released
in 1975 after just seven. He was again sent to prison for
cocaine smuggling in 1997, and died there in 2000.

Apart from being briefly released to attend their mother's funeral in 1982, the twins remained locked up until
their deaths. Ronnie Kray, finally officially certified
insane, was held in Broadmoor Hospital until he died in
1995, aged sixty-one. Reggie Kray – who became a born-
again Christian while in prison – was freed from Wayland
Prison in Norfolk in August 2000, aged sixty-seven, on
'compassionate grounds' due to his suffering from inoper-
able cancer. He died in a Norfolk hotel that October. They
had been the subject of a biographical film – *The Krays*
(1990) – that had starred brothers Gary and Martin Kemp
of the band Spandau Ballet. 'I believe that Ron and I were
predestined to become known, either by fame or infamy,'
Reggie Kray wrote in his autobiography. 'I seem to have

walked a double path most of my life. Perhaps an extra step in one of those directions might have seen me celebrated rather than notorious.'

Gangland UK

The Krays had several rivals for the title of 'top gangster' in the UK, but few ever came close to them in terms of infamy, notoriety or 'achievement'. A London competitor was 'Mad' Frankie Fraser, born Francis Davidson Fraser in 1923. Like the Kray twins' father, Fraser was a deserter from the British Army who participated in the 'black market' supplying rationed goods during the war. He was jailed in 1941 for over a year for burglary, and once complained about Germany surrendering as the end of the war brought an end to his 'easy' criminal enterprises conducted in conjunction with gangster Billy Hill.

In the immediate post-war years, Fraser turned to jewel theft and bank robbery, resulting in another prison sentence and – like Ronnie Kray – a diagnosis of insanity. Back on the streets in the mid-1950s, Fraser later joined the Richardson 'torture gang', rivals to the Krays. Brothers Charlie and Eddie Richardson ran the notoriously violent gang, known for using DIY tools to torture victims. 'Mad Frankie' signed up to function as their 'enforcer' inflicting their unique brand of punishment on those who failed to co-operate. He helped the Richardsons establish a vending machine company that functioned as a front for their criminal undertakings and a useful money-laundering outlet.

Fraser was a suspect in the Great Train Robbery of 1963 that netted the robbers $2.6 million, although he did not take part. However, just three years later he was arrested for the murder of Richard Hart, a member of the Kray gang, at Mr. Smith's Club in Catford, London. When a key witness changed his testimony, Fraser was charged with 'affray' instead and sent to jail for five years. The following 'torture trial' of violent gang members saw another ten years added to his sentence in 1967. In all, Fraser would spend a total of forty-two years in prison, periods often marked by violence against fellow prisoners and wardens.

Released again in 1985, Fraser was the subject of an attempted 'hit' in 1991 when he was shot in the head outside a club in Clerkenwell, London – he always maintained that the police were responsible. 'Mad Frankie' then went on to become a celebrity on British television and radio programmes, some but not all connected with his notoriety as a gangster. He featured in several documentaries on British gangsters and even acted in a gangland movie, *Hard Men* (1996). A ghost-written autobiography became a bestseller. Later in life, Fraser conducted guided tours of London Gangland sites, including the Blind Beggar pub where Ronnie Kray shot George Cornell. Aged ninety, Frankie Fraser was last known to be living in sheltered accommodation for the elderly, where he frequently picked fights with his equally-elderly neighbours.

Scotland also boasted its fair share of well-known gangsters, from the 'Glasgow Godfather' Arthur Thompson to those who participated in the mid-1980s Ice-Cream Van Wars. The popularity of American gangster movies, especially in the West coast city of Glasgow, informed the way many Scottish gangsters acted and perceived themselves.

Arthur Thompson, born in Glasgow's slums in the early 1930s, was credited with creating the 'Tartan Mafia' modelled after the American version established by Lucky Luciano. Initially working as a club bouncer, a bodyguard, and a 'bagman' for other criminals, Thompson created his own syndicate from Glasgow's minor gangsters, keeping them in line through physical intimidation.

He was once said to have held up the Kray twins in their own London headquarters, although that story was likely the result of gangland boasting rather than fact. Thompson's first big score came in moneylending, where those who failed to repay loans promptly suffered

– Thompson was said to 'crucify' defaulters by nailing them to the floor with a nail gun. Protection rackets followed, with Thompson wisely investing a great deal of his money in legitimate businesses as a way of avoiding the attention of the tax man. By the 1980s, Thompson's gang had moved heavily into the illicit drugs trade.

His family suffered, with his daughter Margaret dying of a drug overdose in 1989, and his son Arthur Jr shot to death in the street in 1991, allegedly by former Thompson enforcer, Paul Ferris. Born in 1963, Ferris had worked his way up in the Thompson organization but fell out with the 'Glasgow Godfather' in the summer of 1991. Acquitted of killing Arthur Jr, two of Ferris's friends suspected of involvement in the attack were later killed and his father assaulted by Thompson's men. Ferris was eventually jailed in 1998 for smuggling firearms, although he claimed he'd been framed by corrupt Glasgow police and gangland rivals. Briefly released and then sent back to jail in 2002, Ferris was released again in 2005 and declared he was going to write gangland thrillers, rather than living them for real. That led the Scottish Government to investigate legislation that would prevent criminals profiting from their crimes. A biographical film based on Ferris, called *The Wee Man* and starring Scottish actor Martin Compston, was released in 2013.

There were several attempts made on the life of Arthur Thompson, including a car bombing in 1966 that killed his mother-in-law. Later, he ran the two men he felt were responsible – Patrick Welsh and James Goldie of a rival gang – off the road in their van, killing them. Thompson was charged with murder, but no witnesses could be found to testify. In 1969, Thompson's wife Rita raided the Welsh family home, stabbing Patrick's wife in the chest – she was jailed for three years. Time finally caught up with Arthur Thompson in March 1993 when he died of a heart attack, aged sixty-one. Later rumours stoked mystery by suggesting the 'Glasgow Godfather' had not died at home, but had been placed there after death by paramedics. No motive was ever revealed. Thompson was buried without a headstone to deter grave robbers, but rumours of a $10 million 'buried treasure' – rivalling that of Bugsy Siegel – persist.

In the early 1980s, a full eighty years after the gang wars to control the proceeds of crime in turn-of-the-century New York, a battle erupted in Glasgow between rival gangsters to control the lucrative ice-cream van trade and routes – which fronted for on-the-street drugs sales. It was a struggle that would result in six people dead and two men – ultimately innocent in the eyes of the law – spending two decades locked up in jail.

Rival vans, run by various gangland 'families' were repeatedly raided – as took place in 1920s New York and Chicago, with bootleggers stealing each other's trucks laden with alcohol. Shotguns would be fired at point-blank range into the windscreens of a rival's ice cream van, which appeared disproportionate for a trade in ice lollies, until it was revealed that the vans were also selling drugs at street level. It was a clever way for gangsters to distribute their 'product' while appearing to be pursuing a legitimate trade. The in-fighting between gangs ultimately ruined the lucrative trade for everyone involved.

In 1984, the Glasgow tenement flat of the Doyle family was set alight by arsonists, killing all six Doyle family members inside. The crime – then Scotland's largest mass murder – only made sense when it was discovered that despite threats Andrew Doyle had refused to hand over the family's van route to gangsters. Strathclyde Police arrested six people, including gang leaders Thomas 'T.C.' Campbell and Joseph Steele, all of whom were convicted of the murders. Campbell was said to have confessed that the attack on the Doyle household had only been intended as a 'frightener' that 'went too far'. What followed was a twenty-year legal campaign by Campbell and Steele, which involved in their lawyer's words, 'twenty years of hunger strikes, prison breakouts, demonstrations, political pressure, solitary isolation, prison beatings, [and] legal fight after legal fight'.

The case had been heavily reliant on testimony from informer William Love, who had been granted bail instead of prison in return for his witness statement that Campbell and Steele had planned and carried out the attack. Despite Love having admitted to lying under oath in 1992, the legal battle and campaigns of protest continued: Steele escaped jail in 1993, travelled to London and chained himself to the railings of Buckingham Palace, to draw attention to his case. Eventually, the convictions of Campbell and Steele were overturned on appeal, as the supposedly verbatim evidence from police and witnesses recalling exact detailed conversations was deemed unreliable. Campbell accused rival Glasgow gangster Tam McGraw – an armed robber of post offices and a drug trafficker – of burning the Doyles' house and of attempting to have him killed while in prison. Steele blamed Campbell for dragging him into the conspiracy, claiming he was innocent of any involvement. Officially, the murder of the Doyle family remains unsolved to this day. The original story was the basis for the 1984 Bill Forsyth movie *Comfort and Joy*, starring Bill Paterson, and provided inspiration for the ability of players of the Scottish-produced crime video game *Grand Theft Auto: Vice City* to deal drugs from an ice-cream van.

The other nations of the UK – Wales and Northern Ireland – certainly suffered their fair share of crime and criminal activity, but they produced few notorious gangster figures to rival the Krays, 'Mad Frankie' Fraser or Arthur Thompson. Things were further complicated in Northern Ireland where criminality became entwined with the political struggle against British rule known as 'the Troubles'.

In some cases, funds raised through crime were used to finance violent political action, while in others, the politics of the situation was used as a cover for criminal activity. It is beyond the scope of the present volume to explore the subject in depth, but a few key figures are worth noting.

Bank robber Gerry Hutch, born in Dublin in 1963, named his outfit the Bugsy Malone Gang not after the gangster himself but after the 1976 British film in which all the gangsters and molls were played by children, including a young Jodie Foster. Armoured car raids saw Hutch jailed in the late 1970s, only to be released in the mid-1980s. He became a taxi driver and attempted to fight off Government claims for unpaid taxes (that old ruse still worked), eventually settling with a payment of IR£1.2 million.

Fellow Dublin mobster Martin Cahill, born in 1949 and dubbed 'The General', was said to have made £60 million from his criminal endeavours, which included the theft to order of valuable artworks. Cahill's was a prime case of a would-be gangster becoming embroiled in the Troubles, and he was assassinated – seemingly by Irish Republican Army (IRA) gunmen in 1994. That was typical of others, such as drug smuggler John Gilligan, accused but acquitted of the murder of journalist Veronica Guerin in 1996, and Martin Foley, who attempted to fill the space vacated by Cahill and became caught up in the 'Dublin Gang Wars' of the late 1990s. Rival city gangsters battled each other for control of the drugs trade, resulting in several tit-for-tat murders recalling the gangland internecine warfare of New York in the 1930s. It may not have had the spread or the organization of the American Mafia, but British gangsters still made their mark upon the country's criminal history.

16

EUROPEAN GANGSTERS: JACQUES MESRINE

Gangsters could be found across Europe, from France's very own Dillinger, Public Enemy Number One, in Jacques René Mesrine, to the original Sicilian version of the Mafia, and other prominent gangsters in Spain, the Netherlands and Greece.

Multiple murders, burglaries, bank robberies and kidnappings in France and Canada appear on Jacques Mesrine's rap sheet, while his repeated prison escapes made him something of a French folk hero outlaw. On the run for much of his life, Mesrine had a 'man of a thousand faces' reputation for adopting disguises, and an uncanny ability for evading the forces of the law.

Born in Clichy to a middle-class family in 1936, Mesrine's disruptive behaviour – he once attacked the principal – saw him expelled from two schools. During the war, he was witness to the massacre of French villagers by German soldiers, an event that stayed with him. Much to the annoyance of his upwardly mobile parents, young Mesrine settled into the life of a juvenile delinquent.

He was married at the age of nineteen in 1955, but the union only lasted a year. Drafted into the French Army, he didn't desert like the Krays, but instead volunteered for 'special duty' as a parachutist and commando during the Algerian war. Combat saw Mesrine make his first kill, and he seemed particularly suited to distasteful tasks such as torturing prisoners, counter-insurgency operations and targeted assassinations. He left the army in 1959, with the Cross of Military Valour, but his parents felt the war had changed their son beyond all recognition.

Married again in 1961 (this marriage lasted until 1965 and produced three children), Mesrine was active in the Organisation de l'armée secrète (OAS) that fought an underground war attempting to ensure that Algeria continued as part of France (the country won its independence in 1962). Like many who returned from war with their lives disrupted, Mesrine had difficulty settling back into civilian society and adapting to society's norms. He was soon arrested, with three associates, for attempted bank robbery and sentenced to eighteen months in jail in 1962 – he was paroled the following year.

Steady employment proved elusive for Mesrine, although he attempted to hold down a variety of jobs including one at an architectural practice where he designed models of buildings, a task he seemed quite skilled at. That lasted until 1964, when the company downsized and he was made redundant. An attempt to run a restaurant in the French countryside failed, and Mesrine soon fell into his old criminal habits. The criminal life that brought easy money and equally easy women proved irresistible to him, while his violent background in the French Army saw Mesrine rapidly gain a reputation as something of a tough guy.

Once again he was caught – this time in the villa of the

military governor of Palma de Mallorca, Spain (which was under military rule until 1975). Sentenced to six months in jail, Mesrine complained he was being treated harshly as the Spanish authorities had assumed he was a spy working for French intelligence. Out of Spanish jail by 1966, he once again tried the restaurant business, this time in the Canary Islands. His criminal habits returned, however, and Mesrine staged several robberies from his Canary Islands base, including a jewellery store in Geneva and a hotel in Chamonix.

Following a raid on a store in Paris, Mesrine fled Europe to Canada, along with his girlfriend Jeanne Schneider. The pair found work as cook and chauffeur for millionaire Georges Deslauriers. After a squabble, they were dismissed, but attempted to kidnap Deslauriers, hoping to raise a significant ransom from his wider family. They made a mess of the attempt, though, and were back on the run in the summer of 1969, eventually surfacing in Arkansas, Texas. An elderly woman who gave the pair shelter was found strangled, and Mesrine and Schneider were captured by the US authorities and extradited to Canada.

Mesrine received his longest prison sentence yet: ten years. However, he quickly escaped from prison (within weeks of his arrival), but was recaptured again within a day. This was to set a pattern of repeated escape attempts, periods on the run, and periods back in captivity that would mark out the rest of Mesrine's life, just like Dillinger in the 1930s in the United States. In 1972, Mesrine escaped jail once again, with five other prisoners in tow. He and another escapee, a murderer named Jean-Paul Mercier, held up a series of banks in Montreal, sometimes two in a single day (just as 'Pretty Boy' Floyd had done forty years earlier). Seemingly, his experiences in the army had removed Mesrine's sense of danger, so he staged his robberies with the minimal of planning and aforethought.

Looking to command a larger gang, in September 1972

Mesrine staged a daring attempt to break more prisoners out of the jail he'd been held in. Unfortunately for him, security at the prison had been hugely stepped up following his own escape, and the prison was well guarded. A shoot-out erupted between Mesrine, his accomplice Mercier, and the prison guards, injuring two. Mercier was also injured, but he and Mesrine managed to get away – once again, Mesrine's actions uncannily echoed those of John Dillinger and his gang.

After killing two forest rangers who'd interrupted their target practice in the woods, Mesrine and Mercier headed to Venezuela, as if in an attempt to follow in the South American footsteps of Butch and Sundance. Their sojourn south of the equator didn't last long, and the pair were back in France and once again robbing banks, until Mesrine was caught again in March 1973. Sentenced to twenty years' imprisonment on a long list of charges, he was to be sent to a supposedly 'escape proof' maximum security prison. During sentencing, however, Mesrine recklessly took the trial judge hostage using a revolver that had been supplied to him by an accomplice, and escaped once more.

On the run for four months, Mesrine was nabbed again in a Paris apartment and taken to the high-security cell that was waiting for him at La Santé prison in the Montparnasse district of Paris. While incarcerated, Jacques Mesrine wrote a memoir entitled *L'Instinct de mort* ('Killer Instinct'), which he smuggled out of prison via an accomplice. In the book he claimed responsibility for up to forty murders (possibly a self-aggrandizing exaggeration), but the book's publication led to a new French law that prevented criminals from earning income by cashing in on their crimes.

Inevitably (again, like Dillinger from Crown Point's 'escape proof' jail), Mesrine broke out of prison in May 1978, using a smuggled gun, stolen keys and a grappling iron, and taking three other inmates with him (one of whom was shot dead by a guard during the escape). Outside the prison walls, Mesrine and fellow escapee François Besse hijacked a passing car and became the first men to successfully escape from La Santé prison. The escape would, however, be the beginning of the end for Jacques René Mesrine.

That prison break galvanized the French authorities, who were thoroughly embarrassed that they seemed incapable of holding Mesrine for any length of time. A relentless 'Get Capone' style drive was put into action, with French police in continual pursuit of Mesrine who'd embarked upon his latest, and final, crime spree. He repeatedly evaded capture, sometimes using disguises, sometimes through the use of forged documents that he allegedly acquired from former comrades of the OAS. No bank, casino or jewellery store in France was safe from Mesrine's attention, and he also shook down pimps for money and set up a gun-running operation. Shoot-outs, both with the police and with criminal associates who double-crossed him, were a regular feature of Mesrine's final days.

Mesrine appeared on the cover of *Paris Match* in August 1978 (like Frank Costello on *Time* and *Newsweek*, or Leroy 'Nicky' Barnes on the cover of *The New York Times Magazine*), and in an interview inside he declared war on the French Minister of Justice. Now, as far as the French government were concerned, Jacques Mesrine was 'L'Ennemi public numéro un', Public Enemy Number One. Large sections of the French public nonetheless looked upon Mesrine as nothing less than a Gallic Robin Hood.

Inter-agency rivalries hampered the French authority's attempts to capture Mesrine for many months. The fugitive managed to travel to London, Algeria, Sicily and Brussels, before robbing another bank in Paris in November 1978. His accomplice, Besse, dumped Mesrine when he planned to kidnap a senior judge who'd sentenced him, fearing that the rash action would only cause the fugitives even more trouble. Besse did not share Mesrine's seeming desire for 'revenge' upon the French justice system, recalling Clyde

Barrow's driving force. Besse would be captured and jailed in 1994, and released in 2006.

In a repeat of his previous pattern, in 1979 Mesrine kidnapped a millionaire property mogul – Henri Lelièvre – and then released him in return for a ransom of six million francs, which the family promptly paid. He then targeted, shot and wounded a journalist who'd written unflattering stories about him, revealing that Mesrine was concerned with how his actions appeared to the wider French public, just as Bonnie Parker had been. That same journalist, however, was able to set the police on the trail of Mesrine's then-current girlfriend, Sylvia Jeanjacquot, and through her pattern of movements they were able to track Mesrine to Porte de Cligancourt, on the outskirts of Paris.

On 2 November 1979, Mesrine's luck finally ran out. As he and Jeanjacquot headed for the countryside in their car, they were followed by a van full of police marksmen. The police van blocked Mesrine's car – a not inconspicuous gold BMW – in traffic, and the armed officers fired around twenty shots through the windscreen, supposedly without warning. Mesrine was killed instantly, hit by at least fifteen bullets. Jeanjacquot survived, but lost an eye and the use of her arm. The police operation was hailed as a success by the French President, but much of the public and the media criticized their actions as little more than a summary execution without due process. Mesrine, however, had become such an 'enemy of the state' (Mesrine had said he would never surrender under any circumstances), that those in power felt they had no other option but to end his criminal reign by whatever means they had at their disposal.

Mesrine's publisher, Gérard Lebovici, republished *L'Instinct de mort* in 1984 and, curiously, adopted Mesrine's orphaned daughter. In March 1984, Lebovici was found shot to death in an underground car park, apparently the subject of a 'hit' carried out by a former associate of Mesrine. The first film chronicling Mesrine's life was released in 1984, starring Nicolas Silberg, and it was followed by a later epic two-film retelling of his exploits in *L'Instinct de mort* (*Mesrine: Killer Instinct*) and *L'Ennemi public numéro un* (*Mesrine: Public Enemy Number One*) in 2008, starring Vincent Cassel as Mesrine.

The original Mafia

Mesrine was perhaps the most notorious European criminal, but other countries in Western Europe boasted their own key gangsters. Italy, of course, was the birthplace of the Mafia, although the original Sicilian version bore little resemblance to the later American organization that used the same name. Researchers debate the geographical and temporal origins of the Italian Mafia, placing it anywhere between the thirteenth and nineteenth centuries, as well as the origin of the name, which may be Italian or Arabic.

The first public usage of the word appears in 1865 in a report by Palermo's public prosecutor, followed over a decade later by a report on violent crime by an Italian parliamentary deputy. The word became attached to family or clan organizations in Sicily in the mid to late-nineteenth century, and grew to encompass secret initiation ceremonies (possibly involving murder), a vow of loyalty, a code of honour among members, and a network of contacts put to both social and criminal ends. The first collective action by Mafia members appears to be a stint as armed guards for Palermo citrus growers sometime in the nineteenth century. From there it grew to take in extortion, protection rackets and various internecine turf wars.

Each 'family' (usually an extended family of related people, but not always) had a 'don' or head, who would direct the family 'business' and meet with other dons to plan group strategies. By the time Benito Mussolini was in power in Italy in 1922, the Mafia was a well-established organization, especially strong on the island of Sicily (there were regional variations under different names across Italy, such as the Camorra in Naples). Mussolini set out to assert his own power by wiping out all 'secret societies', including the Mafia, so causing a flight of many young, and some older, mafiosi to the United States.

During the Second World War, the Mafia would be used by United States intelligence to prepare the way for the Allied invasion of Sicily (one-time Commission head Lucky Luciano may have been involved in negotiating this alliance). These Mafia–CIA connections would come back to haunt America in the 1960s [see chapter 11]. In the post-war period the Sicilian Mafia (as distinct from the American version) focused on international drug trafficking, especially Turkish heroin shipped through France to the United States, the so-called 'French Connection' of the 1960s and early 1970s.

For the remainder of the twentieth century and into the twenty-first, the Sicilian Mafia appears to have pursued a series of violent territory wars, with gangs killing each other and innocent civilians alike. Assassinations of politicians who stood in the way of Mafia ambitions continued, while the jailing of several high-profile 'leaders' created a power vacuum which some younger mafiosi were keen to fill. There was also a vogue for 'pentitos', or informers, who spilled the beans on the organization and its activities that led to many convictions following several high-profile trials. Pretty much (corrupt) business as usual, then, for the original Italian branch of the larger, worldwide Mafia family.

New Europeans

Other notable Western European gangsters have included Spain's Laureano Oubiña Piñeiro, the Netherland's John Mieremet, and Greece's notorious Grigorakis family. There were, of course, many others, but these few serve as typical examples of the kind of people involved in organized crime across Europe and the kind of activities they pursued.

In Spain, Laureano Oubiña Piñeiro was widely known as the 'little bird' for his apparent ability to 'fly away' from the agencies of law enforcement pursuing him. Born in 1946, various drug smuggling schemes resulted in his first arrest in 1983 (for trafficking in illegal cigarettes). Later in the 1980s, Piñeiro had established himself as Spain's top drug smuggler with an army of corrupt officials on the take willing to protect him. In 1998 and 1999, however, several huge cargoes of hashish were captured, resulting in Piñeiro being tracked to Greece in 2000, where he was arrested and extradited to Spain. After a series of trials and delays, by 2006 Piñeiro and twenty-two accomplices had been sentenced to several years in prison and hit with huge fines. Piñeiro has repeatedly filed appeals and fought to resume his freedom, but remains jailed in Spain today.

The Netherland's John Mieremet, born in 1961, has long been seen as one of the country's top mobsters. Aligned with various accomplices he got involved in extortion, smuggling and illegal gambling rackets, and gained a reputation for the 'efficient' manner in which he rubbed out any opposition to his criminal schemes. Various members of his criminal gang were attacked and killed, often by rival gangsters wanting a cut of his action, and Mieremet himself was attacked and wounded in 2002. Mieremet publicly blamed property tycoon Willem Endstra for the attack, and Endstra himself was found dead in 2004.

The attacks on Holland's gangster kingpin continued. In February 2006, he was shot at by motorcycle-riding would-be assassins, while eight months later his trusted (crooked) lawyer was bumped off. Two days later, on 2 November 2005, Mieremet himself was the victim, shot in the head by an assassin while his bodyguard reportedly cowered under a desk. Local police put the killing of Mieremet down to the outcome of the long-running Dutch–Yugoslav drug war.

Greece's notorious Grigorakis family ruled Athens for

almost two decades from the 1980s into the twenty-first century. Vassilis Grigorakis established his family-based criminal group in the 1980s, but it began to unravel after his death in a drive-by shooting, despite the bulletproof vest he was wearing. His son, Niko, had been killed by gunmen in Athens a few months earlier. When a car bomb exploded in Athens in May 2001 killing British woman Susan-Mary Aris, local police initially put it down to international terrorism. Upon investigation of her background, it seemed likely she was planting or preparing the bomb herself, as she had married an associate of the Grigorakis family and had become involved in their criminal activities. Theodoros Grigorakis, the last surviving son of family head Vassilis, was convicted of extortion and attempted murder and jailed, although he, too, died in 2002 when he ate a plate of poisoned spaghetti served to him in prison. In September 2003, Vassilis Grigorakis's daughter, thirty-six-year-old Kyriaki, was found dead in her car in Athens – unlikely as it may seem given the family history of violent death, her cause of death was declared natural. Their pursuit of crime as a family enterprise had more or less wiped out the entire Grigorakis clan in just two decades, proving – as though proof were needed – that the wages of gangsterism are, most often, death.

17

CENTRAL EUROPEAN GANGSTERS: THE SERBIANS

The most well-known and notorious gangsters of Central and Eastern Europe tend to be of Serbian origin, although there is much scope for criminals of all nationalities along the porous borders of the European Union member states, the old USSR territories, the south-of-the-Dead Sea state of Turkey, and the countries that border the current Russian Federation.

One of the earliest Serbian gangsters was the outlaw Jovo Stanisavljević Čaruga who died by public hanging in 1925 in front of a crowd of thousands of spectators. Čaruga was another national Robin Hood figure, born in 1897 in the then-Kingdom of Croatia-Slavonia, part of the Austro-Hungarian Empire. He quickly deserted from the Austro-Hungarian Army, then killed a man who made some moves on his girlfriend, followed by his murdering the nobleman who came to arrest him. When finally captured, he was imprisoned, only to escape.

Čaruga joined a gang of fellow deserter-outlaws, and rose to the leadership. They embarked upon a self-serving crime spree, murdering those in their way, but especially any ethnic Slav peasants whom Čaruga despised (a symptom of the ethnic tensions that continue to divide the wider area today). Following the end of the First World War, Čaruga made his way to Croatia's capital Zagreb in 1922, disguised as a merchant. He then returned to Slavonia and regrouped his old gang, and they raided the prosperous Eltz family estate in 1923, killing one person, although another escaped and was able to raise the alarm. The gang also escaped, but were trailed by the police who caught them and put Čaruga on trial. His exploits formed the basis of the 1991 movie *Čaruga*, starring Ivo Gregurević as the gangster.

The Yugoslav conflicts of the 1990s broke apart the former territory that had been artificially formed in the wake of the Second World War under dictator Josip Tito. Ethnic Croats, Serbs, Bosnians and Kosovars fought for their own independent territories, provoking the involvement of NATO. Many war criminals emerged from the conflicts, but the nearest to a typical gangster was 'Arkan', Željko Ražnatović.

Ražnatović, born in 1952, came from Slovenia and was the son of a high-ranking officer in the Yugoslav air force. When his parents divorced, his Communist Party member mother looked after him, although for a while he became the 'ward' of Stane Dolanc, a friend of his father who ran Tito's secret police (known as the UDBA). The young Ražnatović frequently ran away from home and participated in juvenile crime.

By the age of twenty, he was conducting a European-wide crime spree, specializing in armed robbery and notching up arrests in Italy, Germany, Belgium, Austria, the Netherlands, Sweden and Switzerland. He was briefly jailed in Belgium in 1974, but escaped after three years only to be recaptured in the Netherlands in 1979. He broke out once again in 1981, only to find himself on Europe-wide police service Interpol's Top Ten 'Most Wanted' list.

Ražnatović escaped justice frequently thanks to his connections with Stane Dolanc and the UDBA. As well as a career criminal – the very definition of a gangster – Ražnatović doubled up as a hitman for the secret police, assassinating various Yugoslavian exiles and Tito critics. The UDBA facilitated his return to Serbia at the beginning of the 1980s, and his life as a fully-fledged Serbian gangster. After killing a pair of federal police who attempted to arrest him, Ražnatović was sprung from jail in 1983 by Dolanc.

The collapse of Yugoslavian communism at the beginning of the 1980s saw Ražnatović reform his criminal gang as the Serbian Volunteer Guard, a paramilitary force that would play a part in the later Yugoslavian Wars. This private army – known as 'Arkan's Tigers' – gave Ražnatović a power base during the conflict. Supposedly under the command of the Yugoslavian People's Army, Ražnatović went rogue becoming a regional 'warlord' who pleased himself.

In November 1990, he and five others were charged with an attempt to overthrow newly elected Croatian President Franjo Tudjman. The outcome of the secret trial is unknown, but Ražnatović was freed in the summer of 1991, probably due to the intervention once more of Stane Dolanc.

The civil war and 'ethnic cleansing' process of 1992–5 saw Ražnatović build up an army estimated to number around 10,000 and take an active part in the war. His 'Tigers' pillaged and raped their way across the country, wilfully murdering any Muslims they came across. Ražnatović would claim he only killed 'enemy soldiers', but filmed evidence suggested he went far beyond the traditional gangster role and became a full-on evil butcher.

Ražnatović attempted to take a political route to achieve his aims, although his short-lived Party of Serbian Unity

won no parliamentary seats. By autumn 1995, Ražnatović
had been branded a terrorist by Western diplomats and a
hero by Serbian nationalists. He was driven into hiding by
NATO bombing, but emerged later in the 1990s to once
more pursue more traditional gangster crimes of protection rackets, sports corruption and smuggling. Like the
gangsters of old, he invested his illegal funds in restaurants,
casinos, petrol stations, bakeries and – ironically – a security firm. He announced a plan to run for the Presidency
of Yugoslavia in the autumn of 2000, but was assassinated
that January in a Belgrade hotel by a young policeman
with underworld connections, who was himself later sentenced to a near twenty-year prison term for the killing.
Police never discovered who ordered the hit on Arkan,
but it brought to an end a genuine reign of terror that far
surpassed the efforts of most gangsters who pursued their
lives in organized crime.

Turkish delight
The 'Turkish Mafia' is active across Europe and beyond,
and was deemed responsible for 90 per cent of the heroin
smuggled into Britain at the start of the twenty-first century. Broadly following the classic structure of the Sicilian
Cosa Nostra, Istanbul, Turkey's largest city, is divided
between five families who dominate organized crime in
the country. Crime groups are largely made up of ethnic
Turks, although like Lucky Luciano's Italian mob, they are
open to others.

Known as the 'Godfather of the Godfathers', Dündar
Kiliç was the head of the Turkish Mob until his death in
1999. Born in 1935 in Turkey, Kiliç was first arrested at the
age of fourteen, but that didn't dissuade him from a life of
crime. By the 1960s, Kiliç dominated the underworld in
Turkey's capital city, Ankara. Extortion and illegal gambling was his initial focus, gaining him a local reputation
as the 'good Godfather' as he generally only targeted other

criminals. It was, however, through the far more harmful trade in heroin that Kiliç found wealth. Released in 1965 after a few years in jail, Kiliç was said to have become involved in narcotics, gun-running, and to have personally carried out at least three cold-blooded murders. Repeatedly interrogated by police, he always seemed to walk away a free man. Even when he was locked up, he managed to successfully run his criminal empire from behind bars.

He was sent down in 1984 following an anti-crime operation by Turkey's National Intelligence Service (MIT) in conjunction with local police. A total of eleven charges were laid on Kiliç and he was sent to Ankara's Mamak prison. Kiliç's daughter, Uğur, was killed in 1995, seemingly as part of a gang war, but Kiliç did not retaliate, fearing she had spilled his secrets to her husband, rival ganglord Alaattin Çakici, or even the authorities.

Dündar Kiliç died of natural causes in prison in August 1999, leaving behind a reputation as a philanthropic gangster who'd donated (stolen) money to Turkish students and other good causes. His crime empire was inherited by his grandson, Onur Özbizerdik, who had been only twelve years old when he witnessed the killing of his mother, Uğur, in 1995 (he was not Çakici's son, though – that would have been too much of a Mafia soap opera). When Özbizerdik was imprisoned, daily control of their drug distribution network passed to his advisor, Osman Dönmez. It was Dönmez who supposedly killed the chauffeur of Alaattin Çakici, Kiliç's rival ganglord, who had been deemed responsible for the killing of Uğur, probably on Çakici's orders.

Çakici, born in 1953, dominated heroin smuggling in Turkey throughout the 1970s and 1980s, and had been a constant thorn in Kiliç's side, despite marrying his daughter. He was an operative for the Grey Wolves, an ultra-Turkish nationalist and neo-Fascist militia. After the killing of Uğur, Çakici moved to France to escape the authorities, but

was arrested there in August 1998 and extradited back to
Turkey. He was sent to jail for many years on a long list of
charges, but was the constant target of the Ergin brothers'
gang while in jail. They saw him as a 'mob boss' muscling
in on their behind-bars territory. He remains imprisoned,
and as of the time of writing had effectively evaded the
Ergin brothers' deadly knives. Gang feuds between ex-pat
Turks continue to erupt across London from time to time,
mainly over the control of illegal heroin importing.

The Albanian Mafia

Organized crime operated by the Albanian Mafia stretched
beyond Albania itself into neighbouring territories such as
Kosovo, Macedonia, the wider Balkans region and across
Western Europe, even into North America. Traditional in
form, the criminal reach of the Albanian Mafia has been
enormous over the years, considering the size of the country's population of just three million in 2013. Emergence
from Communist-party dominance in 1992 boosted the
country's profile in international criminality. Albanian
organized crime is known for its violence, torture and for
supporting international terrorism. The ethnically driven
crime syndicate is strictly hierarchical and deeply secretive. Starting in the 1980s, they infiltrated New York and
began a conflict with Italian gangs, then went on to control
car theft and vehicle trafficking in Italy, illegal immigrant
smuggling, sex trafficking and the heroin trade in the UK,
and made inroads into Australia and South America.

The 'Macedonian Godfather' Daut Kadriovski personi-
fies the Albanian Mafia in action. Born in 1955 in Macedonia,
Kadriovski dominated the heroin trade from the country
in the 1970s. He involved his relatives in the running of
quasi-legitimate 'front' businesses across the world in the
United States, Italy, Hungary and Germany that covered
for his import-export heroin racket. Kadriovski was rated
by the Yugoslav Interior Ministry to be the boss of one of

the country's Top 15 families of crime and one of Europe's biggest heroin dealers. Based in the United States, and a wanted man in twelve European countries, Kadriovski created a drug pipeline through Albania and Croatia to Sydney and Brisbane in Australia. He was last heard of in Philadelphia.

Not as extensive as the Albanian network, the Bulgarian Mafia have nevertheless made significant inroads into organized crime in Bulgaria, the Balkans and Eastern Europe. They are involved in the usual list of illegal activities, but have a specialism in the trafficking of illegal antiquities and archaeological finds worldwide, and have connections with the original Sicilian Mafia and the new post-communism Russian Mafia. The Bulgarians have a habit of using genuine security and insurance companies as fronts for their illicit activities, laundering money through these companies. Bulgarian immigrants have set up extensions of the Mafia in Belgium and the Netherlands.

Many of the heads of various sub-groups of the Bulgarian Mafia have fallen victim to assassination, especially following the fall of communism in 1989. Widespread corruption of the judicial system means that very few of these 'hits' have ever been prosecuted. Three prime examples are Vasil Iliev, Ivo Karamanski and Konstantin Dimitrov-Samokovetsa. Born in 1955, Iliev was a former sportsman who stole cars for resale in Russia, as well as an exponent of well-worn protection rackets. Through his companies, Iliev would steal cars and then ransom them back to their owners, claiming to have 'protected' them from export to Russia. Soon, drivers were paying in advance to ensure their vehicles were not stolen in the first place and had to display the correct papers to gain immunity from the racket. Iliev was killed in April 1995, while preparing to eat in his favourite restaurant, after gunmen staged a car crash to block traffic so they could rake his car with bullets from silencer-equipped sub-machine guns – a tactic that echoed events in 1930s Chicago. He died instantly at the scene. His brother, Georgi, stepped in to continue the family business.

Ivo Karamanski was born in 1959 and became the Bulgarian 'Godfather' – would-be Mafia Dons were fond of that title following the 1972 Francis Ford Coppola movie. A former national Balkan rowing champion in the 1980s, he claimed he had killed without ever firing a gun. Like Iliev, he was driven into crime when Bulgarian sports subsidies ended along with communism. He was into the same 'protection' rackets as Iliev, but also practised a modern version of the old Italian Black Hand-style intimidation from the nineteenth century. Karamanski was the prime suspect in the slaying of Vasil Iliev, but nothing was ever proven. He died in a drunken, gun-fuelled quarrel with his own bodyguard in 1998.

Konstantin Dimitrov followed his countrymen Iliev and Karamanski to the grave at the age of just thirty-three in 2003, shot dead while window shopping in Amsterdam in the company of a Bulgarian fashion model, who was injured by a ricocheting bullet. He was a minor player in the Bulgarian underworld until the death of Vasil Iliev gave him the opportunity to rise through the criminal ranks. He joined with Iliev's brother, Georgi, in a security company that was a front for heroin trading. A gang war broke out with their rivals, the Marinovs, resulting in bombings and revenge bombings of each other's places of business. Shot to death in a drive-by shooting, Dimitrov's killers were apprehended by members of the public who witnessed his slaying.

One of the results of the fall of Communist rule across all these nations and territories was a huge increase in organized crime, often modelled along the lines of the original Sicilian Mafia. The biggest nation to suffer (or, perhaps, benefit) from this surge in post-Communism crime was Mother Russia herself.

18

RUSSIA: FROM THE SOVIET UNION TO THE OLIGARCHS

Since the fall of the Soviet Union, gangsters have prospered across the vast geographical area of the Russian Federation, and have either influenced or had a direct hand in much international organized crime, from Brighton Beach in New York through locations in Canada, Portugal, Spain, France and elsewhere. It is estimated that over three million people are involved in organized crime throughout Russia, with another 300,000 Russian ex-pats taking part elsewhere in the world, especially in capital cities like New York and London.

Organized crime has a long history in Russia, dating back at least to the time of the pre-revolutionary imperial Tsars. Banditry was rife in the 1700s, often perpetrated by the peasant class against their local overlords. Such groups organized themselves as the 'Vorovskoy Mir' or 'Thieves World', and developed a Sicilian Mafia-like code of conduct, based on clan or ethnic loyalty, and focused on opposition to government, both local and more distant.

The Bolshevik Revolution of 1917 ended the reign of the Tsars. Like Mussolini in 1920s Italy, Communist leader Vladimir Lenin made an attempt to end organized crime across Russia after he was personally 'held up' by a group of highwaymen. However, crime was never stamped out in the Soviet era, whatever the state propaganda might have tried to suggest. The 'workers' paradise' free from crime was little more than a figment of the government's imagination. Communist policies, such as a ban on private property ownership and the making of personal profit, created a ready-made market for the kind of underground economy regularly run by gangsters, just as the Prohibition of alcohol had done in 1920s America. Russian crime groups became more organized during this period, often forming among those held in the gulags (Soviet labour camps), which were filling up under Josef Stalin's dictatorial rule, headed by leaders called 'vory y zakone' or 'thieves-in-law' – a rough equivalent to the Sicilian 'Don'. The position of such leaders was often signified through particular identifying tattoos, a trait still seen in members of the Russian Mafia today. A code of honour developed among such 'thieves' and was policed and imposed throughout the gulags by the criminal groups who prospered there.

An extensive 'thieves' market' operated in Moscow during this time, and was tolerated by the police force. Every so often, though, symbolic raids would have to be made to prove to the wider population that 'the system' was working in their interests. A senior Russian diplomat, Mikhail Florinsky, was jailed by police in 1926 having bought a stolen camera from Russian gangsters – he was used to 'prove' that even the privileged were not above the law. These symbolic prosecutions were few in number, though, in comparison to the huge spread of organized crime across the nation and the increasing numbers of criminal citizens involved. Stalin used known Russian mobsters as a criminal intelligence network, where they would inform on 'traitors' in return for leniency in their criminal matters.

Stalin's accommodations with organized crime caused a split among mobsters. Co-operating with the state was against the thieves' code, so those who informed or even fought for Russia during the Second World War in return for their freedom or a reduced sentence were seen as betraying their criminal comrades (the American Mafia equivalent would be 'snitching' or 'ratting', selling out fellow mobsters). They were regarded as traitors or 'suka', the Russian word for the insult 'bitch'. The period from the end of the war in 1945 through to the death of Stalin in 1953 is known as the 'suka wars' or 'bitch wars' in which gang warfare broke out openly among the various pro- and anti-government factions. Gang fights within the prison system were actively encouraged by the authorities as a way of effectively 'culling' the sometimes difficult to administer, ever-growing prison population.

In the post-Second World War period, after the death of Stalin up to the collapse of the Soviet Union, a thriving black market in goods and services not otherwise provided offered many opportunities for Russia's growing gangster class. When the gulags were opened up, millions of people – not all, but many of them straightforward criminals rather than political prisoners – were released into the Russian economy. For a while, the old 'Thieves World' rules were ignored, and an individualism dominated the criminal classes in which those determined to pursue crime in the 'new' Russia began to establish their bases of influence. Under Brezhnev, corruption in high places increased, and in the opinion of many, Russia itself was being governed by what amounted to a criminal gang.

The arrival of Gorbachev and his 'glasnost' reforms radically changed this state of affairs, opening the doors to private businesses, some of which had their origins in criminal groups. In the post-Soviet era, the unstable governments and loose controls in the former Soviet states saw gangsters move in to take advantage of the situation. It has been estimated that during the 1990s, up to two-thirds of the overall Russian economy was driven by the criminal activities of gangsters, and in the same period the FBI declared the Russian Mafia to be the most serious threat to American national security at that time.

In the early 1990s there arose the 'Red Mafiya', an international organization of criminal groups. Various nationalities, held in check for the lengthy, almost seventy-five-year Soviet period, were now free to travel and participate in regular worldwide activities, in particular crime. Gangsters of all nationalities formerly contained within Communist Russia, such as Chechens, Georgians, Armenians, Azeris and Ukranians, spread their criminal networks worldwide. In other countries across Europe and in the United States, the Red Mafiya found a host of new opportunities and developed new markets for their goods and services, especially illegal drugs imported from their home nations.

Like Luciano's pioneering Commission, Russian mobsters are organized in a 'circle of brothers'. Individual mob leaders meet as a group to discuss their business and resolve inter-clan or inter-gang disputes. The clan leaders are the 'pakhan' or 'Godfather', and each gang is further split into smaller units led by 'brigadiers', while the rank-and-file mobsters are the 'boyeviky' or 'footsoldiers'. To belong to a group, members need to share ethnicity if not strict family connections, and need to have a proven criminal track record, often chronicled in their symbolic prison tattoos.

Many of the Russian gangs follow a broadly para-military set-up, hardly surprising as many of the 'pakhan' are former leaders from the Soviet Army or previously were operatives for the KGB, the Russian secret intelligence service (something they have in common with current Russian leader Vladimir Putin). Former members of the 'Spetznaz' or military special forces – the Russian version of the US Navy Seals or the UK Special Air Service (SAS) – are particularly welcome as members of Red Mafiya gangs for the skills they can offer. Much of the Russian mobs' 'muscle' or enforcers are former Spetznaz officers who have turned to crime to make a living. There have even been tales of former Russian Olympic sharpshooters being employed by the Russian mobs as highly-skilled assassins.

The criminal Russian gangs operate in all the areas covered by most crime syndicates, but they also have a few unique quirks of their own. Beyond the usual gambling, moneylending and drug-running, there is an emphasis on the shipping of stolen vehicles across Europe. Additionally, Russian organized crime has long been rumoured to have captured rogue nuclear warheads seized from temporarily abandoned military arsenals during the political confusion that followed the fall of the Berlin Wall in 1989, but this has never been proven. Human trafficking, whether for the purposes of illegal immigration or sexual slavery, is another specialism of the Russian Mafia.

More perhaps than any other organized crime groups, the Russian Mafia has made use of legitimate business as a way of developing their criminal networks and activities. This grew out of the ban on private ownership of businesses during the Soviet era. Once such ownership was allowed during the 'glasnost' reforms, many of the first to move into the new legitimate fields of business were mobsters who'd previously been carrying out the same activities illegally. By the beginning of the twenty-first century it was estimated that up to 80 per cent of Russian business was either owned by or received substantial investment from the Russian mob. Up to 40 per cent of the nation's entire wealth was estimated to be held in the hands of criminal groups.

During the 1990s, the criminal syndicates that had
developed made a move on the Russian banking system.
Rather than relying on the independent banks to launder
their money, the mob took direct control of several banks
themselves, bumping off any banking executives who
resisted their takeover, and either putting the frighteners
on or bribing those who stayed in post. Almost a dozen
bankers were estimated to have been subject to assassination during this turbulent period. In fact, deaths by
shooting in Russia's capital city, Moscow, are said to be
in the region of 10,000 annually, with about 600 of those
each year estimated to be the direct result of mob contract
killings. According to the Federal Research Division of the
Library of Congress, Russia averaged eighty-four murders
per day in the first four months of 1994, compared to some
periods in the 1930s in Chicago where one murder per day
was considered outrageous.

One of the Russian mob's favourite scams is to skim 20
per cent off the top of profits generated by Russian companies operating abroad, as 'protection' money to ensure
their business is conducted uninterrupted. Like the Eastern
European gangsters, the Russians are also big in the private security field, an extension of their protection rackets,
largely due to the fact that institutional failure and corruption created an opening in the marketplace for the mob to
move in. There are thousands of 'security firms' offering
'protection' to thousands of companies that between them
employ hundreds of thousands of ordinary Russians.

Foreign businesses, and those who run them, operating
within Russia are another target for the Red Mafiya. Those
moving in will either be co-opted by the mob into paying
'protection' money or 'donating' a percentage of their
profits to the syndicate, or they'll be killed as a warning
to others, all good old Chicago tricks. Several prominent
businessmen and investors moving into the Russian markets over the years have lost their lives, including Australian

dancehall owner Richard Hollington; Christopher Kline, the British owner of a department store in Moscow; Israeli entrepreneur Ariel Abramson; as well as a host of others including a Dutch cheese importer, restaurant owners, hotel impresarios and fast food shop owners.

The Red Mafiya has a wide reach, from New York's Little Odessa to Miami, Florida, key areas in London, and elsewhere. They offer money-laundering services for local criminals, muscle-for-hire for those intending to pull off bank heists, and other illegal services. To many, the Russian Federation itself is nothing more than a corrupt oligarchy run by criminals, from the highest to the lowest, at great expense to the ordinary citizens of the country who got a raw deal under communism but may be suffering even harsher conditions under the kind of violent, rampant, raw capitalism practised by the Red Mafiya.

Prominent Russian gangsters

Major figures among the Russian Red Mafiya included Sergei Mikhailov, Vyacheslav Ivankov and the 'Chechen Godfather', Ruslan Labazanov. This trio of Russian Mafia figures encapsulate between them most of the traits that typify the modern Russian gangster.

Born in 1958, Sergei Mikhailov quickly decided that the life of a restaurant waiter was not for him and a life of crime might provide better prospects. Six months in the gulag for fraud and theft in the early 1980s was enough for Mikhailov to build lasting contacts in the Russian underworld. Once out of jail, he founded the Solnsevskaya Bratva, or the Solnsevskaya Brotherhood, named after his home Moscow neighbourhood. The 'Bratva' would, in time, become the largest and most dangerous faction of the post-Soviet Russian Mafia. Anything illegal, the Bratva had a slice of it, irrespective of whether another gang had got there first or not. A series of bloody street battles between Bratva members and other gangsters frequently took place in Moscow. They won most of these turf wars, expanding their business to include gun-running and their membership to over 5,000.

By 1989, Mikhailov was behind bars once more – held for eighteen months before his trial on an extortion charge. The trial, when it came, was anti-climactic as no witnesses could be found to speak out against Mikhailov and his activities, resulting in him walking free from court. His criminal business, alongside some newly established legitimate front businesses, continued, until the collapse of Communism in 1991 changed the political and economic landscape. In the chaos of the time, Mikhailov built up a strong portfolio of genuine businesses, including casinos, banks, car dealerships and even Vnukovo (or Vnoekovo) Airport, the oldest airport in Moscow.

In the mid-1990s, Sergei Mikhailov was to be found in Israel building international links with the American Cosa Nostra, the original Sicilian Mafia, and the newly booming Colombian drug cartels. His enemies around the world were silenced by his highly mobile 'combat brigades' formed by his most trusted, ruthless and violent lieutenants.

Held by the Swiss authorities on a variety of charges in 1996, Mikhailov once again walked free as many of the witnesses who might have testified against him mysteriously vanished, died or changed their minds. Furthermore, he successfully won a case against the Swiss government for two years' wrongful imprisonment, receiving an undisclosed financial settlement of damages. As far as Interpol are concerned, though, Sergei Mikhailov's Solnsevskaya Bratva remains one of the most dangerous criminal organizations in the world.

Born in Moscow, Vyacheslav Ivankov was a member of this Brotherhood who started his professional life as a wrestler before a bar brawl saw him jailed. Once back on the streets, he immediately got involved with the Russian

Mafia, before spending another decade in jail from 1982 for drug trafficking, possession of firearms, forgery and robbery. Like many in the Russian Mafia, he used his time behind bars to build solid links and a ruthless reputation within the organization. His lightly Asian features saw him gain the mob nickname 'Little Japanese'.

Released from jail, Ivankov headed for the United States in 1992 arriving with 'official' papers (recalling that conviction for forgery) that suggested he had a hand in the American film business. He was allowed entry, despite his long criminal record, fuelling later speculation that he may have had ties to either Russian or American intelligence agencies. Despite there being no film business there, Ivankov established himself in the Russian Brighton Beach district in New York.

He was arrested in 1995 and charged with extorting $2.7 million from an investment firm called Summit run by a pair of Russian 'businessmen'. When picked up, he was in possession of multiple passports under various names, thousands of dollars in cash, and a revolver that he'd attempted to dispose of by tossing it out of his window. He was deported to Russia in 2004 to face charges of killing two Turkish nationals in a Moscow restaurant in 1992 – a charge he was acquitted of in 2005.

Four years later, Vyacheslav Ivankov was fatally wounded when leaving a Moscow restaurant. He was in hospital for over two months, but died on 9 October 2009 aged sixty-nine. His funeral attracted gangsters from across Russia who came to pay homage to one of their own, while many local 'Bratva' sent cards and flowers. It was suspected that Ivankov had been killed as part of a gang war between fellow Russian gangster Aslan Usoyan and Georgian crime boss Tariel Oniani.

Ruslan Labazanov, however, died young, at the age of twenty-nine, in 1996, having risen through the ranks to the role of 'Chechen Godfather'. Born in Kazakhstan in

1967, Labazanov taught martial arts to Russian soldiers. Convicted of murder in 1990, he escaped prison during the collapse of the Soviet Union the following year. While on the run, he established a private militia – essentially his own personal army – in Chechnya, which he'd rent out to the highest bidder, regardless of whether the 'work' was political or criminal. Labazanov was killed in an ambush in June 1996, seemingly the victim of a rival Muslim warlord, Shamil Basayev, although some pointed fingers at his own allies.

Russian gangsters in the US

As with the Italians at the turn of the nineteenth century, Russians had emigrated to the United States, and a handful were part of the Prohibition gangster boom of the 1920s and early 1930s. Russian immigration to America boomed, however, when controls were relaxed in both countries in the 1970s and 1980s – and among those coming to America were the unrepentant criminal classes.

Organized Russian crime in the United States expanded across the country from Brighton Beach, just as the New York and Chicago gangs had spread nationwide in the 1920s and 1930s. One of the earliest scams perpetrated by Russian criminals in the 1970s became known as the 'Potato Bag' trick. Russian con men pretending to be legitimate merchants just arrived in America offered to sell batches of 'antique gold' roubles (the Russian currency) cheap and in bulk to the right buyer. Only later would the trusting purchasers discover they had instead been shipped bags packed with worthless potatoes instead of the expected gold roubles.

Leaders emerged among the Brighton Beach gangs, and by the 1980s the local 'pakhan' was Evsei Agron. Born in 1932 in Leningrad, Agron was permitted to leave the Soviet Union in 1971 when he was released from a seven-year jail sentence for murder. He spent time in Hamburg, Germany, managing brothels, before moving on in 1975 to Brighton Beach, where he was already known among the Russian community as a ruthless senior member of the Red Mafiya. He was just one of over 5,000 Russian Jews who fled the country of their birth and arrived in America that year, but he'd make his mark.

Like the nineteenth century Italian Black Hand gangs, Agron preyed on his own community, hitting on Russian immigrants for 'protection' payments otherwise they'd suffer a beating or worse. For those already established in business, he was able to threaten their livelihood if they refused to pay up. One tale has him threatening to kill a fellow Russian's daughter on her wedding day if he didn't hand over $15,000. Agron established a business for himself, selling tax-free motor fuel as oil for home heating, so defrauding the New Jersey local tax authorities of up to $1 billion each year according to some estimates.

Agron's enforcers were two brothers, Benjamin and Boris Nayfeld from Gomel in Russia, who were happy to inflict violence on others, witnesses or not, on behalf of their boss who was known as 'The Little Don'. A defect in Boris Nayfeld's eyes made them appear completely white and was said in the Russian community to prove he was controlled by the Devil. In reality, the Devil in question was the gangster Evsei Agron, not a fallen Angel. His favourite enforcement weapon was an electric cattle prod. However, he managed to create a positive image of himself and his businesses in the local community through control of the local Russian language newspaper.

Reaching the top made Agron a target for assassination by rivals and would-be bosses. In 1980 in Coney Island, the location of so many Italian Mob hits of the past, he was shot and wounded. Sticking with the Russian version of omertà, he refused to identify the shooter – he perhaps took this approach as by this time he'd struck up an alliance with the Genovese Mafia family in New York. Agron provided muscle for some of the Italian Mafia's operations across the US during the 1980s, while he benefited from the Italians' political connections. He was targeted again in January 1984 when he was ambushed approaching his own front door, in the same way the failed hit on Frank Costello had been carried out. This attack on Agron also failed, although he suffered neck and face wounds that changed the way he looked, leaving him with a weird, sinister, off-kilter grin. There was a third failed attack in May 1984.

The main suspect in this trio of attacks was Agron's rival, Boris Goldberg, an ex-military man who'd been aggressively expanding his own Brighton Beach criminal empire. Goldberg's lieutenant David 'Napoleon' Schuster had built up a well-armed mob army that was larger than Agron's own, preventing him from lashing out at his attackers for fear of even worse reprisals. While Agron was planning ways to hit Goldberg, his time ran out. Attempted negotiations between the two went nowhere fast, so one or the other would have to go.

The fatal attack on Evsei Agron came a year after the third attempt, on 4 May 1985. Intending to visit his favourite Turkish bath, the Russian gangster was shot in the street by two hitmen disguised as joggers. He'd made the fatal mistake of establishing a pattern of movements through his regular habits, making him vulnerable to the kind of attack that claimed his life in the end. He died aged just fifty-three, the first – but not the last – Russian 'Godfather' to find success in the United States. The man who most likely ordered Agron's killing, Boris Goldberg, was himself brought to justice through America's Racketeer Influenced and Corrupt Organizations Act (RICO) in 1991. He was sent to jail for a variety of offences, including drug trafficking, armed robbery, extortion, arms dealing and attempted murder.

One of the major concerns to have emerged in Russia in the decades following the collapse of Communism, and especially in the Putin period from 2000, is the seeming impossibility of telling the gangsters who conduct business illegally from the 'legal' Russian oligarchs or politicians. From a certain point of view, modern Russia looks like a state actually run by gangsters who have simply made their way of doing business 'legal' in their own territory. Like the robber barons of old, many modern businessmen and politicians across the Russian Federation are simply old-time gangsters gone legit.

19

LATIN AMERICA: THE COLOMBIAN DRUG LORDS

The heart of organized crime across Latin America has always been the drug trade, especially the exportation of cocaine, marijuana and heroin north to the United States. The Colombian drug lords traffic their 'product' world-wide, with the political corruption engendered by the syndicates making New York's Tammany Hall look like a benevolent society. Beyond mere criminality, beyond even gangsterism, the Latin America drug syndicates have expanded into narco-terrorism, using 'freedom fighters', indigenous guerrilla movements and resistance movements of the left and right to their own ends.

A variety of drug cartels have existed across Latin America, including the Sonora, Juárez, Tijuana, and Guadalajara cartels making their mark in Mexico alone. The most widely known, however, is probably the infamous Medellín Cartel in operation for two decades from the late 1970s until the mid-1990s. It was established by the most notorious of the Mexican drug lords: Pablo Escobar.

Pablo Escobar and the Medellín Cartel

Pablo Emilio Escobar Gavíria started his criminal career as an undistinguished car thief and small-time marijuana dealer. Born in Colombia in 1949, Escobar started selling fake lottery tickets and contraband cigarettes, before graduating to work as a bodyguard in the 1970s. He was then hired by big-time drug dealer Carlos Lehder Rivas, known as Lehder, as 'head of security', essentially an old-fashioned 'muscle' enforcement job.

Having spent time in jail in the United States for auto theft, Lehder had concluded that shipping cocaine to America was an under-exploited criminal opportunity, and he was just the man to take it. Teaming up with two experienced smugglers of marijuana, George Jung and Roman Varone, they developed the ideal routes for smuggling drugs into the US. They began with individual smugglers, such as seemingly innocent American girls hired to pose as holidaymakers who would carry illicit packages from Antigua back to America regularly as human drug mules. The profit made from this early activity saw Lehder buy his first aeroplane, which was used to move cocaine through an island in the Bahamas into Florida. With up to $60 million a month coming in, Lehder soon operated a fleet of small planes. This was the world into which Pablo Escobar stepped in the mid-1970s.

Soon enough Escobar himself was flying planes laden with cocaine from Colombia and Panama into the United States. Escobar was quickly running things, having assassinated rival drug trafficker Fabio Restrepo in 1975 and co-opting all Restrepo's men to his own team. The following year, Escobar was arrested in possession of almost 20 kg of white paste in a return trip to Medellín from Ecuador. The Medellín Cartel operated a policy of 'plomo

o plata', offering officials in law enforcement and government the choice between 'lead' or 'silver', meaning a bullet
to the head (plomo/lead) or plenty of money in bribes
(plata/silver). This 'bend or break' – those who don't bend
and accept bribes will break, meaning be killed – approach
earned big dividends, as Escobar walked away from the
1976 charges thanks to extensive bribery.

This bribery-or-death approach came to be known as
'narco-terrorism', and it dominated the politics of Colombia
throughout the 1980s and 1990s. One high-profile victim
was Colombian Justice Minister Rodrigo Lara Bonilla
who favoured the extradition of drug dealers to face justice in America. He was killed while driving in rush hour
traffic in Bogotá, the Colombian capital, in April 1984,
aged just thirty-seven. His assassination, however, would
lead directly to Colombian President Belisario Betancur
Cuartas instituting a legal order to extradite Carlos Lehder
and to Pablo Escobar's ultimate downfall.

Medellín, Colombia's second largest city, was where
Escobar and his cartel refined the cocaine paste obtained
in Peru or Bolivia into a saleable product. The boom in
demand for cocaine across America from the 1980s, saw
Lehder and Escobar's business succeed beyond their wild-
est dreams. Lehder purchased an island – Norman's Cay
– in the Bahamas that functioned as their central distribution point between South America and the United States.
Between 1978 and 1982, 70 to 80 tonnes of cocaine was
shipped to America every month by this route, bringing
both Escobar and Lehder millions of dollars in personal
profits.

Escobar laundered his money through land purchases,
and in 1982 he entered politics as a representative of the
Colombian Liberal Party in Colombia's Congress. This was
further evidence of the almost completely corrupt nature of
the Colombian system of government at this time. Despite
this, there were those within the judicial system who still

attempted to see proper judicial processes followed, such as Justice Minister Rodrigo Lara Bonilla and others.

Refusing bribes and defying death threats, a group of judges were preparing to approve the extradition of a number of drug traffickers to the US when their Palace of Justice court was raided by armed gunmen in November 1985. The assault, by thirty-five gunmen of the paramilitary group M-19 backed by the Medellín Cartel, killed a total of eleven judges and eighty-four other hostages after a pitched gunfight with the authorities. The cartel publicly denied any involvement in the outrage, but there was evidence linking Lehder at least to the M-19 guerrilla movement.

Ironically, this form of direct action terrorism to free drug traffickers resulted in an even harder crackdown on them and their activities. A joint US–Colombian operation went after Lehder and Escobar. Lehder fled to Nicaragua, before returning to Colombia, where he was captured in 1987. Convicted on multiple charges in America, Carlos Lehder was jailed for 135 years in 1987 (later reduced to fifty-five years in 1992 after Lehder informed on Panamanian President Manuel Noriega's role in the international drugs trade). He remains in jail to this day, although regular rumours suggest he has been released and is living somewhere in America under the Witness Protection Programme.

Pablo Escobar fully took over the Medellín Cartel when Lehder was captured. His illegal business was so financially successful that by 1989 *Forbes* magazine named him as the world's seventh richest man, with a net worth of $25 billion, making him, financially at least, one of the most successful individual gangsters of all time. Up to 80 per cent of the entire world's annual supply of cocaine was estimated to have originated from the Medellín Cartel in the late 1980s, bringing in around $30 billion annually to Escobar's operation. Besides land, the money was invested in fleets of cars and planes, and in financing a private army to protect those involved in the drug-trafficking activity. Despite all that spending, according to a book written by Escobar's brother Robert, there was so much money around – up to $60 million coming in every day – that the gangsters had little choice but to store it stacked in warehouses, where there was a 10 per cent 'write-off' factor to account for the bank notes that were chewed up by rats.

As ever with gangsters, Escobar attempted to play up his Robin Hood credentials with people in South America, putting some of his ill-gotten gains into building public sports facilities like football fields and multi-sports arenas. He was even said to have funded the building of hospitals, churches and schools, although this might just have been personal propaganda as Escobar was a master of public relations. He was still, however, regarded as an important enemy of both the American and Colombian governments, who made him target number one on their list of wanted drug traffickers.

Escobar married and had two children and lived on an extensive estate he dubbed Hacienda Nápoles, or Naples Estate, suggesting that he perhaps looked to prominent Italian gangsters of the past like Lucky Luciano or Al Capone as his role models. He built a zoo on the property, and began work on a Greek-style castle that was never finished. Following his downfall, the property was seized by the government, given to the Colombian people, and ultimately converted into a theme park.

Following the assassination of anti-cartel Presidential candidate Luis Carlos Galán in 1989, even Pablo Escobar realized he was running out of options and probably faced the same fate as Carlos Lehder: extradition and imprisonment in the United States. He tried a very different approach: in 1991 Escobar negotiated his surrender with the Colombian government, but only on his own, unique terms. In return for his surrender, Escobar demanded he only face a maximum prison sentence of five years to be served in Colombia. He was not to be extradited to the United States. Furthermore, he demanded he be allowed to design and supervise the building of his own 'prison', eventually known as 'La Catedral' – essentially a luxurious country club constructed for the pleasure of one man. In addition, he was to be allowed frequent shopping trips in Medellín and be able to meet freely with his former criminal associates.

It sounds like something from a comedy Mafia movie, but it was all granted to him. The Colombian government were so desperate to somehow deal with the 'Escobar problem' that they gave in to all his demands in return for his retirement from his criminal exploits. Swift public outcry against the terms of the ridiculous agreement, however, forced the government to change their approach. Escobar was moved to a more suitable prison, but escaped during transit on 22 July 1992. Finally having had enough of him, the authorities called in military support from US Delta Force and Navy Seal personnel to bring down the world's most wanted gangster. Also on Escobar's trail were 'Los Pepes', a Colombian people's vigilante group who were fed up with Escobar and who wanted to see him brought to justice. However, there was some suspicion that this group may have been funded by the rival Cali Cartel. They were reputed to have killed up to 300 of Escobar's lieutenants during their search for the cartel leader. Also participating in the manhunt was the 'Search Bloc', a specially trained Colombian police faction charged with one job: 'Get Escobar'.

It took fifteen months, but Pablo Escobar was finally tracked down and killed on 2 December 1993 by Colonel Hugo Martinez's Search Bloc squad. The multi-agency, multi-national effort to find and eliminate this one man had cost hundreds of millions of dollars. Escobar was found holed up in a middle-class neighbourhood of Medellín, where a deadly gunfight erupted between him, his bodyguard and his pursuers. Both Escobar and his bodyguard were shot and killed by the Colombian National Police during an attempt to escape across the rooftops. Trophy photographs show Escobar's killers standing or squatting around his dead body. It was never known which of them fired the final shot, and there was some suspicion that Escobar had been killed execution style with a single shot to the head after having been wounded. His family have always maintained that he committed suicide having realized he had no hope of escape.

Following the death of Pablo Escobar, the once formidable Medellín Cartel began to disintegrate. The rival Cali Cartel, run by brothers Gilberto and Miguel Rodríguez Orejuela, took over many of the Medellín's routes and business, until it and its leaders were eliminated by Colombian government action in the mid-1990s. The Robin Hood image and legend of Pablo Escobar lives on in Medellín, but elsewhere he is seen as what he was: a ruthless, violent man who made a huge success of exporting a product that brought suffering and death to millions of people across the United States.

Cartels and drug lords
It was inevitable that South America would become the home of modern gangsters: the vast majority of the world's cocaine is sourced in Colombia, Bolivia and Peru, whereas the biggest markets for the drug are in the United States and Europe. Although drug manufacturing and smuggling cartels existed prior to the Medellín and Cali Cartels, it was only after both those behemoths were dismantled that there was space in the 'market' for a host of smaller, more focused organizations to flourish.

In the 1970s, the Sonora Cartel was a family affair, run by founder Rafael Caro-Quintero with his brothers, Miguel, Jorge and Genaro, as well as their sister, Carmen. Born in 1952, Caro-Quintero focused on smuggling his product across the US–Mexican border into Arizona, California, Nevada and Texas. Rather than focusing on cocaine, however, their primary product was marijuana. The cartel was responsible for the kidnapping and murder of a DEA agent in 1985, but it was Costa Rica that actually jailed Rafael Caro-Quintero for drug trafficking after the American authorities failed to hold him. Although several American states did indict him, Mexico claimed jurisdiction sending Caro-Quintero down for the maximum forty years.

Miguel Caro-Quintero took over, but he too was indicted by Colorado and Arizona for drug trafficking in the late 1980s and early 1990s, but wasn't jailed by the Mexican authorities until 2001, following US claims of political corruption. The other Caro-Quintero brothers and sister Carmen stepped up to continue the operation, but at a much reduced level. There was much surprise and outrage – not least from US President Barack Obama – when Rafael Caro-Quintero was released in 2013 on technicalities related to the original trial. He remains on Interpol's Top 15 list of 'Most Wanted' figures.

The drug kingpin of the south in the 1980s was Miguel Gallardo, head of the Guadalajara Cartel, which controlled the vast majority of the Mexican–United States cross-border trafficking. Their main product was methamphetamine, cooked in secret labs on both sides of the border, although Gallardo had begun with 'softer' drugs like marijuana and opium. Gallardo was one of Pablo Escobar's main conduits in getting his drugs across the border and into the US. Gallardo later split up the trade among several groups, recalling the split Lucky Luciano designed for organized crime in New York in the 1930s. Under Gallardo, the Felix brothers controlled Tijuana, the Fuentes family held the Ciudad Juárez route, the 'Gulf Cartel' remained under its founder Juan García Abrego, and the Pacific Coast would be left to the Sinaloa Cartel, which included notorious drug lord Héctor Salazar.

Into the 21st century, the rival drug cartels of the south fought each other for control of the trade, as well as battling Mexican and American authorities. The Mexican Drug War hit a higher gear in 2006 when it became a 'proper war' thanks to the involvement of the Mexican military in enforcement activities, largely at the behest of the United States, where concern over the cross-border traffic has increased over decades.

With their leadership decimated thanks to arrests in 2007, the Gulf Cartel was split by the departure of Los Zetas, a gang of around 300 – many among them deserters from the Mexican military – led by Heriberto Lazcano. They teamed with the Sinaloa Cartel and declared war on the remainder of the Gulf Cartel, resulting in a bloody conflict over the distribution routes through northeast Mexico. Thousands are suspected to have been killed in the resulting conflict, mainly cartel members, but also civilians including the seventy-two migrants killed in the San Fernando Massacre of 2010. In 2013, the Mexican Navy captured Los Zetas's main boss, Miguel Treviño Morales, who was described in the press as 'the notoriously brutal leader of Mexico's feared Zetas drug cartel'. The forty-year-old had $2 million in cash on him at the time.

Joaquín Guzmán – known as 'El Chapo' – led the Sinaloa Cartel, which itself was battling the Juarez Cartel, which it wiped out and then absorbed several other smaller operations. By 2010, there were allegations that the Sinaloa operation had infiltrated the Mexican government and military, which had aided it in destroying other drug cartels.

La Familia Michoacana was an off-shoot of both the Gulf Cartel and Los Zetas active for about five years between 2006 and 2011. It fragmented in 2010 following the arrest of almost 350 members after a counter-narcotics operation by the US and Mexican governments. By mid-2011, the Mexican Attorney General had enough confidence to claim the entire cartel had been wound up thanks to the actions of law enforcement and the military. Once Mexico's most powerful drug-trafficking operation, the Tijuana Cartel suffered a similar fate, having been weakened thanks to internal schisms in 2009. Although still operating, following the arrests and assassinations of key leaders and members, it is considered to be far less potent than it once was.

While Mexican authorities have focused – with some success – on dismantling the cartels, the United States is more concerned with simply stopping the traffic of drugs into its territory. It is believed that up to 90 per cent of the cocaine entering the United States still makes its way into the country across the Mexican–American border, even with the demise of many of the cartels. It will remain a problem almost impossible to solve for as long as the demand for the drugs exist – as American society discovered almost 100 years ago with alcohol and Prohibition.

20

ASIA: THE TRIADS AND YAKUZA

Of all the active gangs in the Far East, the two most well known are China's Triads and Japan's Yakuza. Many smaller gangster groups operated under the bigger umbrella of both 'secret societies', making them the ideal lens through which to view the origins, growth and spread of organized crime in China, Japan and beyond in the Far East and Asia. Both the Triads and the Yakuza were equally adept at promoting themselves, embracing their own legends and, in later years, modelling themselves after depictions in movies where such gangsters were the last repository of honour, tradition and the sometimes spurious rituals they promoted as being central to their activities.

The Chinese Triads
The roots of the Triad societies, essentially the Chinese equivalent to the Italian or Sicilian Mafia, stretch back to the mid-seventeenth century and the decline of the Ming

dynasty (1368–1644). The last Ming Emperor killed himself in 1644 when his troops failed to hold back invaders from Manchuria during the Battle of Shanghai Pass. That cleared the way for the victorious Manchu dynasty – or Ching/Qing dynasty, as it became – to control China for almost the next 270 years. Despite this victory, resistance continued among the Shaolin monks, and it is in the continued fight-back of the Ming loyalists that the Triads have their origins.

By the 1760s, the remaining representatives of the extinguished Ming dynasty had regrouped as the fraternal organization the Tiandihui, or the 'Heaven and Earth Society', which laboured to overthrow their Manchu rulers. Through time, the original group split into a variety of subgroups, one of which took the form of the Sanhehui, the 'Three Harmonies Society', a title that linked together into a single unity Heaven, Earth, and Mankind. They adopted the triangle as their symbol, usually decorated with additional swords. Their overall aim was the overthrow of the Ching dynasty and the restoration of the Ming dynasty.

It was the arrival of the British that saw these secret societies or gangs given their English language name of Triads, based upon their triangular motifs. In the nineteenth century, British troops and trade organizations forced their way into China, resulting in a series of wars (between 1839 and 1842, and again between 1856 and 1860), which imposed upon the Chinese rulers open trade routes from the West. This trade was both ways and one of the largest exports from the East to the West was opium, which had already captured millions of addicts in China.

For the British in Hong Kong, who were largely unaware of the history, these fraternal organizations or 'secret societies' were seen as potential areas of resistance to British involvement in the region, so they were outlawed as criminal organizations. They were dubbed 'Triads', and members who were caught were to be charged and imprisoned. The Triads themselves remained focused on overturning Manchu rule of China, even though the Manchu themselves were now under an additional layer of British control.

In order to maintain their actions against the Manchu, the Triads needed funding and found a ready source of such funds in criminal activities that prospered in China and Hong Kong under British rule, including gambling, prostitution and opium smuggling. Despite their political purpose, the Triads found a lucrative sideline in organized crime that would, over time, come to be their primary purpose. The colonial governors attempted, without success, to stamp out these secret societies, particularly in Hong Kong and Singapore, where they'd been declared illegal by 1890.

Like many of these criminal groups, new members were required to undergo an initiation ceremony and take the 'thirty-six oaths', which included a pledge of loyalty to fellow members and a vow of silence when it came to society secrets that must never be divulged to outsiders. The penalty for breaking the oaths was 'death by a myriad swords'. By 1911, the Triad aims had been achieved: revolutionaries led by Triad member Sun Yat-sen toppled the Manchu dynasty and he was installed as China's first president. Perhaps that should have seen the end of the Triads, their purpose achieved, but instead the gangs that had formed remained intact, able to focus on the pursuit of their money-making criminal activities free from political distractions. With no more public donations to their political causes, the Triads added extortion to their repertoire of criminal fund-raising schemes.

The Triads spread out beyond China and Hong Kong in search of lucrative new territories, including Portuguese Macau, Malaysia and French Indochina. With 'Chinatowns' of immigrants established in many major cities worldwide, it didn't take long for the Triad gangs to gain a foothold in such places as San Francisco in the United States, as well as in Australia, New Zealand, across Europe and Africa and into Canada throughout the 1920s and 1930s. Most of these largely independent Triad societies were established in the period between the First and Second World Wars. Many of them became known as Tongs, originally meaning 'social club', but their criminal activities were closely modelled on the Triad examples, although lacking the political focus of the earliest Triad activities [see chapter 2].

Founded in a spirit of resistance to 'foreign' rule, the Triads enjoyed a boost in the period following the Second World War when China existed in a state of political uncertainty and British rule was increasingly resented by the population. Gang violence added to the sense of post-war chaos in the area, which finally culminated in the Communist revolution of 1949 that threatened the Triads' very existence (Hong Kong would remain a British 'possession' until 1997).

Just as in Italy where Mussolini had railed against the Mafia, so in Communist China the gangs and gangsters that had enjoyed almost free rein under ineffectual British rule now found themselves to be the subject of a concerted clamp down. Many fled the country's newest rulers, taking up residence – and criminal activity – in Taiwan, which was ruled by Triad member Chaing Kai-shek (who remained in charge until his death in 1975). The Triads would flourish in Taiwan, and the island itself – although officially part of the Republic of China – became a key conduit for drugs sent onwards from the so-called golden triangle of Myanmar, Laos and Thailand. This was the biggest source of heroin since the 1920s, until being replaced by Afghanistan in the twenty-first century.

By the 1950s there were said to be 300,000 members of Triad groups within Hong Kong alone, although the number of distinct gangs in the territory would fall over time from around three hundred to about fifty, of which just over two dozen are still criminally active. Following extensive rioting in 1956, the Hong Kong authorities once more cracked down on the Triads but were unable to eliminate them entirely. As with most gangs, they were largely arranged along geographical lines with each controlling a territory and pledging to stay away from another's area, although incursions often led to Triad gang wars.

Since the 1960s, the Triads have driven the growth of counterfeiting in the East, from currency to music, movies, computer software and video games. Designer clothing, handbags and expensive watches have also been favourite targets, while since the 1970s the gangs have made an effort to move into more mainstream legitimate businesses, whether as a genuine switch of focus or as front organizations to hide their illegal activities from modern surveillance techniques. In Japan in 2012 a quartet of Triad members were arrested amid allegations of a widespread healthcare fraud scheme they were operating. Things had come a long way from the Ching dynasty rebel days.

Triads have been especially active in the major cities of the United Kingdom in the post-war years, ranging from London to Glasgow, Birmingham to Edinburgh, and Liverpool to Dundee. The 14K Triad, named after 14-carat gold and formed in the 1940s as an anti-Communist organization in China, were particularly active, although they were joined by other groups moving in from Hong Kong in the 1980s in anticipation of the handover of Hong Kong to China which was announced in 1984 (but didn't occur until 1997). The Triads would bring heroin into the UK via Hong Kong and Amsterdam, but they moved beyond drug smuggling into VAT fraud and loan sharking and eventually away from heroin to cannabis and so-called 'designer drugs' smuggled from the Netherlands and Germany.

Newly arrived Triad groups such as the Wo On Lok and the Sun Yee On were better organized and more disciplined than the older 14K groups and were often fronted by seemingly 'respectable' Hong Kong businessmen who were nonetheless involved in major tax evasion and money laundering.

While not officially shunning the use of firearms, modern Triads do continue to use their traditional weapons such as the meat cleaver and machete, with gang traitors subject to execution or assassination through 'death by a thousand cuts', known as 'lingchi', or even through being buried alive. Triads are often involved in public confrontations and turf wars, only broken up by the arrival of police. Amid the remnants of other long established gangster organizations in the United Kingdom and the United States, the Chinese Triads nonetheless managed to carve a niche for their own version of organized crime.

The Japanese Yakuza

In keeping with the Chinese Triads, the Japanese Yakuza organizations date back to criminal secret societies of the past, although the name was not actually applied to them until the middle of the twentieth century. The unification of Japan under the first 'shogun' – the de facto ruler of Japan and the highest ranking general – in the early 1600s saw the end of centuries of civil war, but created the conditions for the formation of organized crime groups. Many suddenly master-less samurai warriors (ronin) became outlaws (as in America's Old West, and after the American Civil War in the pre-urban gangster days), leading to the creation of vigilante defence forces based in major towns. The Yakuza can be traced back to the formation of these self-defence groups, with the addition of professional street gamblers (bakuto) and armed salesmen who were government licensed (tekiya). In the aftermath of the Second World War, delinquent street gangs (guerentai, or 'hoodlums') were fed into the mix of characters who made up the Yakuza.

Following the Meiji Restoration in Japan of 1868, the

Yakuza gangs controlled many ultra-nationalist political groups, such as the Black Dragon society and the Dark Ocean society, backing Japanese military expansionism and wider imperial ambition. Such ambitions were curtailed by the Second World War and the defeat of Japan saw the Yakuza aligned with the occupying United States forces and the CIA in disrupting organized labour unions (as the Mafia did in the United States) and suppressing rising left-wing organizations. In return, the Yakuza's criminal activities were largely tolerated by the occupiers. The post-war black market allowed for plenty of criminal opportunities, and saw the Yakuza expand into new criminal activities as well as internationally.

Much like the Mafia, the Yakuza – who look upon themselves as an ancient chivalrous organization – were organized along family principles, in which the boss ruled his gang whose members made up the 'children' in a strict parent–child relationship of authority. A complex hierarchy existed within Yakuza gang organization, with several layers of management separating the ultimate boss (the 'oyabun') from the street-level gang members. Over time the long-ago traditions of the Yakuza have turned into highly detailed (although some are spurious) rituals that must be observed, from initiations involving the drinking of saki (rice wine) and the exchange of cups ('sakazuki' or saki sharing), through to their notorious full-body tattoos ('irezume') which testify to a particular gangster's criminal accomplishments, as well as his bravery and fortitude in enduring the up-to-a-hundred hours such a tattoo takes to complete using fairly primitive traditional bamboo tools.

According to stories, many Yakuza gang members were children abandoned by their parents who were taken in and raised within the gangster structure. Knowing no other life, the codes and rituals of the Yakuza were perfectly normal to them. The tradition of removing finger joints (known as 'yubitsume') as a punishment for offence, betrayal or failure, was widespread in Yakuza gangs and popularized in movies, which mixed with the tattoos was a distinctive physical marker that someone was a gangster. The tradition supposedly emerged from an ancient practice designed to weaken a samurai's sword hand, thus making him increasingly incapable of fighting as an individual and so becoming more reliant on the wider group. A 1993 survey estimated that up to 45 per cent of all Yakuza members were missing at least one finger joint. More extreme punishments would see recalcitrant gangsters shamed into 'seppuku' or ritual suicide by disembowelment.

Although Yakuza membership had been in decline since an anti-gangster decree from the Japanese government in 1992, there are still over 100,000 members active in three main groups (which contain within them many regional sub-groupings). The biggest, with over 50 per cent of all Yakuza personnel, is the Yamaguchi-gumi, made up of around 850 individual family 'clans'. Based in Kobe, it operates across Asia and the United States and is headed by the crime lord Shinobu Tsukasa, the sixth 'kumicho' or 'supreme Godfather' of the organization. Born in 1942 and now in his seventies, Tsukasa is the subject of international sanctions laid against him by the US administration of President Obama in 2012 which also hit three other international crime groups: Los Zetas of Mexico, the Camorra (the Neapolitan Mafia) of Italy, and the Brothers' Circle of Russia.

The second gang is the Sumiyoshi-kai, a confederation of smaller groups headed by Shigeo Nishiguchi, but with a more lax sense of control and hierarchy than other Yakuza gangs. Inagawa-kai is the third organization, made up of around 300 clans and largely based in the Tokyo area. It was one of the first to expand operations beyond Japan and is currently headed by Yoshio Tsunoda. Many other minor gangs join the top three as 'boryokudan' or groups designated by government as particularly harmful to society: there are twenty-two such criminal syndicates in all registered by the Japanese authorities, most dating back to before the Second World War. Where the 'pure' Mafia insisted upon Sicilian heritage (before Lucky Luciano accepted gangsters of Jewish origin like Meyer Lansky), the Yakuza are open to 'foreigners', with around 10 per cent of the overall membership made up of gangsters of Korean origin.

Yakuza activities incorporate the vast majority of those pursued by virtually all organized criminal gangs: extortion, prostitution, the narcotics trade and money laundering, although straightforward theft is frowned upon as being unworthy of Yakuza members. Many Yakuza organizations are almost semi-legitimate, with some for example getting involved in local community relief efforts following the Kobe earthquake of 1995. One uniquely Japanese form of protectionism is for Yakuza members to buy stock in companies to give them access to stockholder meetings, then demand payment so that those meetings are not violently disrupted, an activity known as 'sōkaiya'. The blatant blackmailing of successful businessmen or public figures harks back to the early Italian gangsterism of the Black Hand gangs. Yamaguchi-gumi members are expressly forbidden from getting involved in drug trafficking, echoing Mob boss Frank Costello's desire to stay out of the drug business.

Yakuza funds are laundered through investments in legitimate companies, although few are as large as the purchase of US$255 million of shares of the Tokyo-Kyuko Electric Railway company made in 1989 by Susumu Ishii, then the oyabun of the Inagawa-kai Yakuza. According to the Japanese authorities, around fifty companies listed on the Japanese stock exchange have ties to organized crime groups, with a resolution made in 2008 to expel all those with Yakuza links. Land fraud is also a large part of current Yakuza activities. Bankers who make large loans (often under pressure) to Yakuza-linked groups or individuals generally do not expect to ever see their money repaid.

International connections have seen the Yakuza influence spread widely. In 1999, the Italian-American Bonanno Mafia family member Mickey Zaffarano was said to be involved in an international trade in pornography with Yakuza groups, while the transportation of women, especially from the Philippines, Eastern Europe and Asia, into Japan for the purposes of prostitution is widespread among Yakuza operating across international borders. Across decades, well-intentioned anti-Yakuza campaigns have been largely ineffective, thanks to the gangs right-wing political connections. In fact, some in power see the Yakuza as a force for the prevention of petty street-level crime, with Kobe declared to be one of Japan's safest cities due to Yakuza influence.

In the United States, much Yakuza activity originates from the islands of Hawaii (due to its proximity to Japan), although they have spread not only into the mainland of the Western United States especially California, and the San Francisco Bay area, but also as far across the country as the old American gangster stamping grounds of Chicago and New York. Particularly American Yakuza traits are the trade in methamphetamine into the US and firearms back to Japan. Gambling parlours and brothels in Hawaii are largely Yakuza run.

In California, the Yakuza have made common cause with Chinese Triad gangs, as well as Vietnamese and Korean gangs, with the latter used by the former as violent 'muscle' for enforcement purposes when necessary. In New York, the Yakuza deal with the Mafia gangs by directing Japanese and other Eastern tourists to their gambling dens in return for the payment of 'finder fees'. The FBI class the Yakuza as one of the key sources of money-laundering operations in the United States.

The links between ancient 'friendly societies' or mutual

protection groups, whether it is the Italian or American Mafia, the Chinese Triads or the Japanese Yakuza, are clear. From supportive beginnings among particular ethnic groups, they lost their social or political purposes to become purely criminal enterprises, although still driven by ideas of group loyalty and exclusivity. Eventually, with the spread of such groups internationally throughout the twentieth century, not only did they co-operate within themselves at city or region level, but they formed international pacts and agreements to their mutual benefit. Always, however, the aim was the same: the enrichment and advancement – socially and often politically – of their unique group at the expense of all others.

21

AUSTRALIA: NED KELLY

Edward 'Ned' Kelly was an Australian outlaw (or bush-ranger) on a par with the likes of Billy the Kid or Butch and Sundance in America's Old West: he is one of the figures who set the criminal template for later gangsters, and his tale brings this epic story of the world's gangsters full circle, back to the mid-1800s. His exploits, like those of his American counterparts and near-contemporaries, live on as he is still the subject of books, movies and controversy to this day, over 130 years since he was hanged for his crimes.

Kelly appears to have been born in 1855 in Victoria, Australia to Irish immigrant parents. His father, John 'Red' Kelly had been born in Tipperary, Ireland in 1820 and transported to Tasmania in 1841 as a criminal exile for the theft of a pair of pigs, although the Victoria Royal Commission claimed his crime had been to shoot at his landlord, a claim called 'an unwarrantable piece of propaganda' by an early Kelly biographer.

Freed in 1848 when his sentence expired, John Kelly settled in Victoria, working as a carpenter on a farm. His exploits in searching for gold raised enough funds for him to buy his own homestead – 21 acres for £70 – and by the age of thirty he'd married Ellen Quinn, the eighteen-year-old daughter of his employer. Edward – known as 'Ned' – was born in Beveridge, just north of Melbourne, where his father had built the family a timber cottage. Ned managed well enough at basic schooling, which took place in the local Roman Catholic Church, easily learning to read and write. He became something of a local hero when he saved another boy from drowning at the age of ten in 1865. He was rewarded by the family with a green silk sash, which he was wearing under his armour on the day he was killed.

Ned's father John had sold up the farm in 1864 for £80. The family moved north to Avenel, but John Kelly returned to his earlier criminal ways. He was captured and jailed for cattle rustling in 1865, because he could not pay the £25 fine, and died due to alcoholism (then called 'dropsy') the following year soon after his release. That left Ned, his mother and his many siblings; Ned had left school at twelve to contribute to the support of the now fatherless family.

The family were often suspected of cattle and horse theft, thanks to John Kelly's prior activities, although nothing was ever proven. Among the bush workers, unbranded cattle were treated as currency to be captured and traded. Ned Kelly would later claim to have stolen over 250 horses as a young lad, and although his father had been equally guilty, he held a long-lasting grievance with the police over his father's arrest. During his short life of just twenty-five years, Ned Kelly continued to believe that the treatment of his father while in jail had harmed his health and led to his early death.

Ned's first arrest had come at the age of fourteen in 1869, for assault and robbery against a Chinese trader from a nearby settlement. An altercation turned violent when Kelly beat the man with his own bamboo stick after he supposedly abused Kelly's sister when requesting a drink of water. Ned was locked up overnight, and appeared in court the next morning, but was then held in jail for several days while the court sought a translator for the victim. With no translator proving to be available, the charges were dropped and Ned was finally freed. The police certainly did harass the Kelly family, although they had enough reason to do so. It would take a total of eighteen charges to be laid against family members before Ned himself was declared an outlaw.

Tall and physically imposing, Ned Kelly appeared older than his fifteen years, with many of those whom he encountered assuming him to be nearer twenty years of age rather than a teenager. He would use this physicality to his advantage, both in controlling his trio of gang members and in his personal encounters with the forces of law enforcement, being consistently unwilling to submit to arrest or detention without putting up a strenuous fight.

Kelly's association with outlaw bushranger Harry Power began in 1870 and would bring him nothing but trouble. In March 1870 the pair robbed a man, and in May that same year they were charged, although Ned's charges were dropped as he could not be positively identified. This happened repeatedly, suggesting that the police were targeting Kelly (although in fact he was guilty; just lucky to escape identification three times in a row). The police finally claimed Ned did match the suspect's description, and he was locked up for a month in Melbourne, with no evidence offered and no trial held. Whether, as some suspect, Kelly's relatives intimidated witnesses so they failed to speak out, or whether Kelly was simply being victimized by the police again, he was freed. When Power was subsequently arrested, the suspicion was that Kelly had turned him in, resulting in exclusion by his own community. In desperation, he wrote to his police tormentors asking them to confirm he had nothing to do with Power's arrest. It turned out that Kelly's uncle Jack Lloyd had informed on Power and been rewarded with a payment of £500.

Ned Kelly was, however, locked up again before the end of the year thanks to his involvement in a dispute with a local hawker. He was sentenced to three months' hard labour, further fuelling his resentment of the police and authority figures in general. Later, having borrowed a horse, Kelly was again arrested for having stolen the animal, but was only subdued after a violent encounter with the arresting officer that saw the cop needing nine stitches to his head. Kelly maintained he did not know the horse had been stolen, but was sentenced to three years' imprisonment with hard labour for 'feloniously receiving a horse'. The actual horse thief from whom Kelly had borrowed the stolen horse was only sentenced to eighteen months behind bars, further adding to Kelly's growing persecution complex.

While Ned was locked up, his younger brothers Jim (aged twelve) and Dan (aged ten) had been the continued subject of police harassment, with charges of riding a horse that did not belong to them getting the two boys a night in the cells. Victoria's law-enforcement officers were determined to keep the Kelly clan under their thumb, even before they'd become properly dangerous. Jim Kelly was again arrested aged fourteen, and given a five-year sentence for stealing cattle while the receiver of the stolen goods was released a free man as he was a 'gentleman'. Jim was again sentenced to a decade behind bars from 1877 for stealing horses, before going straight and living a respectable life.

Released in 1874, Ned Kelly tracked down the horse thief who'd sent him to jail and fought and won a bare-knuckle boxing match with him to settle the score. A famous photograph of the then nineteen-year-old Kelly in a boxing pose was taken at this time. He went on to work for two years in the timber trade, before joining his stepfather (his mother having remarried) in the cattle-rustling business once more. Ned and his brother Dan had gone into hiding following more police attention, uniting with Joe Byrne and Steve Hart, two sympathetic outlaws also wanted for horse stealing.

In 1877 the police – who'd been on the constant look out for Ned and Dan Kelly – again had reason to arrest Ned who had been found drunk in charge of a horse. Locked up overnight, he was being escorted by four policemen the following morning when he escaped. The police gave chase and got into a violent confrontation with Kelly in a shoemaker's shop in which he'd attempted to seek refuge. Onlookers complained of the actions of the police, and so violent in his actions was the arresting Constable Lonigan that Kelly threatened to shoot him dead if he ever had the chance.

In April 1878, the Kelly family fell foul of Police Constable Alexander Fitzpatrick who claimed they tried to kill him when he went to the Kelly home to arrest Dan. Although it seems likely that Ned Kelly was not even at the family home, Fitzpatrick, an unreliable drunk later dismissed from the police for drunkenness and perjury, claimed he'd been shot by the outlaw. Ned's mother, his brother-in-law and a neighbour were all arrested and tried for attempted murder. They were convicted and imprisoned for several years, while a £100 bounty was put on the heads of the wanted outlaws Ned and Dan Kelly.

This was the final injustice for Ned Kelly. With his mother in jail on a trumped-up charge, he took to the bush full time in the company of Dan Kelly, as well as Joe Byrne and Steve Hart. In October 1878, the police set off in pursuit of the outlaws determined to bring them in. The 'Kelly Gang' were discovered hiding out at a timber camp in Stringybank Creek, a heavily wooded area. It appears that the police, having located the camp, were surprised by the early return of the gang. A shoot-out ensued,

during which Ned Kelly fulfilled his promise by shooting thirty-seven-year-old Constable Lonigan in the head.
His partner, Constable McIntyre, surrendered to the gang,
but when his colleagues Sergeant Kennedy and Constable
Scanlon (sometimes 'Scanlan') arrived they provoked a
new gunfight. Kelly swiftly killed thirty-three-year-old
Scanlon and fatally wounded Kennedy. He later claimed
to have shot Kennedy a second time as an 'act of mercy'
to put him out of his misery. In the melee, McIntyre managed to escape on horseback to report the killings to the
authorities.

The Kelly Gang were now true outlaws – fulfilling the
image the police already held of them – with the death of
three officers on their heads. On 15 November 1878 the
government of Victoria issued a formal 'proclamation of
outlawry' against Kelly and his associates, offering cash
rewards of £500 for each gang member captured dead or
alive. The 'Felons Apprehension Act' made it lawful for
anyone, whether licensed or not, to shoot and kill anyone
determined officially to be an outlaw – neither arrest nor
trial were required.

Early that December the gang hid out in a sheep station at Faithfull's Creek, taking the twenty-two people
who lived and worked there hostage by locking them in a
store room. Byrne remained to guard the hostages, while
the other three went to nearby Euroa where they robbed
the National Bank, escaping with £2,000 in notes and gold.
That act saw the rewards on each of their heads doubled to
£1,000, dead or alive, and a round-up of as many of Kelly's
friends and family as could be found took place in January
1879 – they were held without charge for up to three months
before public condemnation forced their release.

In early-February 1879, the Kelly gang struck again, robbing a bank in Jerilderie, New South Wales, where they had
locked up two policemen and occupied the police station
over the weekend, before hitting the Bank of New South

Wales on the Monday morning for in excess of another £2,000 in notes and coins. In the process, they rounded up and held hostage up to sixty people in the Royal Hotel next door – the outlaws even had drinks with their captives. Kelly told the hostages his tale of police persecution, gaining some sympathy from the crowd. In an echo of the actions of Jessie James in the United States, Ned Kelly issued a more than 7,000-word manifesto to a bank teller, explaining and justifying his conduct. A further twenty-page letter had been posted to a member of parliament at the end of 1878 outlining Ned Kelly's grievances, but only an extract was ever published. The so-called 'Jerilderie Letter' was not published in full until 1930, long after Kelly and his gang were all dead.

By June 1880, all the warrants relating to the Kelly Gang had expired, along with any rewards offered. Arriving on Aaron Sherritt's farm in an area known as The Woolhead, the gang were planning to rob a nearby bank in Benalla, where Kelly also hoped to cause trouble for the hated police in the town of Glenrowan. Sherritt, a one-time friend of gang member Joe Byrne, was a police informer who had been helping trackers follow the Kelly gang. Byrne wanted revenge, and promptly shot Sherritt dead in his doorway, while the four armed policemen assigned to guard him reportedly hid in a back room.

Later in Glenrowan, the Kelly gang took possession of the local hotel holding all the residents captive – there were around fifty. There, Ned and his gang members donned specially-made armour, skilfully constructed from farming equipment and metal pieces. They expected a response to the killing of Sherritt from the local police, and were prepared to defend themselves. The armour weighed about 44 kilos, and while it left the legs unprotected, jerry-rigged helmets covered the gang members' heads and protected them from flying bullets. Police reinforcements arrived at Glenrowan by train from Melbourne, although they had to

disembark short of the line's end as Kelly and the gang had
wrecked the rail tracks in a bid to stop the reinforcements.

When the police did arrive, there followed a fifteen-
minute shoot-out with the Kelly gang. A police super-
intendent was injured. The resulting stand-off lasted all
night, with the gang holed up in the hotel with their hostages. Intermittent firing resumed from both sides with
first light. Eventually, the hostages were allowed to leave in
small groups, which were carefully checked to ensure the
Kelly gang weren't attempting to escape in disguise. While
this was going on, Ned Kelly had made his way out the
back of the hotel and into the bush.

Kelly then brought the fight back to the police, accosting
them from their rear, firing his weapons and hiding behind
trees to avoid the return fire. Three policemen charged at
Kelly firing their weapons, only to realize they were ineffective against the gangster's improvised armour. Only one
among them – Sergeant Steele – understood the limitations
of Kelly's armour and began firing at the outlaw's unprotected legs. Steele brought Ned Kelly to his knees with two
shots. He was seized when trying to fire his gun again –
Kelly had been wounded in his left foot, right hand, left
arm, and twice in his groin area, but no bullets had pen-
etrated his armour.

Inside the hotel, the three remaining gang members
were still holding out, as Ned Kelly's wounds were being
treated by a doctor. Byrne had been fatally wounded, while
Steve Hart and Dan Kelly continued to trade volleys with
the police. By 10 a.m., a white flag or handkerchief was
displayed and the final remaining hostages released. The
building was then deliberately set alight by the police,
in the hope of driving the remaining outlaws out. When
no one emerged, the vicar-general of Western Australia,
Father Gibney, entered the building. He discovered the
dead bodies of Steve Hart, aged twenty-one, and Dan Kelly,
aged nineteen. They had apparently killed each other in a

suicide pact. A final wounded hostage was evacuated, but died shortly thereafter. Other civilians had been injured or killed in the fracas, including children. Joe Byrne's body was retrieved and strung up on display in Benalla as a warning to others, before being interred in an unmarked grave by the police force.

Ned Kelly survived his gang and was put on trial in October 1880 in Melbourne. He was charged with the murders of the three policemen – Lonigan, Scanlon and Kennedy – as well as three bank robberies, the murder of Aaron Sherritt, and resistance to the police at Glenrowan, plus a host of other more minor charges. He was convicted, and sentenced to death, hanging on 11 November 1880 at the Melbourne jail. Ned Kelly's last words were said to be inaudible, but his 'Jerilderie Letter' survived him and explained much of his motivation. Driven to banditry and crime by police persecution, Ned Kelly – Australia's own Public Enemy Number One – had turned gangster in self-defence.

Kelly's remains were said to have been disposed of within the walls of Melbourne jail, although it was rumoured that police had used his skull as a paperweight for some time. When the jail was closed and demolished in 1929, grave robbers were said to have made off with some of what they believed to have been Kelly's skeleton. Kelly's skull, retained by the police into the 1930s, was then lost and finally rediscovered in an old safe in 1952. It was stolen from a Melbourne jail museum display in 1978. Kelly's true remains were recovered in 2011 from a prison mass grave site, identified after being checked against the DNA of related descendants. In 2013, the remains of Ned Kelly were finally laid to rest in a proper church graveyard, close to the burial site of his mother. His skull remains missing.

Modern gangsters Down Under
Although he is by far the best known, there have been a few other more recent Australian gangsters of note

besides Ned Kelly. Among them were George Freeman, a Sydney gambler and illegal casino operator involved in the drug trade in the 1970s and 1980s, who died in 1990 aged fifty-five of asthma after surviving an attempt on his life in 1979. There was also Lenny McPherson, who controlled organized crime in the Sydney area for several decades, alongside the so-called 'Mr Sin', Abe Saffron, and Freeman. McPherson's fields included illegal alcohol sales, gambling, extortion rackets, prostitution, drug dealing and robbery. By the time he reached his thirties in the 1950s, McPherson had taken to modelling himself directly on Chicago gangster Al Capone, although that did not extend to the Mafia vow of silence, as he also turned informer, keen to help the police put away his gangster rivals. He reportedly murdered at least five rivals in his rise to power over Sydney's gangland, and he even built up direct contacts with the Chicago Mafia over a poker machine racket. Lenny McPherson was jailed in the 1990s for threatening a 'business rival', and died in jail due to a heart attack in 1996, aged seventy-five.

Abraham 'Abe' Saffron lived to a similar old age, dying at eighty-six in 2006. He was a Kings Cross, Sydney nightclub owner and property developer who became a major organized crime figure through trafficking in stolen goods and illegal drugs, before expanding into prostitution, extortion and other illegal activities. As well as 'Mr Sin' he was also variously dubbed the 'Mr Big' of Australian crime, or the 'Boss of the Cross' after the red-light area of Sydney he dominated. Corruption of police officers and bribery of politicians kept Saffron out of jail, until public exposure in the 1980s led to a conviction in 1987 for tax evasion – the rap the US authorities had used to finally nail Al Capone.

Jason Moran, born in Melbourne, Victoria in 1967, was the leader of Australia's Moran crime family, until his death at the age of thirty-five in 2003. Like 'Scarface' Al

Capone, Moran had a long scar along the side of his face. A rising drug dealer in Melbourne, Moran shot and wounded rival gangster Carl Williams during an argument over an unpaid debt in 1999. The result was a long-running gang war between the Moran and the Williams families and a wider Melbourne gangland war, resulting in the deaths of almost forty people. The matriarch of the Moran family, Judy, lost her husband Lewis, two sons Jason and Mark, and brother-in-law Des (whose murder she was later convicted of) to the underworld feud that largely consisted of tit-for-tat hits between gangsters. Carl Williams was held responsible for commissioning the murders of Mark Moran, Jason Moran and Lewis Moran, among others. He, in turn, died of a head injury incurred while in the prison gym when he was struck with an exercise bike by another prisoner. The exploits of the Moran clan provided the basis for the controversial thirteen-episode Australian television drama series *Underbelly* (2008).

Perhaps Australia's only other gangster to rival the notoriety of outlaw Ned Kelly was Mark 'Chopper' Read. He and his 'Overcoat Gang', named after their trademark clothing worn in weather foul or fair, robbed drug dealers and tortured fellow gangsters using blowtorches and bolt cutters to raise 'protection money' for themselves. Read spent time in jail and was later ambushed by members of his own gang, who felt he'd turned 'crazy' after chopping off his own ears in an attempt to escape jail on mental health grounds.

In later memoirs, Read claimed to have killed nearly twenty people, and having attempted to murder a dozen more during his thirty-year career in crime. He was the rival of younger fellow gangster Alphonse Gangitano, known as the Black Prince of Lygon Street after the suburb of Melbourne where he operated, who was assassinated in 1998 at the age of forty. Read was able to turn his notoriety as a gangster into a second career as an author of crime fiction and as a television personality. He was the subject of the 2000 film *Chopper* that starred Eric Bana. Read himself died of liver cancer in October 2008, aged fifty-eight.

Gangsters fought the law, and often the law won, but not always. The heads of various crime organizations in America's major cities in the 1930s and 1940s mainly thrived. They were able to maintain lavish lifestyles, certainly in comparison with most other immigrants to the country, and indulge their every whim. The price paid was eternal vigilance, constant danger and the imminent threat of death (in a shoot-out with the law, or other gangsters) or imprisonment. When gangsters were brought down, it was often for something innocuous, such as Al Capone's conviction for tax evasion, rather than the bank robberies, bootlegging or murders they were actually responsible for.

While some fell early, thanks to the police or the gun, certain others lived on and prospered – Meyer Lansky and Frank Costello were just two who made the most of their lives of crime. The movies of the 1930s gave the public an impossibly glamorous image of the gangsters, although just about all of them ended with the anti-hero getting his comeuppance: in each of *The Public Enemy* (1931), *Little Caesar* (1931) and *Scarface* (1932), James Cagney, Edward G. Robinson and Paul Muni are dead by the end of the picture [see chapter 22]. So it was with many of the real-world gangsters who had a spectacular rise and just as spectacular a fall in many cases, such as John Dillinger, Bugsy Siegel or Bonnie and Clyde, who each met with a hail of bullets.

The 1950s official inquiries revealed to the American people the existence of 'the Mafia', organized crime groups that prospered across the country. Across the world, from South America to Britain, Europe and the Far East, other nations were dealing with their own organized crime problems, networks that produced anti-heroes – like Pablo Escobar – as well as damaging the economies of whole countries. Although organized crime would mutate and change, becoming ever more sophisticated and technological, its origins among the largely Italian immigrants to America who came of age in the 1920s and 1930s remain fascinating to us today.

The real gangsters were brutal, ruthless criminals who enriched themselves and their friends at the expense of others and wider society as a whole. Despite that, people today still have a romanticized, almost glamorized view of the gangsters. They are anti-heroes for a time when America's rulers – presidents, senators and congressmen – failed the people, resulting in the Great Depression of the 1930s. Without that, and the ill-fated experiment of Prohibition, the classic gangster might never have existed as he is now known. There would always have been organized crime, of course, but that unique moment in time created a cultural figure that has transcended the time and place of its origins. Gangsters couldn't be contained, and so lived on as figures of fantasy, as much as of fact. That's why audiences enjoy gangster movies today, new or old, and can endlessly relive the lives of the real gangsters.

PART FIVE: FILM AND TELEVISION GANGSTERS

22

GANGSTERS ON SCREEN

Since the beginnings of cinema there have always been gangster films. Entire books have been dedicated to the subject, so all that's possible here is a summary of the high points and important developments in the field. What's interesting is the places where from the beginning, real gangsters and their cinematic counterparts have crossed over, either in disguised portrayals or, later, in direct bio-pics of various gangster luminaries. Gangsters have been involved in the production of movies, while some gangster movies have had a dramatic impact on the box office and culture, or are noteworthy because of the different approach they've taken to one of the biggest of all film genres.

Early movies charted the activities of criminals, as in *The Burglar on the Roof* (1898) and *How They Rob Men in Chicago* (1900), but they were often semi-documentary films almost devoid of story. The 1903 silent short (only ten minutes) *The Great Train Robbery*, written and directed by

movie pioneer Edwin S. Porter, features an arresting final
shot in which the leader of the bandits (Justus D. Barnes)
points his gun out of the cinema screen and fires directly
at the viewing audience. The gangsters are coming, and the
audience is their target.

New York's real-life gangsters started out in the Five Point
district a few decades before *The Great Train Robbery* was
released – a period chronicled in Martin Scorsese's *Gangs
of New York* (2002) – one of the director's many gangster
pictures, made between *Casino* (1995) and *The Departed*
(2006). Its setting of the mid to late 1800s chronicles the
time before the 1920s gangsters' heyday of Prohibition, an
area few other gangster films have ever explored. Scorsese
drew upon Herbert Asbury's *The Gangs of New York:
An Informal History of the Underworld* (1928), which
he'd read in 1970 before making his first gangster movie,
Mean Streets (1973). Especially praised for its attention to
historical accuracy, *Gangs of New York* starred Daniel
Day-Lewis as crime lord Bill 'The Butcher' Cutting and
Leonardo DiCaprio as Amsterdam Vallon, a member of
Cutting's gang whose father he killed. Vallon is biding his
time before he achieves the one thing more important to
gangsters than criminal success: revenge. The gangster
movie has been a favourite genre of the Italian-American
Scorsese, which include *Goodfellas* (1990), based on the
self-aggrandizing autobiography of the Lucchese family
associate Henry Hill (played with verve by Ray Liotta).

In contrast to *Gangs of New York*, one of the earliest gangster films celebrated a particular proto-gangster.
The Story of the Kelly Gang (1906) featured Frank Mills
as Australian outlaw Ned Kelly, and was written and
directed by Charles Tait. It was released just over a quarter
of a century after Kelly's death, and was the first of many
chronicling his downfall. At an hour in length, it was the
longest narrative film yet made and is often considered the
world's first feature-length film.

The oldest surviving American gangster movie is *The Black Hand* (1906), based upon the real life exploits of the Mano Negra Italian blackmail gangs in New York and Chicago. It makes for an interesting illustration of how such gangs may have operated, from nearer the time they were actually active, and it includes some great New York street footage with deep snow piled high against the sidewalks. A butcher is threatened, and his refusal to pay up leads to his daughter being kidnapped by the gang – it's perhaps the first film to explicitly depict organized crime rather than just opportunistic criminals.

The first true American gangster film was probably *The Musketeers of Pig Alley* (1912), written and directed by D. W. Griffith. Partly shot on location in New York City (in what remained of the Five Points district) as well as in studios in Fort Lee, New Jersey, the movie used real life gang members, giving it extra verisimilitude. The seventeen-minute short follows a struggling young couple after the husband is robbed in the street and they find themselves in the middle of a feud between two gangsters. It's a slight piece, more interesting for its advances in filmic technique than its narrative. However, it is widely regarded as the first genuine gangster film: it grew out of the increasing press coverage given to revelations about police corruption and gangster activities on New York's Lower East Side, where some of the film was shot. The film's gangster, nicknamed 'The Snapper Kid', is portrayed sympathetically as someone who has joined the gang to ensure his own survival on the street. It's the kind of character, perhaps a little older and a little wiser, who would become central to the genre.

Certain directors would become associated with the 1930s boom in gangster movies, key among them Raoul Walsh, director of *Regeneration* (1915), the first full-length American gangster feature film. It tells of a dispossessed orphan who rises through the ranks of the Mob, until his love for a woman sees him change his ways. *Regeneration* was one of the first films to present the rise and fall of a gangster within his criminal milieu as central to the story, but this one doesn't end with his death. Like *The Musketeers of Pig Alley*, real locations and real-life gangsters, prostitutes and homeless people helped give the film dramatic colour. The mix of social realism and crime featured in *Regeneration* would be central to the later crusading Warner Bros. gangster pictures. Walsh would go on to helm various gangster movies, including *The Bowery* (1933), *The Roaring Twenties* (1939) and *High Sierra* (1941) – probably the last true gangster movie before the dawn of film noir in the post-war 1940s – as well as *White Heat* (1949), the classic genre's final lament.

The melodrama *Underworld* (1927), directed by Josef von Sternberg, is another film with a legitimate claim to being one of the first gangster movies, but it is more notable as screenplay writer Ben Hecht's first contribution to a genre he would do much to shape. A Chicago newspaper reporter, Hecht brought his experience chronicling the criminal underworld to his screenplay, which is full of snappy slang and violent events. Hecht would go on to write *Scarface* (1932), a barely-disguised retelling of the Al Capone story – the use of a neon billboard reading 'The World is Yours' links both movies. Moving away from the gritty realism of either *The Musketeers of Pig Alley* or *Regeneration*, *Underworld* focuses on the relationships and jealousies between individual gangsters, and their connections with law enforcement. A key sequence is the 'gangsters' ball', described in an inter-title as the 'Devil's carnival'.

Another Chicago newspaperman wrote *The Racket* (1928), which depicts the operation of corrupt city government in co-operation with organized crime and that was nominated for the first ever Oscars. The central mobster, Nick Scarsi (Louis Wolheim), is a barely disguised Capone figure, while Chicago's corrupt mayor 'Big Bill' Thompson is depicted as 'The Old Man', an authority figure in the pay of gangsters. The film, and the play it was based on, were both banned in Chicago, perhaps because it threw too much light onto the city's situation. The film tells the clichéd story of the pursuit of a criminal by a dedicated cop – but this was one of the earliest times that story was seen, and it was therefore fresh. *The Racket* was the last of the notable silent-era proto-gangster movies: a revolution was coming that would not just change cinema but the very nature of the gangster movie.

The coming of sound would be the making of the gangster film: at last audiences could hear the pithy dialogue, but more especially the roar of the Tommy guns, as yet another villain took a tumble in a rain-drenched street. The noises of the city, the vehicles, crowds and sirens were all important and new, but most important was the fact that the gangsters could now be heard. Warner Bros., the studio most closely associated with the wave of classic gangster films of the 1930s, ripped their stories from the headlines of the day, making central characters out of the men on the make during the era of Prohibition, mixing social realism with the rat-a-tat-tat of frequent gunfire. In the first years of the Depression, anti-heroes who fought against the system became cinema's newest heroes. Between the Wall Street Crash of 1929, the start of the Depression and the death of John Dillinger in 1934, the film gangster would rule the cinema screens of America and beyond.

The starting point of the classic 1930s gangster film cycle is Mervyn LeRoy's *Little Caesar* (1931), which made a star of Edward G. Robinson. Adapted from a novel by W.R. Burnett, it was another disguised Capone-inspired story, although it offered the fatal downfall for Robinson's crime kingpin Rico that Capone never had. Robinson's passing resemblance to the real-life gangster helped sell

Little Caesar as a torn-from-the-headlines tale. Rico's rise to the top, in a shadow world parody of the traditional American rags-to-riches story, and equally dramatic fall, would provide the template for most other movies in the growing genre that followed.

The second Hollywood star created by the gangster movies was James Cagney, unforgettable in *The Public Enemy* (1931). William Wellman's film followed Cagney's Tom Powers, whose rise from the streets to the top of gangland is both the making of him and the death of him. Cagney, although past thirty, brought a youthful vibrancy to the charming hoodlum, a gangster the audience could identify with. These movies were told from the gangster's point of view – it was their world and audiences got to live in it. Famous for Cagney pushing a watermelon in Mae Clarke's face, the film was a box office hit, sealing the popular image of the movie gangster. It created the association of the cinematic gangster with the gang war montage, featuring machine-gun fire and spinning newspaper headlines, dramatic drive-by shootings, bombings and assassinations, culminating in scenes of baffled policeman unable to curb the gangster menace.

Ben Hecht's scripting double bill of *The Beast of the City* (1932) and *Scarface* (1932) provided the model for almost all subsequent gangster movies. Charles Brabin's movie attempted to redress the balance by putting the cops' side of the gangster versus the law story, with Walter Huston as a dedicated police chief who has to become a vigilante to rid his city of the 'beasts' of crime. *Scarface* – subtitled *The Shame of a Nation* in a bid to stay on the right side of the movie censors – is clearly based upon the life and times of the gangsters' own gangster, Al Capone. Paul Muni played Tony Camonte, the ruthless gangster out to wipe out his competition, who is particularly excited by the possibilities of the new Tommy gun. Directed by Howard Hawks and produced by Howard Hughes, *Scarface* features a number

of characters based upon real life Chicago gangland per-
sonalities – including 'Big Jim' Colosimo, Dion O'Banion,
Hymie Weiss, and the St Valentine's Day Massacre of 1929.

Stylishly directed, drawing upon surrealism and
European expressionism for much of its effect, *Scarface*
features a repeated X motif throughout, most often when
someone is killed on or off screen, echoing Camonte's own
X-shaped facial scar. The X pops up everywhere, created
by shadows and lights, or from the way objects are juxta-
posed. It is especially noticeable in the St Valentine's Day
Massacre scene, where a series of seven Xs are lined up,
just like the seven mobsters about to hear the roar of the
'Chicago Typewriter'. The most amusing is perhaps the X
mark made on a bowling alley scorecard just before several gangsters, including Boris Karloff, get rubbed out. It
was a flourish that Martin Scorsese paid homage to in his
later gangster movie *The Departed* (2006), where the background X image reappears in abundance.

When working on *Scarface*, Hecht was supposedly visited by mobsters on behalf of Capone complaining about
the main character's resemblance to their boss. Hecht
claimed that wasn't the case, but the hoods asked him if
that was so, why was it called *Scarface*? 'If we call the movie
Scarface, people will think it's about Capone and come to
see it,' Hecht explained to the none-too-bright hoodlums.
'It's part of the racket we call show business.' Satisfied with
that, they left Hecht alone.

Capone eventually obtained a print of the film, declaring
it to be a personal favourite. The movie faced trouble with
the censors, with critics claiming it glorified the gangster
lifestyle. As a result, in the middle there's a clumsily added
scene in a newspaper editor's office in which various anti-
gangster views are put forward – it's heavy handed and
completely against the style of the movie, and wasn't shot
by Hawks. An alternate ending was also made, in which
Camonte (played by doubles, not Muni) doesn't die in a

hail of bullets but is captured, faces a trial, and is then put to death by the state. The film featured George Raft, who was connected to Los Angeles mobster Mickey Cohen, in a co-starring role. *Scarface* was loosely remade and updated, set in Cuba and Miami, by Brian De Palma in 1983 starring Al Pacino as drug lord Tony Montana.

Although in effect from 1930 onwards, it wouldn't be until the mid-1930s that the Motion Picture Production Code rules would be heavily enforced, with gangster movies the first high-profile casualties. Although *Little Caesar*, *The Public Enemy*, and *Scarface* all carried textual warnings at their openings, and by the end all three of the main protagonists were dead, no longer would the gangster as romantic hero be tolerated. Thanks to such censorship, such characters always had to get their comeuppance – rare was the 1930s movie gangster who hadn't fallen under a hail of bullets by the final scene.

The studios repurposed their gangster stars, Cagney and Robinson, as lawmen and carried on with the same mix of crime, violence and action, although from the other side of the legal divide. Perhaps the original version of the gangster picture died with *Manhattan Melodrama* (1934), the film that John Dillinger watched just before he was gunned down by Melvin Purvis and his 'G-men' of the FBI. What followed was Cagney as an FBI agent battling gangsters in *The G-Men* (1935), but all the generic elements of *Scarface* and the other movies remained intact, despite the Production Code.

Now the heroes were lawmen, or special agents under-cover in the world of gangsters, as with Edward G. Robinson in *Bullets or Ballots* (1936), directed by William Keighley, or the gangsters were played for laughs, again with Robinson spoofing *Little Caesar*'s Rico Bandello as 'Remy Marco' in Lloyd Bacon's 1938 comedy *A Slight Case of Murder*. Another alternative was the prison pic-ture, in which the gangster battled for survival in jail, as in

San Quentin (1937), and innocent-man-in-jail drama *Each Dawn I Die* (1939), with Cagney and Raft. Sometimes, the focus would be from the female perspective of the gangster's life, as in the Bette Davis starring-witness drama *Marked Woman* (1937), which pushes the male roles into the background – a refreshing take on an otherwise macho genre.

In the later 1930s, Humphrey Bogart emerged as the new face of the cinematic gangster, playing the Dillinger-like Duke Mantee in *The Petrified Forest* (1936) and 'Baby Face' Martin in the brilliant social drama *Dead End* (1937). He'd co-star with Cagney in *Angels with Dirty Faces* (1938) in which Cagney's Rocky Sullivan goes to the electric chair faking his cowardice to serve as an example to the neighbourhood kids who look up to him. Bogart was in action beside Cagney again in *The Roaring Twenties* (1939), an effective recapitulation of all the classic gangster movies' greatest hits and a lament for a pre-Code lost age of crime and movie making. Bogart played another variation on Dillinger in *High Sierra* (1941), perhaps the last 'pure' gangster movie before the form mutated into post-war film noir. Both Robinson, as the washed up Johnny Rocco in *Key Largo* (1948), and Cagney, as the defiantly unhinged Cody Jarrett in *White Heat* (1949), each had one last significant swansong in the kind of roles that made them famous.

Critic Robert Warshow wrote of the 1930s movie gangster anti-hero: 'He appeals to that side of all of us which refuses to believe in the "normal" possibilities of happiness and achievement; the gangster is the "no" to that great American "yes" which is stamped so big over our official culture and yet has so little to do with the way we really feel about our lives.' The form would develop and change, but the gangster movie would leave its mark – always punctuated by the sound of the Tommy gun – on American cinema.

*   *   *

In the years after the post-war vogue for film noir, gangster bio-pics became popular again, but filmmakers were
no longer wary of using the protagonists' real names:
there was no need any more for a Rico Bandello or a
Tony Camonte, a simple Al Capone would do. Capone is
perhaps the gangster most often depicted in film and television, whether in disguise or under his own name. Two
films took his name as their titles, 1959's *Al Capone* starring Rod Steiger, and 1975's *Capone* starring Ben Gazzara.
Steiger had initially refused the role, fearing the script
romanticized the gangster, and only agreed to do it after
rewrites 'de-glamourized' the title character. Factually
based and fairly accurate, if broadly dramatic in Steiger's
performance, the 1959 film depicted Capone's rise under
the tutelage of Johnny Torrio. Other real-life gangsters
featured included Dion O'Banion, Hymie Weiss and Bugs
Moran. The documentary-style approach won the movie
plaudits from *Variety* as 'a tough, ruthless and generally
unsentimental account'. The movie prepared the way for
the success of *The Untouchables* (1959–63) on television,
in which Neville Brand played Capone in a handful of episodes (as he would again in the 1961 movie *The George Raft
Story*). The series focused on Robert Stack's overly heroic
Eliot Ness and his police squad rather than the gangsters.

The 1975 *Capone* was an altogether more fanciful low-
budget affair, produced by Roger Corman, with an early
role for Sylvester Stallone as Frank Nitti. Gazzara's Capone
won plaudits, however, and the film included Capone's
years in prison and suffering from syphilis, details most
bio-pics had a tendency to omit altogether. Filmmaker
and actor John Cassavetes (who played maverick detective
Johnny Staccato in his 1950s television series) played Frank
Yale.

Other movie Capones included Robert De Niro in
Brian De Palma's operatic *The Untouchables* (1987, loosely
based on the television series) that focused on Ness and his

crime busters; William Forsythe in the short-lived television revival of *The Untouchables* in 1993–4; and F. Murray Abraham in 1995's counter-factual *Dillinger and Capone* (a later Corman production), which featured Dillinger's brother killed in his place. Five years after the showdown at the Biograph Theatre, Dillinger (Martin Sheen) teams up with Capone to raid a secret vault. The most celebrated Al Capone in recent years has been British actor Stephen Graham in the TV series *Boardwalk Empire* (2010–14). Across its five years, the series featured many of the prime gangsters from the end of the First World War through to the later 1920s in a serious-minded drama.

Capone was just one of four gangster-themed movies produced by low-budget filmmaker Corman (who also made several other general crime movies), beginning with *Machine Gun Kelly* (1958) in which he gave Charles Bronson his first lead role. More explosive was Corman's exploitation movie *The St Valentine's Day Massacre* (1967), an event that also opened the classic Marilyn Monroe comedy *Some Like It Hot* (1959). Jason Robards featured in *The St Valentine's Day Massacre* as a wildly over-the-top Capone (replacing the 'undirectable' Orson Welles), while Ralph Meeker played rival gang leader, Bugs Moran. Bruce Dern was one of the victims, and an uncredited Jack Nicholson appeared as a minor gangster. The film was based on an earlier 1958 *Playhouse 90* television instalment called *Seven Against the Wall*, also written by screenwriter Harold Browne. The movie made No. 7 in a list produced by *Empire* magazine entitled 'The 20 Greatest Gangster Movies You've Never Seen (Probably)'. The fourth Corman gangster flick was *Bloody Mama* (1970), loosely based on the story of Ma Baker – played by an enthusiastic Shelley Winters – and her gangster sons (one of whom is Robert De Niro, pre-*Mean Streets*).

Other notable gangsters given the bio-pic treatment include *Baby Face Nelson* (1957), directed by Don Siegel and starring Mickey Rooney as 'Baby Face'. Budd Boetticher's *The Rise and Fall of Legs Diamond* (1960) dealt with a lesser known gangster, the Irish mobster Jack 'Legs' Diamond – the bootlegger and Arnold Rothstein protégé shot dead in December 1931 by Dutch Shultz – and is an effective, if somewhat bleak, exploitation movie. It was also the source for the 1988–9 theatre musical *Legs Diamond* that played on Broadway. Another Irish gangster, Vincent 'Mad Dog' Coll, was the subject of two movies entitled *Mad Dog Coll* in 1961 and 1992, played by John Chandler and Christopher Bradley respectively.

Leo Gordon had appeared as Dillinger in *Baby Face Nelson*, but the gangster headlined his own bio-pic in John Milius' *Dillinger* (1973) in which Warren Oates played a sympathetic version of the character as an anti-hero in a film that plays fast and loose with the facts. The first movie Dillinger had been Lawrence Tierney in the 1945 film, and Robert Conrad would follow Oates in 1979's *The Lady in Red*, featuring Pamela Sue Martin as the mystery woman who turned Dillinger in. A 1991 television movie also titled *Dillinger* saw later *NCIS* actor Mark Harmon star. Most recently, Michael Mann's *Public Enemies* (2009) starred Johnny Depp as a dapper Dillinger in an adaptation of Bryan Burrough's non-fiction book that chronicled the 1930s rural crime wave.

It took until the 1970s for an actor to portray Charles 'Lucky' Luciano on film: Angelo Infanti in *The Valachi Papers* (1972), based on the testimony of Mob informer Joseph Valachi. That opened the floodgates, with Luciano played by Gian Maria Volonté in *Lucky Luciano* (1973) and Joe Dallesandro taking the role in Francis Ford Coppola's murkily financed *The Cotton Club* (1984). Four competing Lucianos appeared in movies in 1991: Christian Slater in the boisterous if juvenile *Mobsters*; Bill Graham in Warren Beatty's classic *Bugsy*; Stanley Tucci in *Billy Bathgate*; and Robert Davi in the television movie *White Hot: The*

Mysterious Murder of Thelma Todd. Loni Anderson played Todd, and the TV movie pins the blame for her death firmly on Luciano (as did the source biography, Andy Edmonds' *Hot Toddy*). Other actors to have played Luciano include Billy Drago (*The Outfit*, 1993), Andy Garcia (*Hoodlum*, 1997), and Anthony LaPaglia in *Lansky*, a 1999 television movie. In *Boardwalk Empire*, Vincent Piazza played a mercurial Luciano.

Meyer Lansky has been depicted in a fair number of films, but other than the 1991 television movie *Lansky* he was never the title character. The primary depiction of Lansky came in *The Godfather* (1972) and *The Godfather Part II* (1974), in which Hyman Roth, played by Oscar-nominated Lee Strasberg, was closely modelled upon Lansky, including biographical details such as his involvement in Cuba and his attempt to take up residency in Israel. In 1991's *Bugsy*, with Warren Beatty as a sanitized Bugsy Siegel, Lansky was played by an Oscar-nominated Ben Kingsley. Mark Rydell, Patrick Dempsey and Dustin Hoffman all played versions of Lansky in *Havana* (1990), *Mobsters* (1991) and *The Lost City* (2005). A gangster based on Meyer Lansky appeared in *Once Upon a Time in America* (1984), played by James Woods. Various television shows also used Lansky or characters based upon him, usually in supporting roles. As well Warren Beatty's portrayal, Bugsy Siegel was re-imagined as Moe Greene in *The Godfather*, and in *Mobsters* was played by Richard Greico. In *Boardwalk Empire*, Anatol Yusef was Lansky, while Michael Zegen played Siegel. Perhaps one of the more obscure bio-pics of a real-life gangster was *Lepke* (1975), starring Tony Curtis as 'Lepke' Buchalter. It featured both Murder, Inc. and Buchalter's battles with crusading prosecutor Thomas Dewey.

There are several contenders for the position of America's best or most popular gangster movie, but prime among them are comedy-drama *Bonnie and Clyde* (1967), the first two movies in the overrated *The Godfather* trilogy (1972, 1974, 1990), Sergio Leone's stately *Once Upon A Time in America* (1984), and Scorsese's populist *Goodfellas* (1990) – all but the first featuring Robert De Niro. The top three movies in the American Film Institute's (AFI) gangster movie Top 10 are: *The Godfather* (#1), *Goodfellas* (#2), and *The Godfather Part II* (#3). The 1930s classics feature, with *White Heat* (#4), *Scarface* (#6), *The Public Enemy* (#8) and *Little Ceasar* (#9) all making the cut. The final three are *Bonnie and Clyde* (#5), Quentin Tarantino's *Pulp Fiction* (#7), and the 1983 Brian De Palma remake of *Scarface* (#10).

Between them, De Niro and Al Pacino are the modern equivalents of Edward G. Robinson and James Cagney, given their repeated appearances in gangster movies. They both appeared in *The Godfather*, and excluding those films mentioned in the AFI's Top 10 list, De Niro's gangster movies ranged from *Bloody Mama* via *Mean Streets* and *The Untouchables*, to his self-directed *A Bronx Tale* (1993), *Casino*, and his pairing with his Cagney, Al Pacino, on *Heat* (1995), with the actors playing characters on opposite sides of the law. He even appeared in the comedy gangster movies *Analyze This* (1999) and *Analyze That* (2002), and was uncredited as the gangster kingpin of *American Hustle* (2013). For his part, Pacino additionally featured in *Dick Tracy* (1990), the Brian De Palma-directed *Carlito's Way* (1993), *Donnie Brasco* (1997), *Ocean's Thirteen* (2007) and *Stand Up Guys* (2012), among others. Martin Scorsese plans to reunite De Niro and Pacino in *The Irishman*, about a mobster (De Niro) who confesses to killing missing union boss Jimmy Hoffa.

Quentin Tarantino's *Pulp Fiction* made the AFI list at #7, and he'd certainly brought new popularity to the gangster genre in the 1990s with his heist movie *Reservoir Dogs* (1992), which featured real-life gangster Eddie Bunker. However, it was the dynamic *Pulp Fiction* (1994) that really brought a new approach to the older elements of the gangster movie. Where some movies, like *Donnie Brasco*, several Scorsese movies and the Cohen brothers' *Miller's Crossing* (1990) got caught up in the minutia of Mob life, Tarantino breezed through that to focus on the characters caught up in the lives of mobsters. It was a refreshing approach, part of a widening of the genre in the 1990s.

There had always been black gangsters, but beyond the 'blaxploitation' craze of the 1970s there were few black-focused gangster films until the 1990s. Both *Boyz N the Hood* (1991, an African-American version of Scorsese's *Mean Streets*) and *New Jack City* (1991) told the classic rise-and-fall tale through a new filter – a clip from the end of *Scarface* features in *New Jack City*, provoking mirth. Others would follow, such as *Juice* (1992) and *Menace II Society* (1993), but Ridley Scott's *American Gangster* (2007), starring Denzel Washington and telling the true story of drug smuggler Frank Lucas, was the only black-driven gangster film that broke into the American mainstream.

Beyond that, there have been a number of hard-to-classify oddball gangster films, ranging from gangland musical *West Side Story* (1961) to child cast (including Jodie Foster) British musical *Bugsy Malone* (1976). Two very different gangster films have been inspired by comic strips: *Dick Tracy* (1990) and *The Road to Perdition* (2002). Playing up the colourful presentation of the newspaper strips from 1931, *Dick Tracy* starred and was directed by Warren Beatty (in between *Bonnie and Clyde* and *Bugsy*). It followed earlier Dick Tracy serials, B-movies and animated cartoons, but proved to be a faithful encapsulation of Chester Gould's original. In stark contrast, *The Road to Perdition*, based on a graphic novel by Max Allan Collins, starred Tom Hanks and Paul Newman in a moving father–son story wrapped up in a gangster film. The Sam Mendes directed film was packed with all the relevant gangster tropes, but somehow rose above them to create an underrated classic, notable for its silent, rain-drenched Tommy gun-packed climax. Its biggest success was in capturing the atmosphere and dynamics of the comic book page and the original 1930s gangster films together in a modern movie.

British cinema has not produced as many gangster movies as the American industry, but there have been some key films, especially during the late-1990s trend for 'geezer' gangsters. While crime was often a subject for British movies, gangsters rarely featured until the 1940s, partly due to censorship restrictions that meant realistic depictions of, for example, drug culture were impossible, but also because the classic gangster was considered a quintessentially American subject. Alfred Hitchcock's early British crime films paved the way for what is perhaps the first true British gangster movie, *Brighton Rock* (1947), based on a 1938 novel by Graham Greene, itself a response to American gangster movies.

Richard Attenborough reprised his West End stage role of Pinkie Brown, the young hoodlum who comes of age in the south coast town of Brighton. In classic gangster style, Pinkie is the gang muscle who takes over the leadership when the previous gang leader is killed by rivals. Pinkie then marries a young waitress named Rose (Carol Marsh) to prevent her testifying against him – but Rose herself is soon on Pinkie's growing hit list. The original Boulting Brothers production was remade by Rowan Joffé in 2011 with Sam Riley and Andrea Riseborough, as Rose. The original is a gothic-style gangster film, in which Attenborough's Pinkie is a morals-free monster, abusing all those around him.

Loosening censorship rules and the impact of *Brighton Rock* lead to a series of uniquely British neo-noir gangster movies such as war veteran turns gangster story *They Made Me a Fugitive* (1947), prostitution drama *Good Time Girl* (1948), Soho-set gang thriller *Noose* (1948), and *Night and the City* (1950), starring Richard Widmark. By the

1950s, though, the genre incorporated comedy as in the Ealing classics *The Lavender Hill Mob* (1951), starring Alec Guinness as a bank clerk plotting the perfect heist, and *The Ladykillers* (1955), in which a gang of criminals come up against a force they cannot defeat: a little old English lady. Gangsters featured in many British B-movies in the 1950s and 1960s, but more often than not mainstream films played the genre for laughs, as in a series of Peter Sellers-starring comedies including *Two Way Stretch* (1960) and *Crooks in Cloisters* (1964).

Britain didn't produce gangster movie stars to rival Robinson and Cagney or De Niro and Pacino, but arguably Michael Caine and Bob Hoskins came closest. Caine featured in the gangster-driven double bill of *The Italian Job* (1969), built around a Turin bullion robbery, and seedy Newcastle-set underworld revenge drama *Get Carter* (1971). As crime boss Harold Shand, Hoskins headlined *The Long Good Friday* (1980) in which East End gangsters run foul of Irish terrorists in a film that anticipated Thatcher's Britain, and he played lieutenant to Caine's Mob boss in *Mona Lisa* (1986), in which Hoskins' hopeless romantic driver falls for a high-class prostitute.

The gangland bio-pic *The Krays* (1990) harked back to the height of 1960s London gangsterism, and pre-empted a late-1990s spurt of 'geezer' gangster flicks including the Guy Ritchie directed capers *Lock, Stock & Two Smoking Barrels* (1998) and *Snatch* (2000). Films such as *Love, Honour and Obey* (2000) and *Gangster No.1* (2000) followed the Ritchie style, before things turned more serious with *Sexy Beast* (2000), a gangster movie cliché greatest hits compilation with Ben Kingsley as a malevolent gang boss who hunts down his former partner in Spain, and *Layer Cake* (2004), in which Daniel Craig's reluctant hood agrees to 'one last job'. Later, the decade produced more interesting work in *In Bruges* (2008), in which two hitmen await their instructions, and *The Bank Job* (2008), a period piece mixing gangsters with 1960s politics and the darker side of royalty.

Beyond America and Britain, there have been notable non-English language gangster movies that have found dedicated audiences. One of the earliest, which launched a long-running series, was *Dr Mabuse the Gambler* (1922), directed in Germany by Fritz Lang. This silent epic was made up of two feature-length episodes, comprising an almost five-hour duration, following the plots of criminal mastermind Dr Mabuse (Rudolph Klein-Rogge). Mabuse is a master of technology such as the telephone, using it to control the urban environment he has made his criminal playground. The character reappeared in Lang's *The Testament of Dr Mabuse* (1933) and *The Thousand Eyes of Dr Mabuse* (1960), as well as a host of German B-movies.

From France came *Pépé le moko* (1937) in which Jean Gabin's gangster hides out in Algiers after a heist, only to fall in love. It's atmospheric, with its kasbah setting offering a fresh take on the gangster's milleu. In 1955 came heist movie *Rififi* (French slang for 'trouble'), directed by Jules Dassin, who'd been blacklisted and was in exile from US. It's the old story of an ex-con attempting one last job with a new gang, but it is done with such style, including a near silent thirty-minute heist sequence, that it stands with the best of the genre. The following year brought *Bob le flambeur* ('Fever Heat'/'Bob the Gambler', 1956), the first of Jean-Pierre Melville's gangster films, which include *Le Samouraï* (1967), *Le Cercle rouge* (1970) and *Un Flic* (1972). *Bob le flambeur* is another 'final job' movie, built around a raid on a casino.

Japan has a long history of gangster movies, dating back to works by Kurosawa (better known for his samurai dramas) and Ozu. In a series of silent films in the 1930s, including *Walk Cheerfully* (1930), *That Night's Wife* (1930) and *Dragnet Girl* (1933), Yasugiro Ozu paved the way for the exuberant colour films of Seijun Suzuki from the 1960s. Suzuki's films were pop art Japan-style and included *Youth of the Beast* (1963), *Tokyo Drifter* (1966) and *Branded to Kill* (1967). Kurosawa's 1948 film *Drunken Angel* – which follows a world-weary gangster played by Toshiro Mifune as he attempts to leave the yakuza behind – mixed the post-war American influence on Japan and its filmmakers with an authentically Japanese take on the genre. Also worth seeking out is Kinji Fukasaku's *Battles Without Honour and Humanity* (1973), a searing indictment of the yakuza in the post-war era; it led to a series of follow-ups and sequels throughout the 1970s. Another Japanese talent whose best work was often in gangster movies is Takeshi Kitano who forensically dissected the yakuza in *Sonatine* (1993), *Hana-bi* (1997) and *Brother* (2000).

Hong Kong filmmaker John Woo made his mark on the gangster movie before making films in America. Both 1986's *A Better Tomorrow* and 1992's *Hard Boiled* starred Chow Yun-fat in tales of the Triads (and were an influence on Tarantino). In the first, Yun-fat's the criminal fighting his way to the top of the mob, while in the second he's the tough cop attempting to thwart the Triad's arms trade (an on-screen career switch recalling those of Cagney and Robinson in the 1930s). *Infernal Affairs* (2002), a complex tale of infiltration and double cross in which the roles of cop and gangster become confused is a notable film in its own right, as well as the source material for Martin Scorsese's Oscar-winning *The Departed* (2006), a simpler take on the same ideas. Two sequels (the third film being both a sequel and a prequel) followed in 2003. Many other countries have produced notable work – such as Brazil's *City of God* (2002) – but it is only possible to offer a taster of worldwide gangster cinema here.

It appears screen gangsters are here to stay having been thoroughly deconstructed in the epic yet domestic American television series *The Sopranos* (1999–2007), which followed the travails of a present-day New Jersey mobster played by James Gandolfini, and celebrated in the historic drama *Boardwalk Empire* (featuring many of the same creative crew, 2010–14).

In the cinema the stories of the classic gangsters have been retold, such as John Dillinger's wild ride in *Public Enemies* (2009) and the efforts of the LA Police to bring down Mickey Cohen (Sean Penn) in *Gangster Squad* (2012), proving that the gangster genre hasn't been plugged full of lead just yet.

ACKNOWLEDGEMENTS

Thanks as always to my very own 'gun moll', Brigid Cherry, and my regular 'consigliere', Paul Simpson, who both offered much welcome advice on the text as it developed. Also thanks to all at Constable & Robinson, including Duncan Proudfoot, Clive Hebard, Una McGovern and Louise Cullen, and to my agent Chelsey Fox of Fox & Howard.

BIBLIOGRAPHY

Many sources were consulted in researching the lives and times of the famous gangsters, including but not restricted to those listed here.

Tim Adler, *Hollywood and the Mob: Movies, Mafia, Sex and Death* (London: Bloomsbury, 2007)

Cari Beauchamp, *Joseph P. Kennedy's Hollywood Years* (London: Faber & Faber, 2009)

Edward Behr, *Prohibition: Thirteen Years That Changed America* (New York: Skyhorse, 2011)

John Buntin, *LA Noir: The Struggle for the Soul of America's Most Seductive City* (New York: Three Rivers Press, 2009)

Bryan Burrough, *Public Enemies: Bonnie and Clyde, Machine Gun Kelly, Baby Face Nelson, Ma Barker's Gang and America's Greatest Crime Wave* (London: Penguin, 2004)

Patrick Downey, *Gangster City: The History of the New York Underworld 1900–1935* (New Jersey: Barricade, 2004)

Andy Edmonds, *Bugsy's Baby: The Secret Life of Mob Queen Virginia Hill* (New York: Carol, 1993)

Jonathan Eig, *Get Capone: The Secret Plot That Captured America's Most Wanted Gangster* (New York: Simon & Schuster, 2010)

Sid Feder and Joachim Joesten, *The Luciano Story* (New York: DaCapo Press, 1994)

Elliot J. Gorn, *Dillinger's Wild Ride: The Year That Made America's Public Enemy Number One* (Oxford: Oxford University Press, 2009)

Martin A. Gosch and Richard Hammer, *The Last Testament of Lucky Luciano* (New York: Enigma, 2013)

Jeff Guinn, *Go Down Together: The True Untold Story of Bonnie & Clyde* (London: Simon & Schuster, 2009)

William J. Helmer & Arthur J. Bilek, *The St. Valentine's Day Massacre: The Untold Story of the Gangland Bloodbath That Brought Down Al Capone* (Nashville: Cumberland House, 2004)

Nelson Johnson, *Boardwalk Empire: The Birth, High Times and Corruption of Atlantic City* (New Jersey: Medford Press, 2002)

John Kobler, *Capone: The Life and World of Al Capone* (New York: DaCapo Press, 2003)

Paul Lieberman, *Gangster Squad: Covert Cops, the Mob, and the Battle for Los Angeles* (New York: Thomas Dunne Books, 2012)

Jonathan Munby, *Public Enemies, Public Heroes: Screening the Gangster from Little Caesar to Touch of Evil* (Chicago: University of Chicago Press, 1999)

Tim Newark, *Boardwalk Gangster: The Real Lucky Luciano* (New York: St. Martin's Press, 2011)

Michael Newton, *Gangsters Encyclopedia: The World's Most Notorious Mobs, Gangs and Villains* (London: Collins & Brown, 2007)

Daniel Okrent, *Last Call: The Rise and Fall of Prohibition* (New York: Scribner, 2010)

Claire Bond Potter, *War on Crime: Bandits, G-Men, and the Politics of Mass Culture* (New Jersey: Rutgers University Press, 1998)

Charles Rappleye and Ed Becker, *All American Mafioso: The Johnny Rosselli Story* (New York: Doubleday, 1991)

Thomas Reppetto, *American Mafia: A History of Its Rise to Power* (New York: Henry Holt, 2004)

Gus Russo, *The Outfit: The Role of Chicago's Underworld in the Shaping of Modern America* (London: Bloomsbury, 2003)

David E. Ruth, *Inventing the Public Enemy: The Gangster in American Culture 1918–1934* (Chicago: University of Chicago Press, 1996)

Alain Silver and James Ursini (Eds), *Gangster Film Reader* (New Jersey: Limelight, 2007)

Anthony Summers, *Conspiracy: Who Killed President Kennedy?* (London: Fontana, 1980)

Burton Turkus and Sid Feder, *Murder, Inc.: The Inside Story of the Syndicate Killing Machine* (New York: Tenacity, 2012)

Lamar Waldron, *The Hidden History of the JFK Assassination: The Definitive Account of the Most Controversial Crime of the 20th Century* (Berkley: Counterpoint, 2013)

Stone Wallace, *Dustbowl Desperadoes: Gangsters of the Dirty '30s* (Edmonton: Folklore Publishing, 2003)

Francis Wheen, *The Soul of Indiscretion – Tom Driberg: Poet, Philanderer, Legislator and Outlaw* (London: Fourth Estate, 1990)